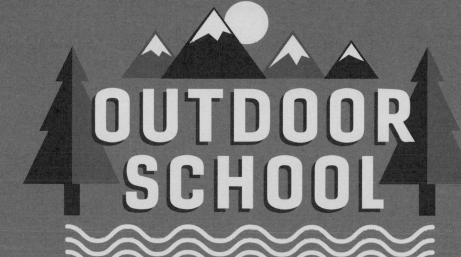

OUTDOOR SCHOOL

TREE, WILDFLOWER, AND MUSHROOM SPOTTING

MARY KAY CARSON

ILLUSTRATED BY
JOHN D. DAWSON

Odd Dot · New York

An imprint of Macmillan Publishing Group, LLC
120 Broadway, New York, NY 10271
OddDot.com
Odd Dot ® is a registered trademark of Macmillan Publishing Group, LLC

Outdoor School is a trademark of Odd Dot.
Text copyright © 2023 by Mary Kay Carson
Illustrations copyright © 2023 by John D. Dawson
Library of Congress Cataloging-in-Publication Data is available.
ISBN 978-1-250-75061-7

OUTDOOR SCHOOL LOGO DESIGNER Tae Won Yu
COVER DESIGNER Caitlyn Hunter
INTERIOR DESIGNER Christina Quintero
EDITOR Kate Avino
ILLUSTRATOR John D. Dawson

Illustration credits: Art from *Golden Guides* series: *Flowers* (New title *Wildflowers*) by Rudolf
Freund; *Trees of North America* by Rebecca Merrilees; *Trees* by Herbert S. Zim; *Butterflies* by
Andre Durenceau; *Seashores* by Dorothea and Sy Barlowe; *Birds, Poisonous Animls*, and *Bird Life*
by John D. Dawson; *Weeds* by Jean Zallinger. Select images from Biodiversity Heritage Library.
www.biodiversitylibrary.org

Our books may be purchased in bulk for promotional, educational, or business use.
Please contact your local bookseller or the Macmillan Corporate and
Premium Sales Department at (800) 221-7945 ext. 5442 or by email at
MacmillanSpecialMarkets@macmillan.com

Printed in China by 1010 Printing International Limited, Kwun Tong, Hong Kong
First edition, 2023

1 3 5 7 9 10 8 6 4 2

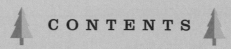

CONTENTS

OUTDOOR SCHOOL

OPEN YOUR DOOR.
STEP **OUTSIDE.**
YOU'VE JUST WALKED INTO
OUTDOOR SCHOOL.

Whether you're entering an urban wilderness or a remote forest, at Outdoor School we have only four guidelines.

→ **BE AN EXPLORER, A RESEARCHER, AND—MOST OF ALL—A LEADER.**

→ **TAKE CHANCES AND SOLVE PROBLEMS AFTER CONSIDERING ANY RISKS.**

→ **FORGE A RESPECTFUL RELATIONSHIP WITH NATURE AND YOURSELF.**

→ **BE FREE, BE WILD, AND BE BRAVE.**

We believe that people learn best through doing. So we not only give you information about the wild, but we also include three kinds of activities:

TRY IT → Read about the topic and experience it right away.

TRACK IT ↘ Observe and interact with the plants, and reflect on your experiences right in this book.

TAKE IT TO THE NEXT LEVEL ↗ Progress to advanced techniques and master a skill.

Completed any of these activities? Awesome! Check off your accomplishment and write in the date.

✓ **I DID IT!** DATE:

This book is the guide to the adventures you've been waiting for. We hope you'll do something outside your comfort zone—but we're not telling you to go out of your way to find danger. If something makes you uncomfortable, don't do it.

Don't forget: This book is **YOURS**, so use it. Write in it, draw in it, make notes about your favorite waterfall hike in it, dry a flower in it, whatever! The purpose of Outdoor School is to help you learn about your world, help you learn about yourself, and—best of all—help you have an epic adventure.

So now that you have everything you need—keep going. Take another step. And another. And never stop.

Yours in adventure,

THE **OUTDOOR SCHOOL** TEAM

PART I

WHAT IS PLANT SPOTTING?

DAWSON

What would
YOU do?

It's a sunny, warm spring day at the park. The budding flowers and trees are so nice that you forget to be mad about babysitting your little cousin. The two of you find a bright green patch of grass and start tossing a ball back and forth.

Oops! The ball goes over your cousin's head and bounces into some weeds. As she runs toward the ball, you remember something your uncle said earlier: "Watch out for poison ivy at the park. She's allergic to it."

Uh-oh. Is that poison ivy surrounding the ball? Or some other weedy plant? How can you tell? Should you stop your cousin from getting the ball? *What would you do?*

CHAPTER 1

Noticing and Identifying Plants

Are you outside? Can you look out a window and see outside? If you can, there's a good chance plants are within sight. Even city sidewalks sprout grass in their cracks, and snowy scenes are striped with dark tree trunks. It's nearly impossible to be outdoors at any time of the year without a leaf, root, twig, or sprout showing up somewhere. How can you *not* be a plant spotter?

MAYFLOWER

WILD GRASS

LONGLEAF BLOLLY

SEA GRAPE

MAGNOLIA

MAPLE

BEECH

OAK

Plants are everywhere: They're easy to find and simple to see. Unlike animals, plants don't run away or hide. That makes trees, grasses, flowers, mosses, ferns, and other plants (as well as mushrooms) ideal targets for spotting and identifying. Plants are so cooperative! Spot a tree you want to identify? You can leave it right where it is and go get this book without worrying about it fleeing or flying away. The tree will patiently wait for your return. Plants are so awesome!

Taking notice of the trees and flowers around you is what plant spotting is all about. Plant identification can turn any ordinary outside moment into a fun treasure hunt. No matter the place—or how many times you've visited—chances are you can't name *every* plant you see. And paying attention to the trees, flowers, ferns, and mushrooms in a place clues you in to that particular habitat, its ecoregion, and where you are on earth. It's true! Crime detectives use plant seeds and pollen to figure out where a suspect has been

before. And recognizing the trees or wild plants in someone's photo clues you in to that person's whereabouts.

Plants are the foundation of ecosystems, fuel most food chains, and come first when defining land biomes. There are no sloths and toucans without rain forest trees and plants, after all. Animals depend on plants for food, homes, nesting sites, and breathable air. The ability to identify the trees and plants around you lets you know what kind of habitat you're in and what other life-forms you can expect to see.

Plant Spotting Skills and Thrills

This book will help you notice and identify trees, wildflowers, mushrooms, ferns, and mosses. Part I gets you up to speed on the basics—plant parts, plant "lingo," ecoregions, and some dos and don'ts of plant spotting. Parts II through V focus in on a particular category of plant or fungi, with details on identifying groups and subspecies within trees, wildflowers, ferns, mosses, and mushrooms.

So what does it actually take to be a plant spotter? It takes patience and all the powers of observation! Fortunately, both are free skills to learn and improve upon with practice. Need proof? Take a quick glance at the nearest tree or plant. Without looking at it again, what do you remember about it? What shape were its leaves? Did it have flowers? How large was it? Look at the tree or plant again, but count to twenty this time. Did you remember more? Of course you did. You're already a plant spotter in training!

Here are some general guidelines about observing and noticing plants so you can become a superb plant spotter:

ZOOM IN AND OUT A tree is a whole thing with its own shape, as well as individual distinctive parts, such as bark, leaves, branches, and roots. Leaves look different when you turn them over, for example. Observing plants involves looking at the big picture and noticing small details.

SMELL, FEEL, AND LISTEN, TOO
Seeing is great, but don't forget to engage your other senses when plant spotting. The smell of flowers or sap can be identification clues. Bark can feel smooth, rough, pebbly, or corky. Listen to whistling pines in the wind, the creaking of trees swaying in the forest, or the rattling of dry leaves. (And don't forget to observe safely—see more in Plant Spotting Rules and Reminders [pages 10-11]!)

LOOK FOR PATTERNS Does an unfamiliar leaf remind you of the leaves of a tree you know? Does a flower's color look like another flower you're familiar with? Do you keep seeing the same plant where the ground stays wet? Put your brain's pattern-recognition skills to work!

BILTMORE CRAB APPLE

THINK WHILE OBSERVING When you see a tree or plant you don't recognize, describe it to yourself: *Marsh plant with waxy apple tree–shaped leaves and long, dangling flowers the color of phlox.* This will help you notice and remember its details.

AMERICAN MOUNTAIN ASH

LOOK IT UP Start with the identification sections in this book, and then perhaps invest in a field guide that is focused on your geographic location or plant type. Libraries have field guides, too.

KING BOLETE

TAKE WILD NOTES Writing down what you observe turbocharges your path to plant spotter extraordinaire. Celebrate a successful plant recognition by checking off the **I SPOTTED IT!** box on the plant's identification page. Congrats! Write in the date and location where you spotted the plant, as well as some notes about the plant you saw.

DRAW IT Whether you consider yourself artistic or not, sketching plants will advance your observation skills. Trying to sketch the details of a leaf or flower takes concentration. That's rewarded by a memory boost. Want to remember what a mushroom looks like? Draw a picture of it!

Not a Plant

Not every nonmoving living thing big enough to spot outside is a plant. Quick quiz! Which of these is *not* a plant?

FLY AGARIC

DOG LICHEN

CODIUM

SEAWEED   **MUSHROOM**   **LICHEN**

Answer: None of these are plants. (It was a trick!) Remember, plants are just one of the kinds of organisms living on earth. Scientists categorize organisms into major groups, called kingdoms. "Plants" is one of those kingdoms, and so is "Animals." Mushrooms belong to a completely separate kingdom called "Fungi." Fungi can't make their own food from sunlight, like plants do, nor can they chew and swallow like animals. Fungi are their own nutrient-absorbing amazing things.

LOCOWEED

HORSE MUSHROOM

PLANTS   **ANIMALS**   **FUNGI**

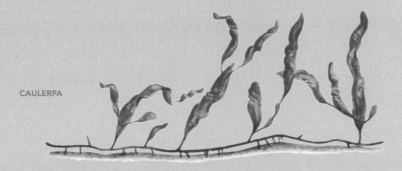

CAULERPA

What about seaweed? Seaweed is a kind of algae, which is another kind of organism that's different (and separate) from plants. And lichen? Hold on to your about-to-be-blown mind, because lichen isn't any single thing. It's a combo organism that grows together as a unit. Most lichens are part fungi and part algae. The fungal part soaks up water and provides a place for the algae to live and make food that the fungi eat. Lichen is super cool, but it's not a plant.

MAP LICHEN

GREEN-SPORED MUSHROOM

RED BELT FUNGUS

BRITISH SOLDIERS LICHEN

This book is about plant spotting, but Part V includes mushrooms, fungi, and lichen. Why? Because fungi are often found near plants. Mushrooms sprout in grass and near tree roots; bracket fungi and lichen grow on tree trunks. You'll come across fungi while out looking for trees, flowers, and ferns. The best way to recognize what it isn't (a plant) is to know what, in fact, it truly is. Besides, fungi are some of the coolest, fastest-growing, fun-to-spot living things around.

Plant Spotting Rules and Reminders

Stay safe and out of trouble while plant spotting outdoors. Here are a few tips:

LOOK BEFORE TOUCHING > Some thorny and sharp plant parts can cause injuries! (See Wild Plants to Avoid on page 37.)

DEVILS-WALKINGSTICK

NO TASTING > The fruits, berries, leaves, and other parts of some plants are poisonous or can cause allergic reactions. Deadly mushrooms don't carry warning signs. Leave the foraging to experts.

POKEWEED

JACK-O'-LANTERN

ASK BEFORE COLLECTING

It's illegal to take anything from most national and state parks, nature preserves, and private property. Find out what's allowed where you're going before taking home seeds or gathering leaves. Ask a park ranger or check the park's website for more information.

AMERICAN BASSWOOD

TAKE OR MAKE PICTURES

Picking wildflowers prevents them from producing seeds. Sketching or taking photographs are great ways to learn their shapes without collecting them and halting their growth.

STAY OFF PRIVATE PROPERTY

Don't enter any outdoor area without permission. Most places are still off-limits, even if there aren't any "No Trespassing" signs around.

PRIVATE PROPERTY NO TRESPASSING

TRY IT → Line Up Some Plants

All different kinds of plants live in backyards and parks. Want proof? Make a line transect, a simple tool that scientists use to record plants in a habitat. Instead of identifying and counting every single plant, a tape or string is laid on the ground in a straight line. Only the plants touching the string are recorded. You can make your own simple line transect to get familiar with the variety of plant life near you. Go ahead, try it!

STEP 1 Tie the string securely to one of the pencils. Measure 1 yard (1 meter) from the pencil along the string and generously mark the spot on the string with the marker pen as shown below.

STEP 2 Wind the string around the pencil up to your 1-yard mark. Repeat Step 1 until you've marked off 10 yards (about 10 meters).

STEP 3 Cut the string a pencil's length past the 10-yard mark. Use the extra length of string to tie on the second pencil. Your line transect is ready!

STEP 4 Find some woods, a weedy lot, a lush park, or a spot in your backyard. Poke the second pencil anywhere into the ground.

STEP 5 Hold on to the first pencil, then slowly back away, unwinding the string as you go. Walk in a straight line, letting the string stretch against a tree trunk or go through a bush—whatever is in your direct path!

STEP 6 When the string runs out, push the first pencil into the ground. Congrats! You've made a 10-yard line transect!

STEP 7 Walk the length of the string, observing the plants that touch the string. Check off the kinds of plants you see below.

☐ trees   ☐ bushes or shrubs

☐ wildflowers   ☐ grasses

☐ ferns   ☐ mosses

☐ mushrooms

☐ other ....

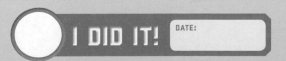

I DID IT! DATE:

TRACK IT ↘ Sample Your Transect

Now record the plants and fungi along the line transect you made.

STEP 1 Start at your first pencil. This is "Meter 0" on the chart on page 15. Note any plants within your hand's width of Meter 0 in the chart. Name all the plants you can, and describe or draw pictures of those you can't.

STEP 2 Go to the next marking on the string (Meter 1) and name, describe, or draw the plants you see on the chart to the right of 1. Keep going until you reach the second pencil (Meter 10).

For example:

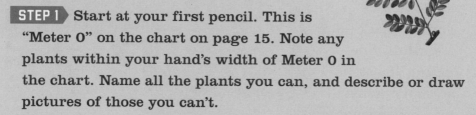

DATE		LOCATION	
	6/22		Central Park

METER	NAMES, DESCRIPTIONS, OR DRAWINGS OF NEARBY PLANTS
1	small tree, sugar maple, tall grass, blue flower, kind of oak, violets, red clover, thin toadstool, rough-leafed fern

METER	NAMES, DESCRIPTIONS, OR DRAWINGS OF NEARBY PLANTS
0 (1st pencil)	
1	
2	
3	
4	
5	
6	
7	
8	
9	
10 (2nd pencil)	

STEP 3 ▸ **How many different kinds of plants were in your sample?** ....

Was that more or less than you expected? ....

Describe this plant community—is it a field, a forest, a lawn? ....

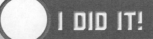

I DID IT!   DATE:

How Plants Live

Your lawn might not seem like a community of advanced life-forms, but plants are complex organisms no matter how small. Plants are made up of four parts: roots, stems, flowers, and leaves. Each part handles a different job thanks to specialized groups of cells called *tissues*. Root tissue soaks up water from the soil, stem tissue holds up the plant, leaf tissue collects sunlight, and so on.

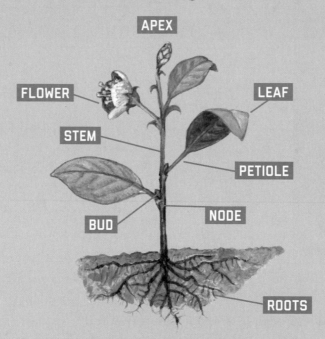

A plant's parts allow it to get the water and nutrients it needs to make food, grow, and reproduce. Luckily for plant spotters, these plant survival tools come in different shapes, sizes, and colors depending on the species. Plant parts like leaves and flowers are what distinguish an oak from an oat or a fir from a fern. They're what make plants identifiable!

Roots, Stems, and Leaves

Plants stay put, living their life in a single place. When a seed *germinates*, or sprouts, a root is one of the first parts to grow. It pushes and extends down into the soil and then soaks up water and minerals for the plant to use. Some plants, like dandelions, have one main large root, called a *taproot*. Grasses have fibrous root systems, with many thin roots that spread in all directions.

TAPROOT   **FIBROUS ROOTS**

Roots draw water out of the soil, and the stem shuttles it out toward the leaves. Water escapes the plant through tiny pores in the leaves called *stomata*. The process of water moving through the plant and out the leaves is called *transpiration*. It's part of earth's water cycle of cloud creation, rain, and evaporation.

LEAF   **LEAF CROSS SECTION**   **STOMA**

Transpiration moves a phenomenal amount of water into the atmosphere. An oak tree can transpire 40,000 gallons (151,000 liters) of water every year. That's why plant-filled places are more humid than others. The plants put water vapor into the air, which creates the excess humidity.

Stems grow from the apex end of the plant. They provide a plant with structure and support for its leaves, flowers, and fruits. *Nodes* are the slightly swollen places along stems where a leaf or another stem bud begins to grow. Some stems are green, while others can be covered in bark. Trees are made up of mostly stems with their trunks, branches, and twigs. But mosses have no stems at all!

NODE

Leaves are plant food factories. They use air, water, and sunlight for photosynthesis. The pigment that makes leaves green, *chlorophyll*, absorbs light energy from the sun. Cells in the leaves use this energy to combine water with carbon dioxide from the air to create food. In other words, plants feed themselves! And while plants photosynthesize food, they give off oxygen. Our planet wouldn't have a breathable level of oxygen without plants.

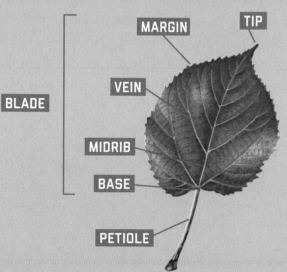

BLADE

MARGIN

TIP

VEIN

MIDRIB

BASE

PETIOLE

Wide World of Leaves

All their different shapes and sizes make leaves crucial for plant identification. But a plant's leaves can also clue you in on how it survives. For example, leaves of desert plants hold water in, while rain forest leaves drain water off.

Leaf Types

BROADLEAF — WITCH-HAZEL

TOOTHED-EDGE LEAF — RED BANEBERRY

NEEDLELIKE LEAF — EASTERN WHITE PINE

SCALELIKE LEAF — NORTHERN WHITE CEDAR

COMPOUND LEAF — CAROLINA ASH

GRASS BLADE — GRASS

WAXY LEAF — SOUTHERN BAYBERRY

LOBED LEAF — RED MULBERRY

PECAN

Broadleaf trees and other flowering plants often have wide, flat leaves that soak up sunlight like a paved parking lot. The veins that run through them shuttle water to the food-making cells—and those cells can burst when frozen! That's why the nonwoody parts of broadleaf plants die or drop their leaves where winters are cold. Needleleaf plants like pine trees can make food all year round. But the tough, skinny needles can't photosynthesize as much food as larger leaves can. That's why hardy evergreens grow at a much slower rate.

NEEDLELEAF PLANT

RED SPRUCE

Carnivorous Plants

Plants make their own food from sunlight, water, and air. But they also need minerals from the soil, like nitrogen. In boggy places with mineral-poor soil, some plants have evolved a way around this problem: They eat bugs!

Digesting trapped insects gives carnivorous plants a nutritional boost. While photosynthesizing its food, the plant gets a nitrogen boost from a decaying fly or beetle, which gives it the extra nourishment it needs to make seeds.

Carnivorous plants have amazing adaptations for trapping insect meals. Some plants, like the Venus flytrap, enclose the bug between its quickly-folding leaves. Pitcher plants drown nectar-seeking insects that shimmy down their tube-shaped leaves. And sundews trap insects with hair-like projections that are covered in their sticky nectar. Watch out, bugs!

PITCHER PLANT

Talk Like a Botanist

Here are some terms to know when you're talking and reading about plants.

ANNUAL a plant that germinates, flowers, seeds, and dies in a single year

BOTANY the scientific study of plants

BUD a compact mass of plant tissue that grows into a leaf, flower, or stem

CHLOROPHYLL a green pigment in plants that absorbs energy from sunlight for photosynthesis

KLAMATH PLUM

CULTIVARS plant varieties created by people through plant production (cultivation) methods like garden plants, fruit trees, and crops

INVASIVE a non-native plant that spreads and causes harm to the ecosystem

NATIVE plants that live in the region where they evolved

NODE the place on a stem where a stem or leaf emerges

NON-NATIVE a plant introduced into a region from another place

PERENNIAL a plant with a life cycle of many years

PETIOLE the stem on a leaf

PHOTOSYNTHESIS a plant's food-making process that combines carbon dioxide and water in the presence of chlorophyll and light to create carbohydrate food and release oxygen

TRANSPIRATION the passage of water from the soil through a plant's roots and out into the atmosphere through its leaves

WEED a plant that grows where people don't want it to live

MILKWEED

Woe Is the Weed

What is a weed, exactly? Simply put, a weed is an unwanted plant, such as grass in cracked sidewalks, dandelions on a golf course, maple seedings in window flower boxes, or little green shoots in a house plant pot. The plants themselves aren't necessarily bad—they're just growing where people don't want them to grow. Whether a plant is a weed or not depends on the weed watcher's perspective. What's a weed to you might be a fascinating find to someone else.

MUSTARD

DANDELION

TRY IT → Watch a Weed

Get up close and personal with an amazing, solar-powered, water-siphoning, self-feeding organism! Find a weed and get to work.

ENGLISH DAISY

WHAT YOU'LL NEED
> A pencil or pen.

STEP 1 Go outside and look for a small weed. (Make sure it is a truly unwanted weed!) Use any plant that you can pull up with its roots intact.

STEP 2 Write information about it here:

DATE	LOCATION

Where was the weed growing? Describe its habitat.

What else was growing around it?

What kind of plant do you think it is?

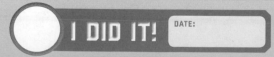
I DID IT! DATE:

TRACK IT ↘ Label a Weed's Parts

Learn the parts of a plant using the weed you collected as an example. Drawing helps your brain notice details and remember them.

> ## WHAT YOU'LL NEED
> ➤ **A pencil or pen, a ruler.**

IRONWEED

STEP 1 Draw the weed you pulled up. Label it with as many of these parts as you can:

ROOTS | STEM | LEAF | BUD | NODE | PETIOLE | FLOWER

STEP 2 Measure specific parts of the plant.

Leaf width:

Plant length (without roots):

Root length:

STEP 3 Write any new ideas about what plant this is and what it needs to grow well.

I DID IT! DATE:

TRY IT → Leaf Survey

PEACHLEAF
WILLOW

Leaves' green color tells you they're equipped and ready for photosynthesis. Leaf attributes come in many variations, which is good news when it comes to plant identification! Get to know some basic leaf types by collecting a few.

WHAT YOU'LL NEED

➤ A pencil or pen.

STEP 1 Revisit the Leaf Types chart on page 19. Go outside and look at some leaves. Check off any of these you see:

☐ broadleaf

☐ scalelike leaf

☐ needlelike leaf

☐ compound leaf

☐ toothed-edge leaf

☐ grass blade

☐ waxy leaf

☐ lobed leaf

STEP 2 Collect and describe three leaves or evergreen sprigs:

LEAF 1	LEAF 2	LEAF 3
DESCRIBE THE LEAF.	DESCRIBE THE LEAF.	DESCRIBE THE LEAF.
DESCRIBE ITS PLANT.	DESCRIBE ITS PLANT.	DESCRIBE ITS PLANT.

I DID IT!   DATE:

TRACK IT ↘

Leaves Up Close

Use a hand lens or magnifying glass to get a closer look at the leaves you collected.

MULBERRY

WHAT YOU'LL NEED

➢ A pencil or pen, a magnifying glass.

STEP 1   Draw a leaf in each Naked Eye section of the chart below.

STEP 2   Use the magnifying glass to get a closer look at the leaves. Draw what you see in the Magnified sections.

LEAF 1	LEAF 2	LEAF 3
NAKED EYE	NAKED EYE	NAKED EYE
MAGNIFIED	MAGNIFIED	MAGNIFIED

STEP 3   What surprised you about what you saw?

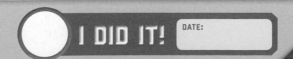

I DID IT!   DATE:

27

See a Plant Exhale

The last step of plant transpiration is when water vapor escapes the leaves into the surrounding air, just like an exhale! Grab a plastic bag and a twist tie. Find a leafy branch or a plant stem with leaves growing in a sunny spot. Cover the leafy end with the bag and use the twist tie to *tightly* close off the bag around the stem. Check back in a couple of hours. Is the bag fogged up with condensation yet? Have water droplets collected? Compare results on different kinds of plant leaves and/or on sunny and cloudy days.

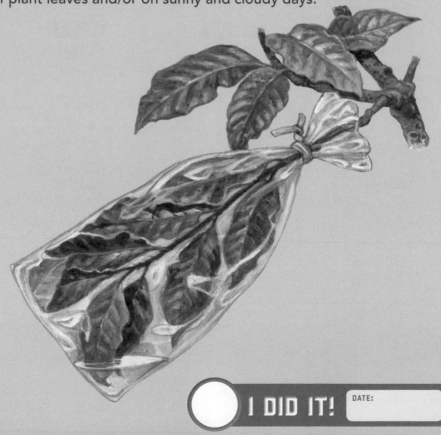

I DID IT!   DATE:

CHAPTER 3

Seeds and Fruits

A tree adorned with acorns gives it away as an oak. Likewise, berries or fruits on bushes, and seedpods on plants, can be helpful for identification. Seeds are how plants get their start and how they reproduce.

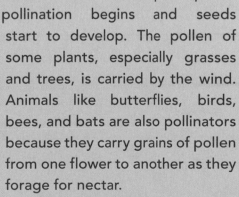

CHAPMAN OAK

A seed contains an *embryo*, which is a tiny, ready-to-grow baby plant. Just like animals, a plant embryo starts out as an egg that's then fertilized by sperm and contains a mix of genes from a male and a female. Unlike animals, many plants have both female and male parts on the same plant and even within a single flower. (See diagram on page 177.)

(See diagram on page 177.)

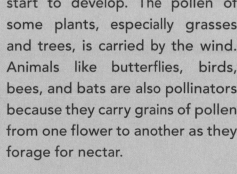

Pollination is how plants are fertilized. Male flower parts (*stamens*) produce pollen. When pollen reaches the female flower part (*pistil*), pollination begins and seeds start to develop. The pollen of some plants, especially grasses and trees, is carried by the wind. Animals like butterflies, birds, bees, and bats are also pollinators because they carry grains of pollen from one flower to another as they forage for nectar.

A seed is a complete package. Inside its protective seed coat is a plant embryo as well as some stored food. It's pretty amazing that a giant redwood tree starts out as a seed about the size of this O!

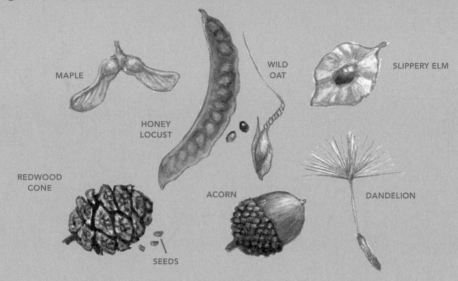

MAPLE

HONEY LOCUST

WILD OAT

SLIPPERY ELM

REDWOOD CONE

ACORN

DANDELION

SEEDS

Seeds come in many variations.

Seeds Travel Around

ROUNDLEAF SERVICEBERRY

The seeds of cone-making plants, like pines and spruces, are bare or naked. Flowering plants and trees make seeds covered in fruit. Now, what a botanist calls a fruit is different from what a grocer calls a fruit. In botany, a fruit is whatever covers a seed. Some fruits are fleshy, like apples or berries, while others are hard, like wheat or acorns. Anything with a seed in it is considered a fruit.

TREE FRUITS AND CONES

Tasty fruits like berries help seeds spread or disperse. While plants don't move, their seeds can. Seed dispersal gives a plant's offspring a chance to grow someplace else. Birds or other animals eat fruits and poop out the seeds elsewhere. Animals like squirrels and ants also help disperse seeds by stashing them away, some of which  germinate long before getting eaten. Burrs and other prickly or sticky seeds grab on to animal fur (or socks) and hitch a ride to some-place else. (Like your washing machine!)

 There are also seeds that travel by floating on water and others that ride along wind cur-rents. Winged maple seeds, called *samaras*, and the fluffy parachutes attached to dandelion and milkweed seeds can drift far away. Plants like jewelweed, witch hazel, and geraniums make fruits that explode as they dry, shooting the seeds into the air. Gravity helps seeds spread, too, by bringing heavy fruit or nuts down to the ground to roll away or be found.

WILD CARROT SEED

WINGED SEEDS

MAPLE TREE SAMARA

COCKELBUR SEED

PITCHFORK SEED

STICKY SEEDS

GERANIUM SEED

FLOATING SEEDS

MILKWEED SEED

EXPLODING SEEDS

TRY IT →   Be an Animal

People are animals, too—even when it comes to seed dispersal. And while few seeds stick to bare skin, clothing (like socks!) often catches burrs and other clingy seeds.

STAR-THISTLE
SEED

> ### WHAT YOU'LL NEED
> ➢ Two large old socks, a magnifying glass.

STEP 1 Choose old socks large enough to go over your shoes. If the insides are fuzzier, turn them inside out. Put a sock over each of your shoes and lower legs.

STEP 2 Walk through a weedy patch, old field, or overgrown wood—anyplace with lots of seeds!

STEP 3 Remove the socks and use the magnifying glass to look closer at the seeds you've collected. Can you tell which seeds came from trees? Which were made by wildflowers or grasses? What similarities and differences are there between seeds from trees, wildflowers, and grasses?

I DID IT!   DATE:

BROME

TRACK IT ↘   Seed Search and Log

RED MAPLE

Find 4 seeds and fruits and determine how they travel. Remember that anything that covers a seed is a fruit.

WHAT YOU'LL NEED

➢ A pencil or pen.

STEP 1   Go for a hike in a place with a variety of plants. Collect 4 fruits, berries, seedpods, grass seedheads, or anything else that holds a seed.

EASTERN COTTONWOOD

STEP 2   Think about how your seeds travel away from their parent plants. Write the location where you found each seed in the charts. Then draw them below and on the next page.

STEP 3   What dispersal method do you think moved your seeds to a new home? Note your answers under "Dispersal Method" and your reasonings under "Why?"

STEP 4   Try your best to determine the plants your seeds come from, then write your guess in each chart.

SEED 1 LOCATION:

SEED SKETCH

DISPERSAL METHOD:

WHY?

PARENT PLANT:

SEED 2 LOCATION:

SEED SKETCH

DISPERSAL METHOD:

WHY?

PARENT PLANT:

SEED 3 LOCATION:	**SEED 4** LOCATION:
SEED SKETCH	SEED SKETCH
DISPERSAL METHOD:	DISPERSAL METHOD:
WHY?	WHY?
PARENT PLANT:	PARENT PLANT:

I DID IT! DATE:

TAKE IT TO THE NEXT LEVEL ↗

Solve Seedy Mysteries

Find a seed that's a complete mystery to you. You may have no idea about the plant that created it. Solve the mystery by growing it into a recognizable plant! Place some potting soil in a pot, push the seed just under the soil, water it, and wait. It might take a while to grow, but then you'll know.

Did you find something on your hike that you're not sure is a seed? See if it'll sprout into a plant! Place the possible seed on a moist, folded paper towel inside a plastic sandwich bag. Then leave it someplace warm and wait. What happens?

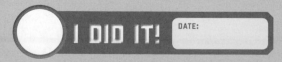

I DID IT! DATE:

CHAPTER 4

Plant Powers and Problems

You recognize a cactus when you see one. It's hard to miss those spines. And a sure sign of a honey locust tree is a trunk covered in thorns. Spines and thorns are helpful clues for plant identification. But for the plant, being prickly or spiny is all about survival.

SAGUARO

Plants are a food source for most everything, from microbes to elephants. To discourage larger munching animals from eating them, many plants have adaptations, like thorns, spines, and prickles. Leaves covered in a waxy coating or with stiff hairs fend off hungry caterpillars and other insects.

WAXY MANGROVE

Plants also engage in chemical warfare. Lots of plants are full of bad-tasting, harmful, and even poisonous toxins. Leaves with a strong smell when crushed, plants with milky or gluey sap, or roots that smell like rotten eggs are all signs that a plant is at war with those who eat it.

But getting eaten isn't the only problem plants have. Plant damage happens when insects lay eggs under bark, when birds drill holes to make nests, and when diseases destroy plant tissue. It's good to know what common kinds of plant damage look like. You don't want to mistake red bumps on leaves or ball-like swellings, called *galls*, on twigs as normal parts of a tree. Nor will you be able to name a plant correctly if thinking that rust, a fungus, is part of a plant's regular coloring. Plus, particular plants are more prone to specific pests than others, so recognizing them can help with plant identification.

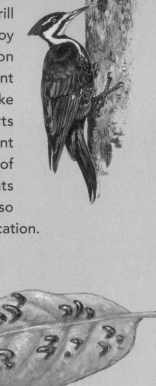

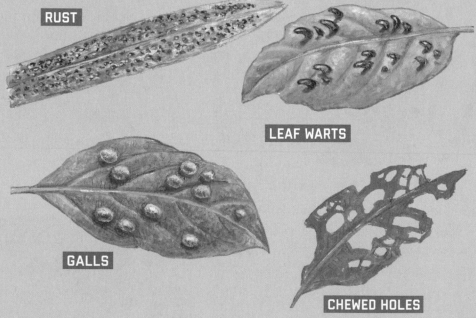

RUST

LEAF WARTS

GALLS

CHEWED HOLES

No Touching! Wild Plants to Avoid

Plant defenses don't just work on bugs and birds. They can hurt you, too. Lots of plants are poisonous if you eat them. Never taste an unfamiliar berry or chew on a random stem. Here are some plants you don't even want to touch:

→ Poison ivy, poison oak, and poison sumac (from the *Toxicodendron* species) all contain *urushiol*. This oily sap oozes out from the leaves, stems, and roots. If it gets on your skin, urushiol can cause a painful, itchy rash that turns into sores that can last for a week or more. Some people are more sensitive to the sap than others, but avoid these plants as much as you can. If exposed, rinse skin with luke-warm, soapy water or rubbing alcohol to remove the urushiol and lessen the reaction.

POISON IVY

The leaflets of poison ivy and oak grow in clusters of three. As the saying goes, "Leaves of three, leave it be." They can grow as a vine, ground cover, or small bush. Poison sumac is a woody shrub with compound leaves of 7–13 leaflets and green berries.

POISON SUMAC

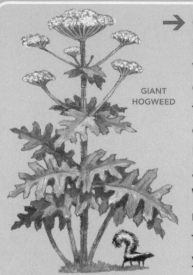

GIANT HOGWEED

→ Giant hogweed (*Heracleum mantegazzianum*) is a giant non-native weed with umbrella-like white flower clusters that grows about 6.5–13 feet (2–4 meters) tall. Its sap can cause blisters and scars on the skin. If exposed, wash the area with soap and cold water as soon as possible. While hydrocortisone cream may reduce blister pain, see a doctor if the reaction is severe or if sap got in your eyes.

→ Stinging nettle (*Urtica dioica*) is a plant whose leaves and stems are covered in brittle hairs full of chemicals. The hairs will inject their toxic brew into anything that brushes against them. The burning sensation and skin rash doesn't last long, thankfully. Rinse the skin with water to relieve the rash if you come in contact with this plant.

STINGING NETTLE

→ Tread-softly (*Cnidoscolus stimulosus*) is a wildflower whose name is a warning—watch where you're walking! The leaves, stems, seeds, and even the pretty white flowers of this small plant are covered in stinging hairs. Covering the affected area with a baking soda paste can help neutralize the burning acid released by the hairs. (As will pee.)

TREAD-SOFTLY

TRY IT →

Plant Defenses Search

What kinds of plant defenses can you find?

SAGURO

WHAT YOU'LL NEED

≫ A pencil or pen.

STEP 1 Take a walk through an area with a variety of trees and plants.

STEP 2 Check off any plant defenses that you spot.

☐ thorns   ☐ spines   ☐ waxy leaves
☐ hairy leaves ☐ other ....

 I DID IT!   DATE:

TRACK IT ↘

Record the Plant Defense

Make an in-depth observation of one of the plant defenses you saw.

WHAT YOU'LL NEED

≫ A pencil or pen.

WAXY MANGROVE

STEP 1 What kind of plant defense did you see?

DATE   LOCATION

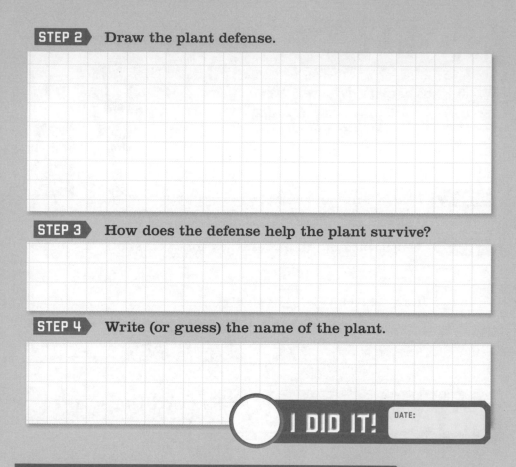

STEP 2 Draw the plant defense.

STEP 3 How does the defense help the plant survive?

STEP 4 Write (or guess) the name of the plant.

I DID IT!   DATE:

TAKE IT TO THE **NEXT LEVEL** ↗

Local Problem Plants

Do you know which of the Wild Plants to Avoid on page 37 live in your area? Are there problem plants in your area beyond those mentioned? Find out by asking local hikers or gardeners, or doing some internet research. Research treatment for the plant defenses as well.

I DID IT!   DATE:

CHAPTER 5

Where Plants Live

Plant spotting is more than just identifying the trees and wildflowers you see. It's also about finding patterns and connections among the kinds of plants that grow in a particular place.

PALM BROADLEAF CONIFER

Do ferns grow where prairie grasses thrive? (Not usually.) Do oak trees and mushrooms share forests? (Sometimes.) Why don't redwood trees grow in Texas? (It's too dry.)

EAGLE
FERN

Habitats determine which plants grow in a particular place. Each species of plant needs a particular set of environmental conditions to thrive. Recognizing habitats is a huge help in identifying plants. Knowing that you're trying to name a desert flower or a tree that likes swamps narrows down the identification possibilities.

Temperature, precipitation, and sunlight are big factors in suitable plant habitats. Spruces can tolerate below-freezing temperatures, but palm trees do not. This is also true for rainfall and sunlight amounts.

EASTERN WHITE PINE

Delicate wildflowers that grow in moist, shady woodlands aren't going to survive long droughts or the strong desert sun.

Soil type is another habitat requirement for plants. It's often classified into one of four basic types: sandy, clay, silty, or loamy. Sandy soil doesn't hold water and is mostly small bits of broken-down rocks. Clay soil is sticky and heavy, and cracks when dry. Silty soil is made of broken-down rock and mineral particles that are larger than clay but smaller than sand. Loamy soil is the dark stuff of fertile farm fields and bagged potting soil. It has a mix of the other three soil types as well as decomposed leaves, plants, and other organic material called *humus*. Even within a habitat, some plants will grow better on sandy hilltops while others will prefer loamy valleys. This makes plant spotting endlessly fascinating! Each nook and cranny of a habitat you explore has unique plants to discover.

SOIL TYPES

SANDY   CLAY   SILTY   LOAMY

Garden Plants and Green Invaders

A native plant is one that grows naturally in a region and wasn't introduced by people. This includes forest trees, prairie grasses, and wildflowers. But all sorts of everyday plants you'll find aren't native to that area. Most lawn grasses and garden flowers, ornamental trees and bushes, fruit tree cultivars, and food crops are non-native plants.

PURPLE LOOSESTRIFE

Orange trees, tulips, and wheat were brought to North America on purpose, but they don't grow by themselves in the wild. Other invasive non-native plants have escaped, reproduced, and spread, causing problems in the ecosystem where they landed. Invasive plants are green invaders, which quickly reproduce and take over natural habitats. They outcompete and replace the native plants that the wildlife depends on for food. Do any of these invasive plants live where you do?

KUDZU

ENGLISH IVY

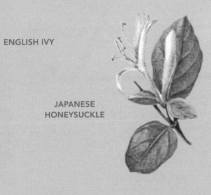

JAPANESE HONEYSUCKLE

Biomes

While habitats are local and specific to individual plants, biomes are general and global. See the map below for the important land biomes for North American plant communities. Read about more specific biome information on the following pages.

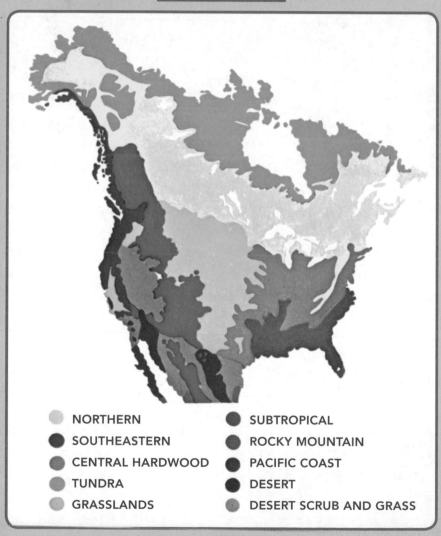

PLANT BIOMES MAP

- ⬤ NORTHERN
- ⬤ SOUTHEASTERN
- ⬤ CENTRAL HARDWOOD
- ⬤ TUNDRA
- ⬤ GRASSLANDS
- ⬤ SUBTROPICAL
- ⬤ ROCKY MOUNTAIN
- ⬤ PACIFIC COAST
- ⬤ DESERT
- ⬤ DESERT SCRUB AND GRASS

BOREAL FORESTS have long, cold winters and short summers. They are in northern regions or high mountains. Evergreen conifer trees like spruces, pines, and firs live here. Their pointy tops shed snow, and the needlelike leaves make food throughout the whole year.

TEMPERATE CONIFEROUS FORESTS have mild, wet winters and warm summers. Many of these forests are found along the Northern Pacific coast and feature giant redwood and Douglas fir trees. In the southeastern United States, pine trees dominate the coniferous forests. Ferns, wildflowers, and mushrooms grow on the forest floor beneath the pines, redwoods, or firs.

DECIDUOUS FORESTS have warm, wet summers and cold winters. Broadleaf trees that lose their leaves in autumn grow here, such as beeches, maples, oaks, ashes, and hickories. The forest floor supports wildflowers, smaller understory trees, and shrubs.

GRASSLANDS have rich soil and seasonal rain. Grasses of many kinds grow here, with cottonwood, oak, and maple trees concentrated near streams or rivers.

CHAPARRALS have hot, dry summers and cool, wet winters. Small trees such as scrub oaks grow here, as well as thick shrubs and seasonal wildflowers.

DESERTS have little rain and hot summers. The plants are tolerant of drought, such as cacti, sagebrush, and creosote bush. Wildflowers bloom only when rain falls.

Grow Zones

The identification pages in this book include a RANGE section to identify where the plant (or fungus) species normally grows. This covers both the geographical region, such as "eastern United States," as well as its growth zones. The zones come from the United States Department of Agriculture (USDA) Plant Hardiness Zone Map. The map is based on extreme temperatures—the coldest and hottest it gets in a place. It's a map made for gardeners, landscapers, and foresters—not a description of biomes. But this map is still handy for understanding the general environment in which a plant thrives.

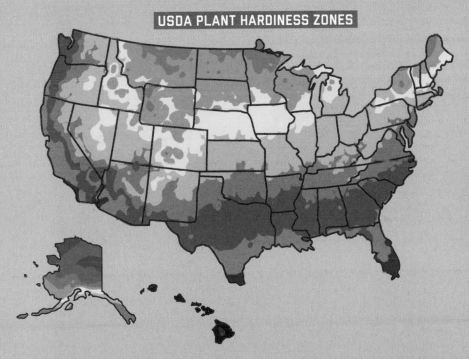

USDA PLANT HARDINESS ZONES

ZONE 1 ■   ZONE 4 ■   ZONE 7 ■   ZONE 10 ■

ZONE 2 ■   ZONE 5 ■   ZONE 8 ■   ZONE 11 ■

ZONE 3 ■   ZONE 6 ■   ZONE 9 ■

Discover how climate and soil conditions determine which plants thrive in two different places.

STEP 1 Go to a natural area with varied habitat, like a park with trails that go through the woods and also through an open field. A streamside area and a hilltop, or a grove of trees and a weedy patch works, too.

ENGELMANN SPRUCE

STEP 2 Look around at the trees, plants, wildflowers, grasses, ferns, mosses, and mushrooms around you.

STEP 3 What differences in plant (and fungal) life do you notice in the two separate places?

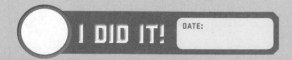

I DID IT! DATE:

TRACK IT ↘

Compare Two Plant Habitats

Record your observations of the two plant habitats.

WHAT YOU'LL NEED

➢ A pencil or pen.

PLACE A

DATE

LOCATION

HABITAT TYPE

- [ ] forest
- [ ] field
- [ ] streamside
- [ ] wetland
- [ ] hill/mountaintop
- [ ] scrub
- [ ] other

GROWING CONDITIONS

Sunlight Available to Plants

- [ ] full sun
- [ ] shade
- [ ] sun & shade

Soil Moisture

- [ ] dry
- [ ] damp
- [ ] wet
- [ ] soggy

Soil Type

- [ ] sandy
- [ ] silty
- [ ] clay
- [ ] loamy

What color is it?

Exposure to Wind
- [ ] protected
- [ ] exposed

49

PLACE A CONT.

PLANTS OBSERVED

Trees	☐ none	☐ few	☐ many
Shrubs/bushes	☐ none	☐ few	☐ many
Wildflowers	☐ none	☐ few	☐ many
Grasses	☐ none	☐ few	☐ many
Ferns	☐ none	☐ few	☐ many
Mosses	☐ none	☐ few	☐ many
Mushrooms	☐ none	☐ few	☐ many

Other:

Identified plants:

PLACE B

DATE

LOCATION

HABITAT TYPE

☐ forest   ☐ field   ☐ streamside

☐ wetland   ☐ hill/mountaintop   ☐ scrub

☐ other

GROWING CONDITIONS

Sunlight Available to Plants

☐ full sun   ☐ shade   ☐ sun & shade

PLACE B CONT.

Soil Moisture

☐ dry   ☐ damp   ☐ wet   ☐ soggy

Soil Type

☐ sandy   ☐ silty   ☐ clay   ☐ loamy

What color is it?

Exposure to Wind ☐ protected ☐ exposed

PLANTS OBSERVED ▸

Trees	☐ none	☐ few	☐ many
Shrubs/bushes	☐ none	☐ few	☐ many
Wildflowers	☐ none	☐ few	☐ many
Grasses	☐ none	☐ few	☐ many
Ferns	☐ none	☐ few	☐ many
Mosses	☐ none	☐ few	☐ many
Mushrooms	☐ none	☐ few	☐ many

Other:

Identified plants:

What differences are there between the growing conditions at the two places? How is the plant life different? What connections between the kinds of plants and growing conditions did you observe and record?

I DID IT! DATE:

PART II

TREES
AND
SHRUBS

V. DAWSON

What would YOU do?

The basketball game went into over-time, and now you're late meeting friends for a hike. By the time you get to the trailhead, no one is there. They left without you! *Ding!* Oh good, they sent a text.

Take the trail by the big sycamore tree. Meet you down by the creek!

Awesome! You head off on the trail, walking quickly to catch up to your friends. As you come to the top of a hill, there's a bench. You sit and catch your breath. From here, the trail splits into two directions. Which way should you go? You read the note again, but there are big trees next to both trails! Which tree is a sycamore? How can you tell? Which trail should you take? *What would you do?*

CHAPTER 1

Spotting Trees

Quick! Name a tree that grows in your yard or neighborhood. Trees are terrific targets for plant spotters. Why? They're big, easy to see, and stay around for a long time. That makes them great for identification. Trees are like family members or old friends. You get to know them over the years and seasons.

SHRUB

TREE

Trees are magnificent plants. They are some of the world's oldest and biggest living things. Trees can be taller than buildings, wider than cars, and live longer than people. But for a grown-up plant to be considered a true tree, it needs to be at least fifteen feet (four and a half meters) tall and have a thick, woody stem. A trunk makes a tree! Shrubs and bushes also have woody stems but aren't usually as tall as trees.

Tree Types

There are more than one thousand species of trees in North America. Botanists, foresters, dendrologists (tree scientists), and other tree experts use different names for tree groups. This book's tree identification pages are divided into two main groups: broadleaf trees and conifer trees.

BROADLEAF   **CONIFER**

BROADLEAF TREES (also sometimes called hardwoods), as their name hints, have broad, flat leaves. The group includes maples, oaks, ashes, elms, walnuts, and fruit trees. Most broadleaf trees that live in habitats that experience winter shed their leaves in autumn. This means they are *deciduous*. Broadleaf trees are a kind of flowering plant, or *angiosperm*. They have flowers that make seeds surrounded by some sort of fruit. (See page 30.)

CONIFER TREES (also sometimes called softwoods) have needlelike or scalelike leaves and include pines, redwoods, spruces, firs, cedars, and junipers. They are *evergreen* (not deciduous), and most species keep their hardy needles all year round. Conifer trees are a kind of nonflowering plant called *gymnosperms*. They produce cones with naked seeds, not fruits.

Tree Parts

Trees have three main parts: a crown, a trunk, and roots. The crown is the leaf-filled part of a tree. It includes the system of branches and twigs that hold out the leaves to soak up sunlight and make food. The trunk supports the crown and is covered in bark. The roots are often hidden underground, but don't be fooled! The root system is as massive as the tree's crown. Tree roots not only soak up water and minerals, but they also anchor the tree in the soil.

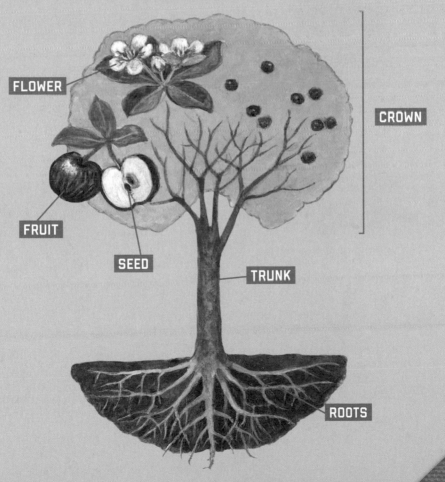

PARTS OF A TREE

FLOWER

FRUIT

SEED

CROWN

TRUNK

ROOTS

Tree Shapes

While all trees have trunks and crowns, trees come in a variety of shapes. Different kinds of trees tend to have a specific shape. Think of a pine tree and a maple tree. They are not the same shape! Overall shape is a useful clue for tree identification. Some basic tree shapes are oval, triangular, wide-spreading, vase-shaped, and irregular.

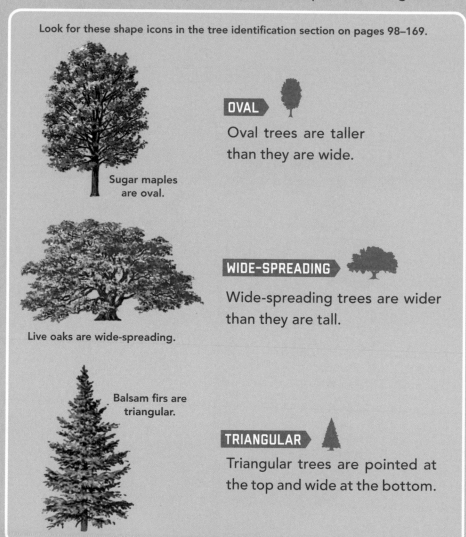

Look for these shape icons in the tree identification section on pages 98–169.

Sugar maples are oval.

OVAL

Oval trees are taller than they are wide.

Live oaks are wide-spreading.

WIDE-SPREADING

Wide-spreading trees are wider than they are tall.

Balsam firs are triangular.

TRIANGULAR

Triangular trees are pointed at the top and wide at the bottom.

American elms are vase-shaped.

VASE-SHAPED

Vase-shaped trees have a crown that's wider at the top with branches that spread out like a fan.

IRREGULAR

Irregular trees don't grow in a uniform shape, or they have big gaps between their branches.

Joshua trees (left) and some kinds of pine trees are irregular-shaped.

These tree shapes are general guidelines to help with identification. Not every sugar maple has the exact same shape, and some live oaks are wider than others. Where a tree grows makes a difference in its overall shape. These shape guidelines are for trees that are more or less out in the open, with room and sunlight to grow

into their characteristic shape. A tree that grows in a crowded forest will be thinner and have more leaves at the top to reach the sunlight. Growing up against a building, on a windy cliff, or where there's a lot of snow affects a tree's ultimate shape, too.

Talk Like a Dendrologist

Here are some terms to know about trees.

ANGIOSPERM a plant that makes flowers

BARK the protective outer covering of a tree or woody shrub

BRANCHLET a small branch of prior year's growth

BUD a compact mass of plant tissue that grows into a leaf, flower, or stem

BUD SCALES the protective covering of buds

COMPOUND LEAF a leaf made up of more than one leaflet

CONE a seed or pollen-bearing part of a conifer tree

CONIFERS trees with cones, naked seeds, and usually needlelike or scalelike leaves; evergreen tree; does not produce flowers

CROWN the leaves and branches of a tree or shrub

DECIDUOUS TREES trees that shed their leaves in autumn

DENDROLOGY the study of woody plants, including trees and shrubs

EVERGREEN TREES trees that don't shed leaves in autumn; not deciduous

FRUIT the seed-containing part of a flowering plant ——

GYMNOSPERM a plant that makes seeds but not flowers

LEAF SCAR the mark left on a twig or stem where a leaf once grew

LEAFLET an individual, leaflike part of a compound leaf

LENTICEL a pore on bark, branches, or twigs

LOBED LEAF a leaf with deep indentations in its edge

MARGIN the outer edge of a leaf

PETIOLE the stem of a leaf

SAMARA a dry, winged fruit from trees like maples or ashes

SHRUB a woody plant smaller than a tree, usually with more than one main stem growing from the ground

SIMPLE LEAF a leaf with a single blade

TERMINAL BUD the growing end of a twig

TERMINAL BUD SCAR the bumpy ring where the prior year's terminal bud grew on a branchlet

TRUNK the woody stem of a tree

TWIG the growing end of a woody plant branch

WOODY PLANT a tree, shrub, or vine covered in bark

TRY IT →   How Tall Is That Tree?

Tree height is hard to measure without a very tall ladder. Most tree spotters estimate tree height instead. Try it yourself!

WHAT YOU'LL NEED

➢ A pencil or pen, a piece of chalk, a ruler, a yardstick or measuring tape.

STEP 1 Find a tall tree in an open area that's not hilly. Use the measuring tape or yardstick to measure 5 feet (about 1.5 meters) up the trunk from the ground. Mark the spot with chalk. (Can't reach? Ask a taller friend to chalk the spot.)

STEP 2 Hold the ruler vertically out in front of you so the 12-inch (almost 30.5 centimeter) measuring line is at the top. Keep it at eye level with your arm outstretched and elbow straight. Close one eye and look at the chalk mark on the trunk while holding the ruler straight and upright.

STEP 3 Back away from the tree until the ground lines up with the ruler's 0-inch line, and where the tree's chalk mark lines up with the ruler's 1-inch (2.5 cm) line.

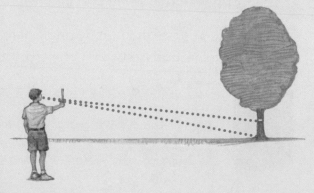

STEP 4 Stay in the same exact place and draw a line on the ruler where the top of the tree meets the ruler. How many inches up from 0 is the top of the tree?

STEP 5 Multiply your tree height in inches by 5 to estimate the height in feet (because 1 inch of ruler = 5 feet of tree). For example, if you measured 8 inches on the ruler, the tree is about 40 feet tall.

How tall is your tree in feet? (Multiply feet by 0.3 to get height in meters.)

I DID IT!   DATE:

TRACK IT ➘   Shape Up a Tree

Now that you know the height of the tree, what's its shape? Drawing it will help you decide.

WHAT YOU'LL NEED

➢ A pencil or pen.

Draw your tree on the next page with these tree-drawing tips:

→ Start from the ground up. Begin at the trunk base and then split the trunk into branches, or add the branches onto the trunk, depending on their shape.

→ The crown comes next: Start with the general shape, then add details.

→ Include leaves, bark patterns, and other details to help with later identification.

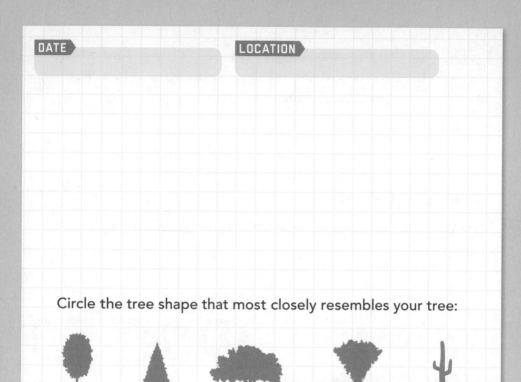

Circle the tree shape that most closely resembles your tree:

I DID IT! DATE:

TAKE IT TO THE NEXT LEVEL ↗

Trees of Every Shape

Find an example for all five tree shapes! Hint: Look in all different sorts of places, like parks, neighborhood yards, forests, or along roadways, to find all the tree shapes. Create a three-dimensional model out of clay, twigs and dried leaves, or other materials for every tree shape you find!

I DID IT! DATE:

CHAPTER 2

Read Tree Leaves

Imagine traveling in a car along a highway. You look out the window and see trees in the distance. Some are dark, triangular evergreens, while others have long trunks and leafy crowns. But recognizing tree type and shape only gets you so far. Tree identification usually calls for a closer look at the tree's leaves!

VARIETY OF MAPLE LEAVES

Leaves are the go-to identifier for nearly all trees because each species has leaves with unique sizes and shapes. There are about a dozen species of maple trees in North America. While they all share a general "maple leaf" shape, no two species are identical. The endless variation in leaf sizes, shapes, colors, textures, and traits is what makes leaves identification gold.

Broadleaf Tree Parts and Arrangements

The leaves of broadleaf trees have some basic parts in common. (Learn about conifer leaves on page 91.) A leaf's stem, or petiole, attaches it to the tree. An individual leaf starts where its petiole attaches to a twig. Sounds obvious, but not all leaves are simple like maple or oak leaves. For example, ash and buckeye trees have compound leaves. One individual compound leaf is made up of multiple leaflets growing out from the petiole.

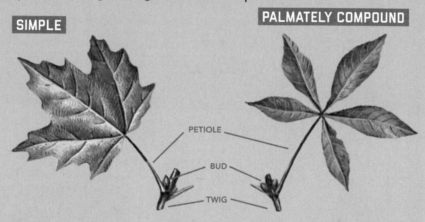

SIMPLE

PALMATELY COMPOUND

PETIOLE

BUD

TWIG

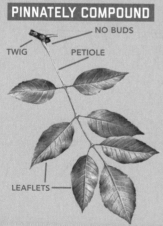

PINNATELY COMPOUND

NO BUDS

TWIG

PETIOLE

LEAFLETS

Compound leaves are either *palmate*, like the example above (a buckeye leaf), or *pinnate*. A palmately compound leaf has leaflets that spread out from a central point. (Think fingers from the palm of your hand to help you remember.) A pinnately compound leaf has leaflets along both sides of a stalk, like sumac, walnut, or ash leaves.

How a simple or compound leaf attaches to the twig helps identify the tree, too.

Leaves grow from nodes. Trees whose nodes sprout single leaves create alternate (or unpaired) leaves. Nodes that produce paired leaves create opposite leaves. Three or more leaves that sprout from a single node create a whorled arrangement.

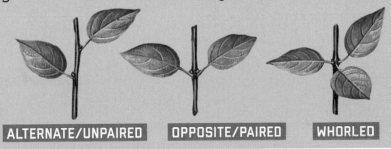

ALTERNATE/UNPAIRED   OPPOSITE/PAIRED   WHORLED

Leaf or Leaflet?

It's not always easy to distinguish a simple leaf or leaflet of a compound leaf. Lots of oval leaflets look like oval simple leaves, and some leaflets have stemlike stalks, too (called *petiolules*).

To be sure which it is, look where the leaf or leaflet attaches. There is a bud alongside the spot where a leaf's stem, or petiole, attaches to the twig. Sometimes the bud is tiny, but it's there. There is no bud where a leaflet attaches to the leaf stem. Snap off some leaves and leaflets and look closely. You'll find the bud next to the leaf scar on a simple leaf. But there won't be anything next to the leaflet scar. The bud next to a compound leaf is at its petiole base on the twig. Happy leaf snapping!

SIMPLE LEAF

SEVEN-LEAFLET COMPOUND LEAF

BUD

NO BUDS

Leaf Edges and Teeth

NORTHERN RED OAK

Think about the overall shape of a tree leaf or leaflet. Imagine tracing a leaf shape. Many are a uniform shape, such as oval, round, heart-shaped, triangular, or fan-shaped. But others have a less uniform outer shape, like a hand, star, or mitten. These deep indentations in leaf edges are called *lobes*.

The edges of lobed leaves have deep indentations.

The *margin*, or outer edge, of a leaf can have small indentations, too, called *teeth*. There are leaves and leaflets with smooth edges, toothed edges, and double-toothed edges.

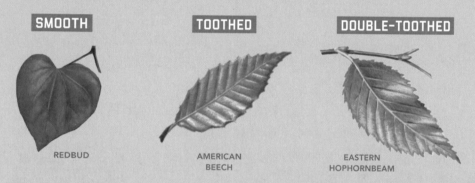

SMOOTH

REDBUD

TOOTHED

AMERICAN BEECH

DOUBLE-TOOTHED

EASTERN HOPHORNBEAM

Leaf Sides

Color isn't that useful for identifying leaves, unless it's autumn in the region you're in. (See Falling Colors on page 69.) Tree leaves are usually shades of green—shiny dark green, dusty light green, yellowish pale green, etc. But texture *does* matter. The thick, leathery, shiny leaves of a magnolia tree give it away for identification. Some trees have leaves that look different underneath than on top. When you're examining a leaf, always turn it over. Its underside could have a different

SILVER MAPLE

color, could be covered in hairs, or could be unlike the top of the leaf in some other way that clues you in to its identity.

Leaves are such terrific identifiers of trees. Each species has its own combination of leaf shape, size, edge, texture, and color characteristics that make it distinct. Now get outside and identify some tree leaves! The TRY IT section on page 70 is a great place to start.

Look for these leaf icons in the Broadleaf Trees Identification section on pages 100–154.

 OVAL **LOBED** **PALM** **NEEDLES** **COMPOUND**

Falling Colors

If you live somewhere with a winter season, there are likely trees that hand out helpful identification hints when the weather turns chilly. Deciduous trees drop most of their leaves in the fall. The water inside the leaves turns icy once temperatures drop below freezing and the leaves no longer make food. As days grow shorter and cold sets in,

SCARLET OAK

trees cut off the supply of water to their leaves. No water means that photosynthesis stops and the green chlorophyll in the leaves is no longer replenished.

It's all a fancy way to say that the leaves start changing colors. Once the green chlorophyll is gone, other colors show through on the leaves.

WITCH HAZEL

Some of those colors are characteristic of the kind of trees the leaves belong to. The leaves of aspen, birch, cottonwood, hickory, and witch hazel trees shine in yellow. Black gum, scarlet oak, red maple, and sumac go full-out red. Orange is the color of autumn sweet gum, sugar maple, and sassafras.

VINE MAPLE

TRY IT →

Tree Leaf Scavenger Hunt

Put all your newly learned leaf knowledge to the test!

STEP 1 Go to a park or nature area with a variety of trees.

STEP 2 Look at tree and shrub leaves. Find as many of these leaf characteristics as possible, then check them off when you do.

LEAF TYPES

☐ simple

☐ palmately compound

☐ pinnately compound

LEAF ARRANGEMENT

☐ opposite/paired

☐ alternate/unpaired

☐ whorled

LEAF SHAPE

☐ lobed

☐ toothed edge

☐ smooth-edged

LEAF SIDES

☐ leaf that looks different underneath

How?

I DID IT!

DATE:

TRACK IT ↘ Draw and Describe Tree Leaves

Record the distinguishing details of two different tree leaves.

STEP 1 Collect two different tree leaves. (Make sure you have permission to take them.) Record each leaf's location and check off the correct leaf arrangement on the chart on the next page.

STEP 2 Draw each leaf.

STEP 3 Record each leaf's characteristics with a detailed, field guide–like description. Include:

→ Leaf type (simple or compound, and if compound, palmately or pinnately)

→ Leaf shape (lobed, smooth or toothed edge)

→ Other unique details, such as hairs, texture, differences between top and underneath, etc.

CALIFORNIA LIVE OAK

RED BAY

STEP 4 Identify the tree that Leaf A or Leaf B came from using the Broadleaf Trees Identification section on pages 100–154. Nice work! Write the tree names on the chart, check off its I SPOTTED IT! box, and fill in the blanks.

LEAF A DATE	LEAF B DATE ....
LOCATION	LOCATION ....
Arrangement:	Arrangement:
☐ opposite ☐ alternate	☐ opposite ☐ alternate
☐ whorled	☐ whorled
DRAW THE LEAF:	DRAW THE LEAF:
Describe it:	Describe it:
What tree is it from?	What tree is it from?

I DID IT! DATE:

TAKE IT TO THE NEXT LEVEL ↗

Start a Leaf Specimen Collection

Press and save your sample leaves! Lay the leaves flat between two sheets of paper. Stack heavy books or rocks over the top paper. Dry the leaves for a week or two, depending on the humidity in your area and the leaves' sizes. Once dry, glue the leaves into a notebook for safekeeping. Figure out which trees the leaves came from, then write their names underneath each leaf!

→ Use your collection as flash cards to learn leaves and their tree names. Cover up the names and start quizzing yourself!

I DID IT! DATE:

CHAPTER 3

Identify Bark

There's something special about a winter hike through the woods. But the lack of leaves can make identifying bare trees a challenge. Luckily, trees are wrapped in a covering that provides clues to their identity. Bark! That's right, tree bark is used for recognizing different species of trees. And while especially helpful in winter, bark can be an important clue for tree identification all year round. After all, bark is always at your eye level, whereas leaves are sometimes too high to easily see. Plus, some trees have bark so distinctive that it practically screams the tree's name. Shagbark hickory (page 109) is a good example of having distinct bark—it's shaggy!

What Bark Is

Trees are plants that have wood stems. Bark is the outer protective layer of that wood. Like skin or shells, bark traps in moisture and protects trees from bugs and other gnawing creatures. Like a shirt, bark keeps out the cold and shields trees from scorching sun. Bark allows trees to live and grow in a single spot out in the open, surviving whatever nature delivers for decades to centuries. Bark is tough stuff!

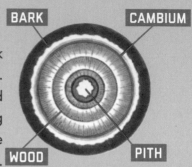

Underneath a tree's bark is the newest growing layer, or *cambium*. The *pith* is the oldest and softest part of the trunk.

A tree's bark is particular to its species. Beech bark is smooth and gray, while pine bark is dark and furrowed. The different textures, thicknesses, colors, and patterns of tree bark are useful for identification, but they also tell you about where the tree lives and how it survives. Insects have a harder time chewing into smooth bark. Thick bark holds in more moisture than thin bark. Trees with bark that sheds in strips or flakes are able to get rid of mosses and lichens that grow on them. Just like roots, leaves, and seeds, the bark on a tree adapts to its habitat and life cycle.

Bark Colors and Textures

Bark covers the stems, roots, branches, and twigs of trees, shrubs, and woody vines. But for tree identification, look for the bark that covers a tree's trunk. Both the Broadleaf and Conifer Trees Identification sections (pages 100–169) include descriptions and illustrations of each tree's bark.

AMERICAN SYCAMORE BARK

Bark characteristics vary mostly in texture and color. When you look at a forest of tree trunks, most of them will have brown or gray bark. But when you look closer, you'll notice some are pale gray while others are blackish brown, white, or even rusty red. Color patterns also give clues. A sycamore tree's trunk has splotchy cream, tan, and brown bark like a camouflage shirt. And many smooth-barked trees have prominent horizontal pores, called *lenticels*, that look like dashes going around the trunk.

LENTICELS

Smooth-barked trees have elastic bark that stretches as the tree gets larger, while other trees have bark that breaks as the tree matures. The outer bark layers crack and become rough with ridges and furrows. Below are eight common descriptive terms for bark textures:

SMOOTH	**FURROWED**	**SCALY**	**PLATED**
AMERICAN BEECH	BLACK OAK	WHITE PINE	PONDEROSA PINE
Stretched & sometimes has lenticels	Vertical valleys & ridges	Resembles overlapping scales or flakes	Divided into flat-topped plates
WARTY	**SHAGGY**	**FIBROUS**	**PAPERY**
COMMON HACKBERRY	SHAGBARK HICKORY	REDWOOD	PAPER BIRCH
Covered in irregular bumps	Curls & peels in vertical strips	Can be thick & looks like rope	Smooth & peels in horizontal bands

Old Bark, Young Bark

Using bark to identify a tree is trickier than using leaves. For example, red oak leaves have the same shape no matter what tree they came from. That's not always true with bark. It can vary from tree to tree of the same species because of environmental conditions like drought, insect infestations, and pollution.

SOUTHERN RED OAK

Age is a big variable in bark, too. A young tree or sapling's bark looks very different from that of a fully grown tree. The bark of super-old trees looks different, too. The bark of very old trees often becomes gnarled, thicker, scarred, and discolored over time. Bark identification works best on mature (but not ancient!) trees.

The bark of a young black cherry tree (left) is smooth, but mature trees have scaly bark (right).

YELLOW BIRCH

TRY IT → Explore Tree Bark

Find some tree trunks to see how different bark can be.

RIVER
BIRCH

> ## WHAT YOU'LL NEED

> ➤ A pencil or pen, a crayon, paper.

STEP 1 Walk around an area with different trees in a variety of habitats.

STEP 2 Look at mature tree trunks. How many kinds of bark can you find? Check off those you see.

BARK TYPES

- ☐ smooth
- ☐ furrowed
- ☐ scaly
- ☐ plated
- ☐ warty
- ☐ shaggy
- ☐ fibrous
- ☐ paper
- ☐ other ....

STEP 3 Make crayon rubbings on paper of a few different bark types you find.

I DID IT! DATE:

TRACK IT ↘ Tree Bark Type Comparison

Take a closer look to compare the bark of two different trees.

WHAT YOU'LL NEED

➢ A pencil or pen, scissors, tape.

STEP 1 Choose two different types of bark rubbings from the previous TRY IT activity to compare.

STEP 2 Fill in the chart below (and on the next page) for each tree.

→ Cut out a section from each of your bark rubbings that are big enough to show the recognizable bark patterns. Tape them onto the blank spaces.

→ Include color and texture in the description. Record any and all details about the thicknesses, patterns, lenticels, and any other observations.

BARK #1 DATE .... LOCATION ....

Bark Type:

Describe it:

Bark rubbing pattern:

What tree is it?

BARK #2 DATE.................... LOCATION ....

Bark Type:

Describe it:

Bark rubbing pattern:

What tree is it?

STEP 3 Identify the tree that either bark belongs to using the Broadleaf Trees Identification section on pages 100–154, then check off the I SPOTTED IT! box and fill in the blanks.

I DID IT! DATE:

TAKE IT TO THE **NEXT LEVEL** ↗

Bark Up Your State Tree

Research your state tree, then go find one! Pay attention to its bark, then make a crayon rubbing of it. Now describe the bark. Can you recognize the tree from just its bark?

YELLOW BUCKEYE

I DID IT! DATE:

TRY IT →

Observe Age: Count Tree Rings

Act like a tree scientist (or dendrologist) by counting its growth rings.

STEP 1 Find a tree stump or a cut log at a park or hiking trail, since crews often clear fallen trees from trails.

STEP 2 Once you find a trunk cross section, get counting! Here are some tips:

ONE GROWTH SEASON

→ Use the magnifying glass to help you see and count the dark rings.

→ Each dark ring marks the end of a growth season, so it is equal to one year in time. (The light part is what it grew that year.)

→ Start counting from the outside near the bark and work inward toward the center.

→ If there are many rings, mark each decade with the pencil. Then you won't have to go back and start all over if you lose count.

→ About how many years did the tree live?

I DID IT! DATE:

80

TRACK IT ↘

Measuring a tree's circumference, or girth, gives you a rough estimate of its age without cutting it down! Different species grow at different rates, and environmental conditions also affect size, so the age you calculate is only an estimate.

WHAT YOU'LL NEED

➢ A pencil or pen, a measuring tape with inches.

STEP 1 Record the tree's location and describe it. If you know what kind of tree it is, write it down.

STEP 2 Measure 4 feet off the ground. Wrap the measuring tape around the tree at this height. This length around the tree is its girth, or circumference. Write it down below.

STEP 3 Estimate the tree's age.

If the tree is out in the open and not shaded by other trees, the circumference in inches is its estimated age in years.

80 inches in girth = 80 years old

If the tree is in a shady forest, double the circumference (x 2) to get an estimate of its age.

80 inches in girth (x 2) = 160 years old

DATE

LOCATION

Tree description:

Type or species of tree?

Circumference in inches:

Estimated age:

I DID IT! DATE:

CHAPTER 4

Decoding Twigs and Buds

Bark isn't the only tree identification clue when leaves aren't around. The growing ends of tree branches—twigs—are another. Tree twigs, and the buds that grow on them, are characteristic of their species. Ash tree twigs look different from hickory tree twigs, and tulip tree buds aren't the same as maple buds. Observing and knowing about twigs and buds can tell you a lot about any tree. Twigs tell a tree's history and future!

From Twig to Branchlet

What most people call a twig and what a dendrologist calls a twig aren't necessarily the same thing. To tree experts, a twig isn't just any small stick. A twig is the very end of a tree or shrub branch. A twig is only the part that grew *this year*. Last year's growth is called a branchlet. (So this year's twig is next year's branchlet.) How can you tell where a branchlet ends and this year's twig starts? The spot is marked by a ring around the bark, an encircling *terminal bud scar*. The scar is where last year's terminal bud started sprouting.

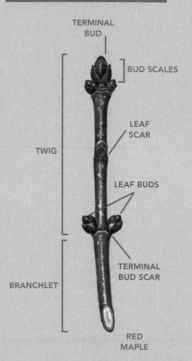

PARTS OF A WINTER TWIG

TERMINAL BUD

BUD SCALES

LEAF SCAR

TWIG

LEAF BUDS

TERMINAL BUD SCAR

BRANCHLET

RED MAPLE

This year's terminal bud is the very tip of the twig. At the end of the growing season, new, distinctive bark will cover the tip and become next year's terminal bud scar. See how branchlets and twigs record the past? You can also find leaf scars, which mark where last year's leaves were attached before dropping off in the fall. Leaf buds are found next to leaf scars, waiting to sprout into this year's leaves. If a tree has opposite leaves, like maples, its leaf scars and leaf buds are opposite. This is one way twigs provide clues to a tree's identity.

Color and Shape

The twigs of different tree species come in a variety of thicknesses, shapes, and even colors. Branchlets are usually gray-brown in color if they are on their way to becoming branches. Twigs, on the other hand, sprout bright green in the spring and can stay greenish, yellowish, or reddish into the winter. Many species of willows and dogwoods have colorful winter twigs.

COLORFUL WINTER TWIGS

DOGWOOD   RED MAPLE   WILLOW   ASPEN   YELLOW BIRCH   BEECH   BLACK CHERRY   RED OAK

Twigs of trees with opposite leaves are often straight, while twigs from alternate-leafed trees are more crooked or zigzag. Some shrubs and trees sprout small, short side twigs called *spur twigs* that often grow flower buds. Birch, Osage orange, apple trees, and even rosebushes have spur twigs.

ASH

LOCUST

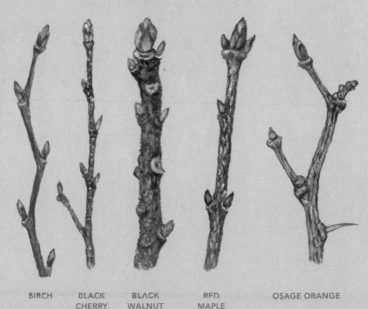

OSAGE ORANGE

Whether or not a twig is covered in small spots, called *lenticels*, is another characteristic that can help with identification. These are pores that some trees, like birches and cherries, have on their bark, too.

BIRCH   BLACK CHERRY   BLACK WALNUT   RED MAPLE   OSAGE ORANGE

Buds

You can also get a hint of the tree's identity by looking at the shapes and sizes of a twig's buds. A bud holds an immature stem, leaf, or flower that will soon sprout and grow. It's how twigs foretell the future! The terminal bud is at the very end of a twig. Many terminal buds are covered in protective coverings called *scales*. The size and shape of the terminal bud and its scales differ among trees. Horse chestnut trees have sticky terminal bud scales. Other trees have velvety scales or none at all.

TERMINAL
BUD

BUD SCALES

SHAGBARK
HICKORY

HORSE CHESTNUT

Leaf buds on the sides of twigs are usually smaller and pointier than rounder, bigger flower buds. Leaf and flower buds are also often covered in scales. The shapes, sizes, configurations, and characteristics of buds are other ways that species of trees differ and can aid in identification. This is especially true when trees are bare and leafless.

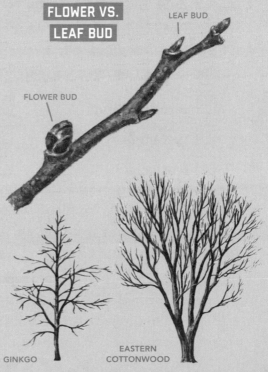

FLOWER VS. LEAF BUD

LEAF BUD

FLOWER BUD

GINKGO

EASTERN
COTTONWOOD

TRY IT → Winter Twig Walk

Learn about a tree's past and future by reading twigs! Late winter (February in the South or March in the North) is often the best time of year for twig watching. That's when last year's leaves are gone and buds are grown, but not yet open. Any time of year is great for finding terminal bud scars and lenticels, however. Get out there and try it!

WHAT YOU'LL NEED

➤ A pencil or pen, binoculars (optional).

RED
OAK

STEP 1 Go for a walk in a place with a variety of shorter deciduous, or broadleaf, trees.

STEP 2 Find a tree twig at the very end of a living branch. (Binoculars can help you spy on the twigs of tall trees.)

STEP 3 Look for these parts on a twig and check off the ones you see. (The diagram on page 82 will help.)

- ☐ terminal bud
- ☐ leaf buds
- ☐ lenticels
- ☐ bud scales
- ☐ leaf scars
- ☐ terminal bud scar

STEP 4 Find a twig from a different kind of tree. Circle the names of the parts you find on the list above. Did the second twig have the same parts as the first?

STEP 5 Identify either of the trees whose twigs you observed using the Broadleaf Trees Identification section on pages 100–154. Then check off its I SPOTTED IT! box and write a twiggy description in the notes.

I DID IT! DATE:

TRACK IT ↘ Decode a Twig

Dive into a closer study of one of the twigs you found.

WHAT YOU'LL NEED

➢ A pencil or pen, a magnifying glass.

STEP 1 Draw a branchlet and its twig you observed below. Label its parts, including: terminal bud, bud scales, leaf buds, leaf scars, lenticels, and terminal bud scar.

STEP 2 Color or shade in your drawing to differentiate last year's growth (branchlet) from this year's growth (twig).

RED MAPLE

DATE

LOCATION

TWIG DRAWING

STEP 3 Write a detailed, field guide–like description.

Include:

→ Twig color and shape (thick or slender, straight or zigzag)

→ Leaf buds' configuration (opposite or alternate)

→ Leaf buds' size and shape (pointy or round)

→ Terminal bud and scales description

AMERICAN SYCAMORE

RED ALDER

BLACK WALNUT

TWIG DESCRIPTION

I DID IT! DATE:

TAKE IT TO THE NEXT LEVEL ↗

Adopt a Branch

Is there a deciduous tree near you with an easy-to-see, low branch? Maybe one in your yard, out a window, or along a street that you pass by most weeks? Choose a day of the month. Then visit the branch on that day every month for a year. Make a sketch or snap a photo each time you go. Marvel at the changes its buds, leaves, and twigs go through during the year.

I DID IT! DATE:

CHAPTER 5

Know Your Conifers

CALIFORNIA
TORREYA

Not all trees are bare in winter. Most conifers are ever-green trees that hold on to their needlelike leaves all year round. And that makes these hardy leaves ideal for identification. (Needle-shedding bald cypress and larch trees are the exception. They're deciduous conifers.)

Conifers are trees that make cone-shaped seeds. Pines, firs, spruces, hemlocks, redwoods, cedars, larches, cypresses, yews, and junipers are all conifer trees. Conifers don't make flowers or fruits, either—they're gymnosperms. The word *gymnosperm* means "naked seed." Naked is exactly what the seeds are inside a cone—the seeds are bare and uncovered by any sort of pod, husk, or other kind of fruit. Flowering plants and trees are *angiosperms*, which means they have covered or encased seeds.

Cones allow conifers to reproduce. Both the male and female cones usually grow on the same tree. Male cones are soft and make pollen. Wind carries this pollen to the female cones, where fertilization happens and seeds grow.

GYMNOSPERM FAMILIES

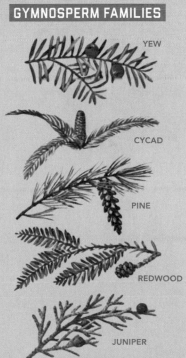

YEW

CYCAD

PINE

REDWOOD

JUNIPER

The female cones are larger and often woody. The seeds attach to structures on the cone called *scales*.

NAKED SEED

SCALE WITH SEED

SEED CONE

Ancient Giants

Conifer trees were around for millions of years before the first flower ever bloomed on earth. These ancient trees are some of the longest-living and tallest organisms on the planet today. Think giant sequoia and redwood trees—talk about big and tall! There are also bristlecone pines more than 4,700 years old.

But not all conifers are ancient or giant, and most have straight trunks, narrow branches, and tough, needle-like leaves. Conifers dominate the forests in northern climates and at high altitudes, but nearly all ecoregions have iconic conifers—such as desert junipers, rain forest hemlocks, and swamp bald cypresses.

GIANT SEQUOIA

Needles and Cones

Can you tell a pine from a spruce? Or a fir tree from a hemlock? Identifying conifers is all about paying attention to their leaves and seed cones. Here are the differences among the four most common needleleaf conifers.

EASTERN WHITE PINE

PINES Needles grow in long bundles of two or more. Cones have thick, woody, overlapping scales that grow from a central stem.

SPRUCE

SPRUCES Needles are short, stiff, and sharp (all S words, like *spruce*). Needles grow as singles all around a branch. Plucked needles leave a rough surface on their twig. Spruce cones hang downward and are filled with thin, paperlike, overlapping scales that grow from a central stem.

WHITE FIR

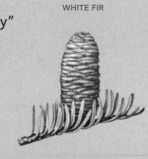

FIRS Needles are flexible, flat, and "friendly" (they won't poke you)—all words that start with F, like *fir*. Needles grow as singles all around a branch. Plucked needles leave round, smooth scars on their twig. Cones sit up on branches and have thin, papery scales.

HEMLOCK

HEMLOCKS Needles grow in singles with pale lines underneath, often on opposite sides of the twig like a feather. Cones are small and grow at the tips of drooping branches.

Scales and Berries

Not all conifers have needles. Some of them, like cedars and junipers, have scalelike leaves that are tiny, flat, and wrap tightly around the twig.

ATLANTIC WHITE CEDAR

PORT ORFORD CEDAR

NORTHERN WHITE CEDAR

WESTERN JUNIPER

Most cedars have small, wood cones, while junipers have soft cones, often called "berries."

NOTE While the common eastern red cedar tree (*Juniperus virginiana*) is the source of aromatic "cedar" wood, it is not a cedar. It has "berries," not cones, and is a kind of juniper tree.

EASTERN RED CEDAR

TRY IT → Check Out a Conifer

Find some evergreen trees near you!

WHAT YOU'LL NEED
➢ A pencil or pen.

STEP 1 Walk through your neighborhood or a nearby park. Look around for a tree or shrub with needlelike or scalelike leaves.

STEP 2 Fill in the chart below for an evergreen you find:

DATE

LOCATION

SIZE ☐ tree ☐ shrub

SHAPE ☐ triangular ☐ vase-shaped ☐ oval
☐ wide-spreading ☐ irregular

LEAVES ☐ scalelike ☐ needlelike

Sketch the needles or scalelike leaves:

Check off the species of conifer if you know it, or circle your best guess:

☐ pine ☐ fir ☐ spruce ☐ hemlock ☐ redwood
☐ cedar ☐ larch ☐ cypress ☐ yew ☐ juniper

What characteristics make you think it's the above type of conifer?

I DID IT! DATE:

93

TRACK IT ⭣   Identify a Conifer

Conifer leaves can look a lot alike. Sometimes, a leaf type key can help in conifer identification. An identification key is a step-by-step tool that helps determine which kind of plant or animal you're observing. Try this one out!

WHITE
SPRUCE

STEP 1 Find a conifer in a natural place. This key won't work for every living conifer, so a native tree is best.

STEP 2 Start with #1 on the key. Decide which description under #1 fits your tree best. Follow the key to the next number (#2 or #3). Keep going until you get to a conifer type in capital letters. That's your tree!

STEP 3 Determine the species of your conifer. Find your tree in the Conifer Trees Identification section on pages 155–169. Having trouble finding what you saw? Retrace the steps of the key to check your decisions. Once you're certain you've got the right tree, check off its I SPOTTED IT! box and fill in the blanks.

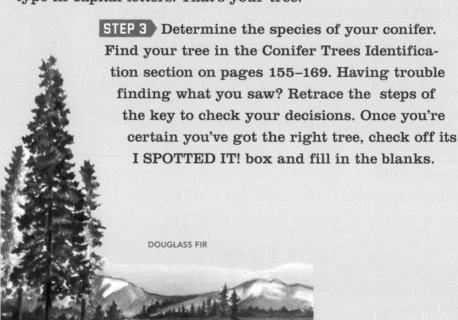

DOUGLASS FIR

Conifer Key

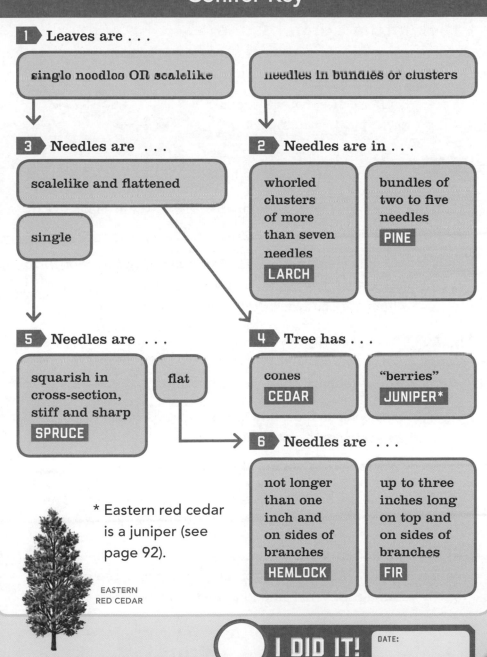

1 Leaves are . . .

single needles OR scalelike

needles in bundles or clusters

3 Needles are . . .

scalelike and flattened

single

2 Needles are in . . .

whorled clusters of more than seven needles
LARCH

bundles of two to five needles
PINE

5 Needles are . . .

squarish in cross-section, stiff and sharp
SPRUCE

flat

4 Tree has . . .

cones
CEDAR

"berries"
JUNIPER*

6 Needles are . . .

not longer than one inch and on sides of branches
HEMLOCK

up to three inches long on top and on sides of branches
FIR

* Eastern red cedar is a juniper (see page 92).

EASTERN
RED CEDAR

I DID IT!

DATE:

Crack into a Conifer Cone

Open up some cones yourself to see the seeds inside!

> **WHAT YOU'LL NEED** >
>
> ➣ Conifer cones, tweezers, paper towel, plastic sandwich bag.

LARCHES

STEP 1 Collect some mature, still-closed cones from a place where you have permission, like a relative's property. (Don't collect open cones with wide-open scales—their seeds are likely already gone.)

STEP 2 Set the cones in a warm, dry place until they open up, which may take a few days. While you are waiting, use the cones to identify the trees they came from.

STEP 3 Find the seeds on the inside of the scales once the cones open. Look closely! Use your tweezers to pull out the seeds without tearing their papery wings.

STEP 4 Do the seeds look like what you expected? What do you think their dispersal method is?

☐ wind   ☐ water   ☐ animals

STEP 5 Watch the conifer seeds sprout by placing them on a dampened paper towel inside a plastic sandwich bag.

STEP 6 Want to go back in time? Place one of the opened cones in a jar filled with water, and then close the lid so it stays submerged. What happens as the cone rehydrates?

I DID IT! DATE:

Plant Spotter Deep Dive: Profile a Tree

Ready to put all your expert tree knowledge together and dive deeper? Pick a favorite tree and profile it!

DATE

LOCATION

What's its shape?

How tall is it?

Age estimate:

Is it a conifer or a broadleaf tree?

What kind of leaves does it have?

Does it have fruit, flowers, or cones?

Describe its bark color and texture.

What kind of habitat does it live in?

Draw the tree: Draw a leaf:

What kind of tree is it?

Make sure to check off the I SPOTTED IT! box in the identification section and fill in the blanks. Superior effort, tree spotter!

I DID IT!   DATE:

TREE AND SHRUB IDENTIFICATION

Welcome to your Tree and Shrub Identification guide!

Here are some tips to get started, and where in the book you'll find more information:

→ The two main tree categories are broadleaf and conifer trees. Learn more on page 56.

→ Both trees and woody (bark-covered) shrubs are included under conifer and broadleaf trees.

PARTS OF A TREE

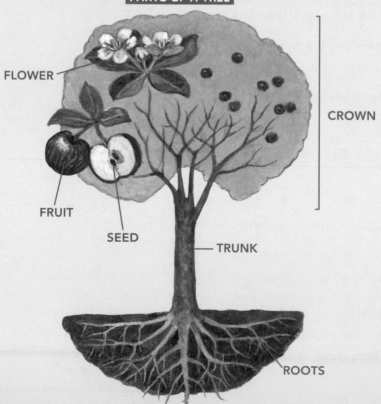

FLOWER

CROWN

FRUIT

SEED

TRUNK

ROOTS

Remember that the shapes, heights, and leaf and fruit sizes in these pages are averages. Fruits are often smaller during drier years, an oak tree in an open field has a wider shape than one in a crowded forest, and not every leaf on a branch is identical.

HEIGHT ranges are for mature trees that are old enough to make seeds and reproduce. In general, small trees are 30 feet (9 meters) tall or less; medium trees are 30–70 feet (9–21.5 meters) tall; and large trees are more than 70 feet (21.5 meters) in height.

SHAPE refers to the tree's overall crown shape (pages 58–59).

OVAL   TRIANGULAR   WIDE-SPREADING   VASE-SHAPED   IRREGULAR

LEAVES are identified by size and shape (pages 66–69). General shapes:

OVAL   LOBED   PALM   NEEDLES   COMPOUND

BARK describes the bark from the mature tree's trunk (pages 74–75).

FRUIT is whatever covers the seed—husk, nutshell, pod, samara, etc. (Pages 30–31.)

RANGE refers to the United States Department of Agriculture (USDA) Hardiness Zones (page 47).

American Sycamore

(Platanus occidentalis)

OVAL LOBED

REGIONAL NAMES American Planetree, Buttonball Tree

HEIGHT 60–100 feet (18.5–30.5 m)

SHAPE Tall, thick trunk, with a wide crown.

LEAVES 4–8 inches (10–20.5 cm) long and wide; large-toothed with 3–5 shallow lobes; alternate, simple.

BARK Mottled tan, gray, white, and green with peeling flakes.

FRUIT 1–1.5 inches (2.5–4 cm) long; single, round, bristled balls on long stems made up of hairy seeds.

HABITAT Moist and wet soils along streams, rivers, and bottomlands.

RANGE Eastern United States. Zones 4–9.

POINT OF FACT It's the most massive tree east of the Rocky Mountains, with trunks that reach widths of 10 feet (3 m).

WINTER

I SPOTTED IT!

WHEN I SAW IT
DATE

WHERE I SAW IT
SPECIFIC LOCATION, INCLUDE STATE

NOTES

Tulip Tree
(Liriodendron tulipifera)

OVAL   LOBED

REGIONAL NAMES Yellow Poplar, Tulip Poplar

HEIGHT 50–100 feet (15–30.5 m)

SHAPE Tall with a thick, straight trunk.

LEAVES 3–7 inches (7.5–18 cm) long; 4–lobed; alternate, simple.

BARK Gray with ridges and lighter gray furrows.

FRUIT Cone-shaped cluster of paper-thin, light brown samaras on the ends of twigs.

HABITAT Damp forests and parks with moist soil.

RANGE Eastern United States. Zones 4–9.

POINT OF FACT It earned its name because of its leaves with pointed tips in a tulip-like shape, as well as its large, cup-shaped flowers.

I SPOTTED IT!

WHEN I SAW IT
DATE

WHERE I SAW IT
SPECIFIC LOCATION, INCLUDE STATE

NOTES

....

....

Sassafras

(Sassafras albidum)

OVAL

LOBED

REGIONAL NAMES White Sassafras, Cinnamon Wood, Mittenleaf

HEIGHT 10–50 feet (3–15 m)

SHAPE Small to medium with many thick branches and sparse leaves.

LEAVES 4–6 inches (10–15 cm) long; dark green with a shiny top and dull underneath; oval or 2–3 lobes; alternate, simple.

BARK Rough, deep furrows.

FRUIT Dark blue berries on red stalks.

HABITAT Forest edges and understories, old fields, and hedgerows.

RANGE Eastern United States. Zones 4–9.

POINT OF FACT Sassafras roots provided the original flavoring for root beer. Crush a leaf to smell its aromatic oil!

I SPOTTED IT!

WHEN I SAW IT
DATE

WHERE I SAW IT
SPECIFIC LOCATION,
INCLUDE STATE

NOTES

Sweet Gum

(Liquidambar styraciflua)

OVAL   LOBED

HEIGHT 50–120 feet (15–36.5 m)

SHAPE Medium to tall with a straight trunk.

LEAVES 5–8 inches (12.5–20.5 cm) long; star-shaped, 5–7 lobes; alternate, simple.

BARK Gray-brown with ridges.

FRUIT 1 inch (2.5 cm) long; long-stemmed, woody, prickly ball.

HABITAT Swamps, bottomlands, old fields, and parks.

RANGE Eastern United States. Zones 5–9.

POINT OF FACT Its spiky brown fruits, called gumballs, fall to the ground in winter, which some people use as Christmas decorations.

I SPOTTED IT!

WHEN I SAW IT
DATE

WHERE I SAW IT
SPECIFIC LOCATION,
INCLUDE STATE

NOTES

American Elm

(Ulmus americana)

VASE OVAL

REGIONAL NAMES Soft Elm, White Elm

HEIGHT 60–100 feet (18.5–30.5 m)

SHAPE Medium to tall with a straight trunk that divides into two or more trunks; V shape with arching branches.

LEAVES 4–6 inches (10–15 cm) long; toothed edges; pointed oval shape; dark green; alternate, simple.

BARK Furrowed in narrow, interlacing scalelike ridges with light patches on the cross section.

FRUIT 0.5 inch (1.5 cm) long; round, hairy-edged wafers with notches at the tips.

HABITAT Near rivers, streams, towns, and parks.

RANGE Eastern United States to Rocky Mountains and Southern Canada. Zones 3–9.

POINT OF FACT An introduced fungal organism called Dutch elm disease killed most of these large trees in the twentieth century, which used to be common shade and street trees.

◖ I SPOTTED IT! ▷

WHEN I SAW IT
DATE

WHERE I SAW IT
SPECIFIC LOCATION,
INCLUDE STATE

NOTES

....

....

Common Hackberry

(Celtis occidentalis)

WIDE-SPREADING   OVAL

REGIONAL NAMES Northern Hackberry, Sugarberry Tree, False Elm, Beaverwood

HEIGHT 60–100 feet (18.5–30.5 m)

SHAPE Medium with a straight trunk and a wide crown, with messy branches tipped in twig clumps called witches' brooms.

LEAVES 3–5 inches (7.5–12.5 cm) long; pointed ovals; toothed edges and a lopsided base; alternate, simple.

BARK Dark gray with many warty knobs.

FRUIT 0.5 inch (1.5 cm) long; dark, red-brown berry that wrinkles as it dries.

HABITAT Floodplains and along streams, river valleys, and woods.

RANGE Eastern and Central United States. Zones 3–9.

POINT OF FACT It's a wildlife restaurant! Its "sugarberries" are energy-filled food for birds and other animals, and its leaves are snacks for numerous kinds of butterfly caterpillars.

I SPOTTED IT!

WHEN I SAW IT
DATE

WHERE I SAW IT
SPECIFIC LOCATION, INCLUDE STATE

NOTES

Osage Orange
(Maclura pomifera)

WIDE-
SPREADING   OVAL

REGIONAL NAMES Hedge Apple, Bois-d'Arc

HEIGHT 40–60 feet (12–18.5 m)

SHAPE Medium with a short trunk and a wide, dense crown.

LEAVES 3–6 inches (7.5–15 cm) long; smooth-edged ovals with pointed tips; alternate, simple.

BARK Deeply split into furrows and peeled strips that reveal orange underneath.

FRUIT 5 inches (12.5 cm) long; bumpy and heavy green balls.

HABITAT Woods, old fields, and moist soils.

RANGE Eastern and Central United States. Zones 4–9.

POINT OF FACT Ranchers planted this thorny tree to make living barbed-wire fences, extending the tree's range far beyond its native region in Texas and Oklahoma.

I SPOTTED IT!

WHEN I SAW IT
DATE

WHERE I SAW IT
SPECIFIC LOCATION,
INCLUDE STATE

NOTES

....

....

Red Mulberry

(Morus rubra)

WIDE SPREADING   OVAL

REGIONAL NAMES American Mulberry

HEIGHT 35–50 feet (10.5–15 m)

SHAPE Small to medium with a short trunk and a wide, thick crown.

LEAVES 4–10 inches (10–25.5 cm) long; dark green and rough on top with toothed edges; wide oval or 2–3 lobed shape and a pointed tip; alternate, simple.

BARK Brown with red tint and wide, scalelike ridges.

FRUIT 1 inch (2.5 cm) long; purple to black berry on a long stalk.

HABITAT Edges of woods and fields and moist backyards.

RANGE Eastern United States. Zones 5–9.

POINT OF FACT This tree's sweet, juicy fruits resemble blackberries and are sought after by birds, groundhogs, and pie makers alike.

◖ I SPOTTED IT! ▷

WHEN I SAW IT
DATE

WHERE I SAW IT
SPECIFIC LOCATION, INCLUDE STATE

NOTES

....

....

Black Walnut

(Juglans nigra)

OVAL COMPOUND

HEIGHT 50–90 feet (15–27.5 m)

SHAPE Tall with a straight trunk and a rounded crown.

LEAVES 12–24 inches (30.5–61 cm) long with 15–23 toothed, pointy-tipped leaflets between 2–4 inches (5–10 cm); alternate, compound.

BARK Dark brown to black with rough furrows in a diamond pattern.

FRUIT 2 inches (5 cm) long; dense, green ball with a strong smell.

HABITAT Moist forests, yards, and parks.

RANGE Eastern United States. Zones 4–9.

POINT OF FACT The dark oil of the husks can be turned into dye, ink, and shoe polish—it stains hands, too.

◉ I SPOTTED IT!

WHEN I SAW IT
DATE

WHERE I SAW IT
SPECIFIC LOCATION,
INCLUDE STATE

NOTES

....

....

Shagbark Hickory

(Carya ovata)

OVAL COMPOUND

HEIGHT 60–90 feet (18.5–27.5 m)

SHAPE Medium to large with a straight trunk and a rounded crown.

LEAVES 8–12 inches (20.5–30.5 cm) long with 5 toothed, hairy-edged leaflets about 5 inches (13 cm) long; compound, opposite.

BARK Gray with long, shaggy, curling strips.

FRUIT 1.5 inches (4 cm) long; pale green, nearly round fruit that splits open when the nut inside is ripe.

HABITAT Hillsides, streams, and river valleys.

RANGE Eastern United States. Zones 4–8.

POINT OF FACT Its shaggy bark sets in when the tree is mature enough to produce its tasty nuts.

I SPOTTED IT!

WHEN I SAW IT
DATE

WHERE I SAW IT
SPECIFIC LOCATION,
INCLUDE STATE

NOTES

....

....

American Beech

(Fagus grandifolia)

OVAL   OVAL

REGIONAL NAMES Gray Beech, Carolina Beech

HEIGHT 60–80 feet (18.5–24.5 m)

SHAPE Tall with a short trunk and thick branches.

LEAVES 2–4 inches (5–10 cm) long; sharp-pointed, toothed edges; alternate, simple.

BARK Gray and smooth.

FRUIT 0.75 inch (2 cm) long; brown, prickly pod with 1–3 triangular nuts inside.

HABITAT Mixed forests, hillsides, and moist woods.

RANGE Eastern United States. Zones 4–9.

POINT OF FACT It holds on to some of its faded, straw-colored leaves throughout the winter. Beechnuts are edible and sought after by birds, mammals, and other wildlife.

I SPOTTED IT!

WHEN I SAW IT
DATE

WHERE I SAW IT
SPECIFIC LOCATION,
INCLUDE STATE

NOTES

Box Elder
(Acer negundo)

WIDE-SPREADING

COMPOUND

REGIONAL NAMES Ash-leaf Maple, Three-leaf Maple, Manitoba Maple

HEIGHT 30–70 feet (9–21.5 m)

SHAPE Medium with a short trunk and rounded crown.

LEAVES 4–10 inches (10–25.5 cm) long; 3–5 smooth, jagged-edged leaflets, 3.5 inches (9 cm); compound, alternate.

BARK Gray–brown with furrows.

FRUIT 1.75 inches (4.5 cm) long; V-shaped, paired, papery-winged samaras.

HABITAT River bottoms and near ponds, streams, and moist woods.

RANGE United States and Southern Canada. Zones 3–9.

POINT OF FACT Its name comes from its leaflets, which look like elder bush leaves, and from its soft wood, which is useful for box making.

I SPOTTED IT!

WHEN I SAW IT
DATE

WHERE I SAW IT
SPECIFIC LOCATION, INCLUDE STATE

NOTES

....

....

Silver Maple

(Acer saccharinum)

OVAL   LOBED

REGIONAL NAMES Swamp Maple, River Maple, Soft Maple, White Maple

HEIGHT 40–100 feet (12–30.5 m)

SHAPE Medium to large with a short trunk and wide crown.

LEAVES 5–7 inches (12.5–18 cm) long; 5–lobed with large teeth; pale green on top with silver underneath; opposite, simple.

BARK Dark and gray-brown with long, narrow, scalelike strips that become shaggy with age.

FRUIT 1.75 inches (4.5 cm) long; bright green V-shaped, paired, and papery-winged samaras.

HABITAT Wet areas and near rivers, swamps, and ponds.

RANGE Eastern United States. Zones 3–9.

POINT OF FACT It's named for its leaves' silvery undersides, which catch light and glint when the wind blows.

I SPOTTED IT!

WHEN I SAW IT
DATE

WHERE I SAW IT
SPECIFIC LOCATION, INCLUDE STATE

NOTES

....

....

Sugar Maple
(Acer saccharum)

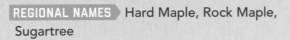

OVAL   LOBED

REGIONAL NAMES Hard Maple, Rock Maple, Sugartree

HEIGHT 70–100 feet (21.5–30.5 m)

SHAPE Medium to tall with a straight trunk and rounded crown.

LEAVES 4–6 inches (10–15 cm) long; 5–lobed with sparse teeth; opposite, simple.

DARK Gray-brown with furrows.

FRUIT 1 inch (2.5 cm) long; paired, papery-winged samaras.

HABITAT Woodlands, parks, and yards.

RANGE Eastern United States and Canada. Zones 4–8.

POINT OF FACT Its sweet sap is the source of most maple syrup.

◗ I SPOTTED IT!

WHEN I SAW IT
DATE

WHERE I SAW IT
SPECIFIC LOCATION, INCLUDE STATE

NOTES

....

....

Flowering Dogwood
(Cornus florida)

WIDE-SPREADING   **OVAL**

HEIGHT 15–40 feet (4.5–12 m)

SHAPE Small with a short trunk and spread branches.

LEAVES 3–6 inches (7.5–15 cm) long; smooth-edged oval shape; curving veins; opposite, simple.

BARK Gray with small, square, and scalelike blocks.

FLOWER Small, greenish cluster surrounded by large, showy white bracts.

FRUIT 0.5 inch (1.5 cm) long; clusters of football-shaped, bright red berries called drupes.

HABITAT Woodland hillsides and understories.

RANGE Eastern United States. Zones 5–8.

POINT OF FACT Its beautiful springtime "flowers" are actually white, petal-like, notch-tipped bracts, which are the opened leaves that enclose the tiny flowers inside.

I SPOTTED IT!

WHEN I SAW IT
DATE

WHERE I SAW IT
SPECIFIC LOCATION, INCLUDE STATE

NOTES

Honey Locust
(Gleditsia triacanthos)

VASE   COMPOUND

REGIONAL NAMES Thorny Locust, Sweet Locust

HEIGHT 30–80 feet (9–24.5 m)

SHAPE Medium with a straight trunk and wide crown.

LEAVES 6 inches (15 cm) long; 15–30 dark green leaflets, 1 inch (2.5 cm); alternate, pinnately compound.

BARK Dark gray-brown with wide ridges that peel on the sides.

FRUIT 8 inches (20.5 cm) long; dark red-brown pods with a sweet pulp and seeds inside.

HABITAT Woods, old fields, parks, and yards.

RANGE United States. Zones 4–9.

POINT OF FACT In the wild, this tree grows sharp thorns on its branches and trunk up to 12 inches (30.5 cm) long. The thorns likely discouraged browsing by mastodons and other now extinct giant mammals.

I SPOTTED IT!

WHEN I SAW IT
DATE

WHERE I SAW IT
SPECIFIC LOCATION,
INCLUDE STATE

NOTES

Northern Catalpa
(Catalpa speciosa)

OVAL   OVAL

REGIONAL NAMES Cigar Tree, Caterpillar Tree, Catawba Tree

HEIGHT 40–60 feet (12–18.5 m)

SHAPE Medium with stout branches and a wide crown.

LEAVES 6–12 inches (15–30.5 cm) long; dull green and heart-shaped; opposite or whorled, simple.

BARK Dark gray-brown and scaly.

FLOWER 2 inches (5 cm) long with a tubular shape; white with purple spots in the center.

FRUIT 10–20 inches (25.5–51 cm) long; brown bean-like capsule.

HABITAT Moist woods, edges of woods and fields, yards, and parks.

RANGE Eastern United States. Zones 4–8.

POINT OF FACT It's also called the "caterpillar tree" because catalpa sphinx moth larvae eat the tree's leaves.

I SPOTTED IT!

WHEN I SAW IT
DATE

WHERE I SAW IT
SPECIFIC LOCATION, INCLUDE STATE

NOTES

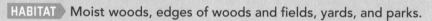

American Basswood

(Tilia americana)

OVAL OVAL

REGIONAL NAMES American Linden, Basswood

HEIGHT 60–80 feet (18.5–24.5 m)

SHAPE Medium to large with a short trunk and rounded crown.

LEAVES 5–8 inches (12.5–20.5 cm) long; dark green, wide, and heart-shaped with pointy tips; alternate, simple.

BARK Dark gray with interlaced ridges.

FRUIT 0.25 inch (0.5 cm) long; round nuts that hang in clusters.

HABITAT Moist forests and lowlands.

RANGE Eastern and Central United States. Zones 3–8.

POINT OF FACT As its name suggests, this tree's wood is used to make instruments.

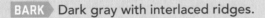

◗ I SPOTTED IT! ▷

WHEN I SAW IT
DATE

WHERE I SAW IT
SPECIFIC LOCATION,
INCLUDE STATE

NOTES

....

....

Northern Red Oak

(Quercus rubra)

OVAL LOBED

REGIONAL NAMES Red Oak, Gray Oak

HEIGHT 60–100 feet (18.5–30.5 m)

SHAPE Medium to large with a tall trunk and wide crown.

LEAVES 4–9 inches (10–23 cm) long; tapered edges with red stalks; 7–11 toothed, pointed, shallow lobes; alternate, simple.

BARK Dark brown to black with long, wide, smooth ridges and shallow furrows.

FRUIT 1–1.5 inches (2.5–4 cm) long; tightly capped greenish acorn that turns brown after dropping.

HABITAT Woods, hillsides, valleys, parks, and yards.

RANGE Eastern United States. Zones 3–7.

POINT OF FACT Once introduced into Europe in the 1700s because of its timber value, this tree has since been labeled an invasive species in some areas.

◗ I SPOTTED IT! ▸

WHEN I SAW IT
DATE

WHERE I SAW IT
SPECIFIC LOCATION, INCLUDE STATE

NOTES ▸

....

....

Live Oak
(Quercus virginiana)

WIDE-SPREADING   **OVAL**

REGIONAL NAMES Southern Live Oak, Encino, Coastal Live Oak, Virginia Live Oak

HEIGHT 50–80 feet (15–24.5 m)

SHAPE Small to large with thick, horizontally spread branches and a huge crown.

LEAVES 2–4 inches (5–10 cm) long; ovals; dark, shiny green on top and silver underneath; sometimes toothed; alternate, simple.

BARK Dark, rough, scalelike blocks.

FRUIT 0.5–1.5 inches (1.5–2.5 cm) long; slender acorn on a long stalk.

HABITAT Open woods, edges of wetlands, yards, and roadsides.

RANGE Southeastern United States. Zones 8–10.

POINT OF FACT This evergreen oak stays covered in leaves all winter long due to its warm climate.

I SPOTTED IT!

WHEN I SAW IT
DATE

WHERE I SAW IT
SPECIFIC LOCATION, INCLUDE STATE

NOTES

White Oak

(Quercus alba)

WIDE-SPREADING **LOBED**

REGIONAL NAMES Stave Oak, Forkleaf Oak, Eastern White Oak, Ridge White Oak

HEIGHT 60–100 feet (18.5–30.5 m)

SHAPE Medium to large with a wide, irregular crown.

LEAVES 5–7 inches (12.5–18 cm) long; dull green; shallow, rounded lobes with smooth edges; alternate, simple.

BARK Dark peeling ridges or small blocks.

FRUIT 0.5–0.75 inch (1.5–2 cm) long; green acorn with a short stalk.

HABITAT Woods, yards, and parks.

RANGE Eastern United States. Zones 3–9.

POINT OF FACT Its wood is used to make staves, which are the narrow strips in a wooden barrel that are held together by metal hoops.

I SPOTTED IT!

WHEN I SAW IT
DATE

WHERE I SAW IT
SPECIFIC LOCATION, INCLUDE STATE

NOTES

....

....

Valley Oak
(Quercus lobata)

WIDE-SPREADING   **LOBED**

REGIONAL NAMES Weeping Oak, California White Oak, Water Oak

HEIGHT 40–60 feet (12–18.5 m)

SHAPE Medium to large with a short trunk, thick, drooping branches, and a wide crown.

WINTER

LEAVES 2–4 inches (5–10 cm) long; 7–11 deep, rounded lobes; alternate, simple.

BARK Dark gray and scalelike with furrows.

FRUIT 1–2 inches (2.5–5 cm) long; brown, pointy acorn.

HABITAT Grasslands, valleys, and low hills.

RANGE California. Zones 8–10.

POINT OF FACT One famous tree, the Henley Oak in Mendocino County, may be more than five hundred years old and is as tall as the Statue of Liberty.

I SPOTTED IT!

WHEN I SAW IT
DATE

WHERE I SAW IT
SPECIFIC LOCATION, INCLUDE STATE

NOTES

....

....

Bur Oak
(Quercus macrocarpa)

WIDE-SPREADING   **LOBED**

REGIONAL NAMES Mossy–Cup Oak, Blue Oak, Burr Oak

HEIGHT 50–100 feet (15–30.5 m)

SHAPE Small in northern ranges, but medium to large in others.

LEAVES 6–12 inches (15–30.5 cm) long; many deep lobes; alternate, simple.

BARK Pale gray, chunky, rectangular blocks.

FRUIT 1–2 inches (2.5–5 cm) long; large acorn covered in a rough cap with shaggy, mosslike bristles.

HABITAT Wet bottomlands, sandy ridges, yards, and parks.

RANGE South Central Canada and Central United States. Zones 3–8.

POINT OF FACT It has the largest acorn of any native oak species, and its species name, *macrocarpa*, means "large fruit" in Greek.

I SPOTTED IT!

WHEN I SAW IT
DATE

WHERE I SAW IT
SPECIFIC LOCATION, INCLUDE STATE

NOTES

Paper Birch
(Betula papyrifera)

OVAL   OVAL

REGIONAL NAMES Canoe Birch, White Birch, Silver Birch

HEIGHT 50–70 feet (15–21.5 m)

SHAPE Medium with a slender trunk and narrow crown.

LEAVES 2–4 inches (5–10 cm) long; double-toothed edges; pale underneath; alternate, simple.

BARK Peeling and white with thin, dark, horizontal lines.

FRUIT 1 inch (2.5 cm) long; stout, cone-like shape that's brown and dry.

HABITAT Open woods and forest edges.

RANGE Northern United States and Canada. Zones 2–6.

POINT OF FACT Humans have used its waterproof bark to make canoes, baskets, and shelters for centuries.

I SPOTTED IT!

WHEN I SAW IT
DATE

WHERE I SAW IT
SPECIFIC LOCATION,
INCLUDE STATE

NOTES

Red Alder

(Alnus rubra)

OVAL   OVAL

REGIONAL NAMES Oregon Alder

HEIGHT 30–80 feet (9–24.5 m)

SHAPE Medium with a straight trunk, slender branches, and a narrow crown.

LEAVES 3–6 inches (7.5–15 cm) long; smooth green on top and pale green with red hairs along veins underneath; double-toothed margin with rounded teeth.

BARK Smooth gray with light splotches and dark branch scars.

FRUIT Small, woody, brown, and cone-like.

HABITAT Open areas, woods, and sides of streams.

RANGE Pacific Northwest and Coast from Alaska to California. Zones 6–8.

POINT OF FACT A fast-growing pioneer tree, it's often the first to grow after a fire or forest clearing.

I SPOTTED IT!

WHEN I SAW IT
DATE

WHERE I SAW IT
SPECIFIC LOCATION, INCLUDE STATE

NOTES

American Plum

(Prunus americana)

WIDE-SPREADING **OVAL**

HEIGHT 15–30 feet (4.5–9 m)

SHAPE Small tree or shrub with a short trunk; thorny and thicket–forming.

LEAVES 2–4 inches (5–10 cm) long; sharp, double-toothed edges with a pointed tip; alternate, simple.

BARK Brown and scaly.

FRUIT 1 inch (2.5 cm) long; red or yellow smooth-skinned balls.

HABITAT Woods, old fields, and sides of streams.

RANGE Central and Eastern United States. Zones 3–8.

POINT OF FACT A member of the rose family, its white flowers are lovely to see—but not always smell. They have a sickly sweet, pungent scent.

I SPOTTED IT!

WHEN I SAW IT
DATE

WHERE I SAW IT
SPECIFIC LOCATION,
INCLUDE STATE

NOTES

125

Black Hawthorn

(Crataegus douglasii)

WIDE-SPREADING   OVAL

HEIGHT Up to 25 feet (7.5 m)

SHAPE Short and shrub-like with tangled, thorny branches.

LEAVES 1–2 inches (2.5–5 cm) long; dark green; wide, toothed, and sometimes lobed; alternate, simple.

BARK Gray, rough, and scaly.

FRUIT 0.5 inch (1.5 cm) long; shiny black balls.

HABITAT Mountains, valleys, streams, and pastures.

RANGE Southwestern Canada and Western United States. Zones 3–9.

POINT OF FACT There are as many as one hundred species of hawthorn in North America.

WINTER

I SPOTTED IT!

WHEN I SAW IT
DATE

WHERE I SAW IT
SPECIFIC LOCATION,
INCLUDE STATE

NOTES

Curl-Leaf Mountain Mahogany

(Cercocarpus ledifolius)

WIDE-
SPREADING   OVAL

REGIONAL NAMES Desert Cercocarpus, Curl-Leaf Cercocarpus

HEIGHT Up to 25 feet (7.5 m)

SHAPE Shrub or small tree with stout branches.

LEAVES 0.5–1 inch (1.5–2.5 cm) long; leathery, evergreen, spear-shaped, glossy green on top, and fuzzy below; smooth, curled-under edges; alternate, simple.

BARK Dark with narrow ridges.

FRUIT Small, woody capsule with a feathery 2-inch (5-cm) long plume.

HABITAT Dry mountains.

RANGE Western United States. Zones 3–8.

POINT OF FACT Winds catch and carry off the feathery-tailed seeds in the summer.

I SPOTTED IT!

WHEN I SAW IT
DATE

WHERE I SAW IT
SPECIFIC LOCATION,
INCLUDE STATE

NOTES

Hercules' Club

(Zanthoxylum clava–herculis)

OVAL COMPOUND

REGIONAL NAMES Toothache Tree, Devil's Walking Stick, Southern Prickly-Ash

HEIGHT 15–25 feet (4.5–7.5 m)

SHAPE Shrub or small tree with a short trunk and spiny twigs.

LEAVES 6–8 inches (15–20.5 cm) long; red stalks with thorns; 7–17 pointed, toothed leaflets, 1–2.5 inches (2.5–6.5 cm); alternate, odd-pinnately compound.

BARK Gray with spiny knobs.

FRUIT Small, dark red berries in clusters that turn black as they ripen.

HABITAT Forest understories, fencerows, and along streams and rivers.

RANGE Southeastern United States. Zones 7–9.

POINT OF FACT It's called the "toothache tree" because its bark was once used as an anesthetic.

I SPOTTED IT!

WHEN I SAW IT
DATE

WHERE I SAW IT
SPECIFIC LOCATION,
INCLUDE STATE

NOTES

....

....

Common Sumac
(Rhus glabra)

VASE COMPOUND

REGIONAL NAMES > Smooth Sumac

HEIGHT > 10–20 feet (3–6 m)

SHAPE > Shrub or thin tree with vase-shaped branches.

LEAVES > 12–18 inches (30.5–45.5 cm) long; 11–31 narrow, pointed, and toothed leaflets; alternate, pinnately compound.

BARK > Gray, thin, and smooth.

FRUIT > Small red berries in pointy clusters.

HABITAT > Fields and roadsides.

RANGE > Across the United States. Zones 3–9.

POINT OF FACT > Birds and mammals eat the seeds in winter, and it's the host plant of many hairstreak butterflies.

I SPOTTED IT!

WHEN I SAW IT
DATE

WHERE I SAW IT
SPECIFIC LOCATION,
INCLUDE STATE

NOTES

American Holly

(Ilex opaca)

TRIANGLE   OVAL

REGIONAL NAMES White Holly, Christmas Holly

HEIGHT 20–50 feet (6–15 m)

SHAPE Shrub or small cone-shaped tree.

LEAVES 2–4 inches (5–10 cm) long; stiff, shiny dark fronds with pointed, toothed edges; alternate, simple.

BARK Pale gray and smooth.

FRUIT Clusters of red berries, 0.25–0.3 inch (0.5–1 cm) long.

HABITAT Understories of open woods, coastal plains, and yards.

RANGE Eastern United States. Zones 5–9.

POINT OF FACT Only the female trees make the berry fruits, which need to be pollinated by a nearby male tree.

I SPOTTED IT!

WHEN I SAW IT
DATE

WHERE I SAW IT
SPECIFIC LOCATION,
INCLUDE STATE

NOTES

American Hornbeam

(Carpinus caroliniana)

VASE   OVAL

REGIONAL NAMES Musclewood, Ironwood, Blue Beech, Water Beech

HEIGHT 20–35 feet (6–10.5 m)

SHAPE Small, vase-shaped tree with a short trunk and low branches.

LEAVES 2–4 inches (5–10 cm) long; double-toothed edges with pointed tips; pale green underneath; alternate, simple.

BARK Smooth, blue-gray with muscle-like, rippling bulges.

FRUIT Three-lobed papery-winged samaras.

HABITAT Understories of woods, along streams, and swamps.

RANGE Eastern and Central United States. Zones 3–9.

POINT OF FACT Pioneers called it "ironwood" because its tough wood dulled their axes and saws.

I SPOTTED IT!

WHEN I SAW IT
DATE

WHERE I SAW IT
SPECIFIC LOCATION, INCLUDE STATE

NOTES

Ginkgo
(Ginkgo biloba)

OVAL   OVAL

REGIONAL NAMES Stinkbomb Tree, Golden Fossil Tree

HEIGHT 40–80 feet (12–24.5 m)

SHAPE Medium to large with a rounded crown.

LEAVES 3 inches (7.5 cm) long; wide and fan-shaped, often with a single notch; alternate, simple.

BARK Pale gray with furrows and flat ridges.

FRUIT 1 inch (2.5 cm) long; orange, foul-smelling oval balls on a long stalk.

HABITAT Yards, parks, and roadsides.

RANGE Non-native, but widely planted across the United States. Zones 4–8.

POINT OF FACT This 270 million-year-old "living fossil" deciduous gymnosperm tree is not a conifer.

WINTER

I SPOTTED IT!

WHEN I SAW IT
DATE

WHERE I SAW IT
SPECIFIC LOCATION,
INCLUDE STATE

NOTES

Black Willow

(Salix nigra)

WIDE-SPREADING   **OVAL**

REGIONAL NAMES › Swamp Willow, American Willow

HEIGHT › 30–60 feet (9–18.5 m)

SHAPE › Medium with more than one trunk, irregular, wide-spreading branches, and clumpy twigs.

LEAVES › 3–6 inches (7.5–15 cm) long; narrow and fine-toothed; pale underneath; alternate, simple.

BARK › Dark brown with rough ridges.

FRUIT › Pointed, cone-shaped, green capsules with cottony seeds inside.

HABITAT › Wet areas near water, stream banks, riversides, swamps, and lakes.

RANGE › Eastern United States. Zones 4–9.

POINT OF FACT › It's often planted to stop erosion along streams and rivers because of its soil-grasping roots.

I SPOTTED IT!

WHEN I SAW IT
DATE

WHERE I SAW IT
SPECIFIC LOCATION, INCLUDE STATE

NOTES

Sandbar Willow

(Salix exigua subspecies)

WIDE-SPREADING   OVAL

REGIONAL NAMES Narrowleaf Willow, Coyote Willow

HEIGHT 6–20 feet (2–6 m)

SHAPE Shrub or small tree that grows in thickets.

LEAVES 2–6 inches (5–15 cm) long and very narrow; wide-toothed; yellow-green with a pale underside; alternate, simple.

BARK Dark red-brown and scaly.

FRUIT Pointed, cone-shaped, green capsules with silky seeds inside.

HABITAT Along rivers and streams.

RANGE United States and Canada. Zones 4–7.

POINT OF FACT Basket weavers weave its flexible twigs into baskets and its bark into string.

◉ I SPOTTED IT!

WHEN I SAW IT
DATE

WHERE I SAW IT
SPECIFIC LOCATION,
INCLUDE STATE

NOTES

Quaking Aspen
(Populus tremuloides)

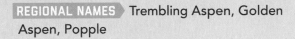

OVAL   OVAL

REGIONAL NAMES Trembling Aspen, Golden Aspen, Popple

HEIGHT 40–60 feet (12–18.5 m)

SHAPE Medium with a straight, slender trunk and rounded crown.

LEAVES 1.5–3 inches (4–7.5 cm) long in a rounded oval to wide triangle shape; fine-toothed with pointed tip; alternate, simple.

BARK Smooth and light green-gray.

FRUIT Narrow, pointed capsules with tufted seeds.

HABITAT Forests, old fields, and mountains.

RANGE Northern United States and Canada. Zones 1–6.

POINT OF FACT Its leaves flutter, or quake, in any wind speed.

I SPOTTED IT!

WHEN I SAW IT
DATE

WHERE I SAW IT
SPECIFIC LOCATION,
INCLUDE STATE

NOTES

....

....

Eastern Cottonwood

(Populus deltoides)

OVAL   OVAL

REGIONAL NAMES Necklace Poplar, Southern Cottonwood

HEIGHT 80–100 feet (24.5–30.5 m)

SHAPE Tall, thick trunk with a wide crown.

LEAVES 3–8 inches (7.5–20.5 cm) long; triangular with rounded teeth; pale underneath; alternate, simple.

BARK Dark gray with deep furrows.

FRUIT Small capsules with cottony seeds inside.

HABITAT Moist lowland forests and along streams and rivers.

RANGE Eastern and Central United States. Zones 3–9.

POINT OF FACT Seeds burst out of their ripe fruit while still attached to the cottony threads that disperse with the wind.

WINTER

I SPOTTED IT!

WHEN I SAW IT
DATE

WHERE I SAW IT
SPECIFIC LOCATION,
INCLUDE STATE

NOTES

Sweet Crab Apple
(Malus coronaria)

WIDE-SPREADING   LOBED

REGIONAL NAMES Garland-Tree, Allegheny Crab

HEIGHT 10–30 feet (3–9 m)

SHAPE Small with a short trunk and wide crown.

LEAVES 3–4 inches (7.5–10 cm) long; fine-toothed; alternate, simple.

BARK Red- and gray-brown with rough scales.

FRUIT 1 inch (2.5 cm) long; round, yellow-green balls on long stalks.

HABITAT Forest edges, old fields, and yards.

RANGE Eastern United States. Zones 4–7.

POINT OF FACT Its fruit is sour but is traditionally made into jellies.

I SPOTTED IT!

WHEN I SAW IT
DATE

WHERE I SAW IT
SPECIFIC LOCATION, INCLUDE STATE

NOTES

Eastern Redbud

(Cercis canadensis)

WIDE-SPREADING   **OVAL**

REGIONAL NAMES Judas Tree, Redbud

HEIGHT 15–30 feet (4.5–9 m)

SHAPE Sometimes has multiple small, short trunks; rounded crown.

LEAVES 5–8 inches (12.5–20.5 cm) long; heart-shaped, smooth-edged; alternate, simple.

BARK Gray to red–brown with small scales.

FRUIT 2–3 inches (5–7.5 cm) long; flat bean-like pods.

HABITAT Moist woods, yards, and roadsides.

RANGE Eastern United States. Zones 4–9.

POINT OF FACT In early spring, before its leaves sprout, small, pink flower clusters grow along its branches and trunk.

◗ I SPOTTED IT! ▷

WHEN I SAW IT
DATE

WHERE I SAW IT
SPECIFIC LOCATION, INCLUDE STATE

NOTES ▷

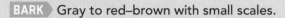

Honey Mesquite

(Prosopis glandulosa)

WIDE-SPREADING

COMPOUND

REGIONAL NAMES Mesquite

HEIGHT 20–30 feet (6–9 m)

SHAPE Small tree or shrub with one or many trunks.

LEAVES Pairs, 5–10 inches (12.5–25.5 cm) long; drooping leaves made of many feathery, narrow leaflets, 1 inch (2.5 cm) long; alternate, double compound.

BARK Dark red–gray with ragged ridges.

FRUIT 4–10 inches (10–25.5 cm) long; pale brown, lumpy pods.

HABITAT Deserts and dry grasslands.

RANGE Southwestern United States. Zones 7–9.

POINT OF FACT It defends itself from browsing animals with twigs covered in paired spines.

I SPOTTED IT!

WHEN I SAW IT
DATE

WHERE I SAW IT
SPECIFIC LOCATION,
INCLUDE STATE

NOTES

....
....

Gregg Catclaw
(Acacia greggii)

WIDE-SPREADING

COMPOUND

REGIONAL NAMES Devil's Claw, Wait-a-Minute Tree

HEIGHT 15–20 feet (4.5–6 m)

SHAPE Shrub to small tree with many trunks that often form thickets.

LEAVES 1–2 inches (2.5–5 cm) long; many feathery, dark gray-green leaflets; alternate, double or triple compound.

BARK Gray-brown and scaly or furrowed.

FRUIT 2–5 inches (5–12.5 cm) long; flat, twisted brown pods.

HABITAT Deserts and dry riverbeds.

RANGE Southwestern United States. Zones 7–9.

POINT OF FACT Sharp, curved, and clawlike spines on its branches and twigs earn the tree its name.

I SPOTTED IT!

WHEN I SAW IT
DATE

WHERE I SAW IT
SPECIFIC LOCATION,
INCLUDE STATE

NOTES

White Ash
(Fraxinus americana)

OVAL COMPOUND

REGIONAL NAMES American Ash, Biltmore Ash

HEIGHT 60–80 feet (18.5–24.5 m)

SHAPE Medium to large with a long, straight trunk and dense crown.

LEAVES 8–12 inches (20.5–30.5 cm) long; made of 5–9 (typically 7) smooth or fine-toothed, dark green leaflets, each about 4 inches (10 cm) long; pale underneath; opposite, pinnately compound.

BARK Gray with diamond-shaped ridges.

FRUIT 1–2 inches (2.5–5 cm) long; narrow, single papery wings that hang in clusters.

HABITAT Moist woods, hillsides, yards, and parks.

RANGE Eastern United States. Zones 4–9.

POINT OF FACT Wooden baseball bats are often carved out of its tough interior.

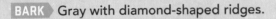

I SPOTTED IT!

WHEN I SAW IT
DATE

WHERE I SAW IT
SPECIFIC LOCATION,
INCLUDE STATE

NOTES

....

....

Pacific Madrone
(Arbutus menziesii)

WIDE-SPREADING **OVAL**

REGIONAL NAMES Coast Madrona

HEIGHT 25–60 feet (7.5–18.5 m)

SHAPE Shrub-size to medium, often with multiple short trunks.

LEAVES 4–6 inches (10–15 cm) long; dark green; leatherlike, evergreen with smooth or fine-toothed edges; alternate, simple.

BARK Thin and red-brown that peels to reveal green underneath.

FRUIT 0.5 inch (1.5 cm) long; small orange-red berries in hanging clusters.

HABITAT Canyons, forests, and yards.

RANGE Southwestern Canada and West Coast of United States. Zones 6–8.

POINT OF FACT Fire control measures prevent periodic losses of competing conifers, making this tree's range decline over time.

I SPOTTED IT!

WHEN I SAW IT
DATE

WHERE I SAW IT
SPECIFIC LOCATION,
INCLUDE STATE

NOTES

Red Mangrove

(Rhizophora mangle)

WIDE-SPREADING **OVAL**

REGIONAL NAMES American Mangrove

HEIGHT 20–40 feet (6–12 m)

SHAPE Shrub-like tangle of arching roots and branches.

LEAVES 3–5 inches (7.5–12.5 cm) long; evergreen and leatherlike; opposite, simple.

BARK Gray-brown and scaly with furrows.

FRUIT 1 inch (2.5 cm) long; cone-shaped with rough, brown skin.

HABITAT Coastal waters, tidal creeks, and estuaries.

RANGE Coastal South Florida and Texas. Zones 10–11.

POINT OF FACT A green sprout can grow from a fruit up to a foot (30.5 cm) long before dropping from the tree.

I SPOTTED IT!

WHEN I SAW IT
DATE

WHERE I SAW IT
SPECIFIC LOCATION, INCLUDE STATE

NOTES

Pacific Rhododendron

(Rhododendron macrophyllum)

WIDE-SPREADING   **OVAL**

REGIONAL NAMES Coast Rhododendron

HEIGHT Up to 25 feet (7.5 m)

SHAPE Short shrub to small tree with thin branches.

LEAVES 3–10 inches (7.5–25.5 cm) long and narrow; evergreen and leatherlike with smooth, rolled-under edges; alternate, simple.

BARK Smooth and red-brown.

FRUIT 0.5 inch (1.5 cm) long; red-brown capsules.

HABITAT Temperate rain forests.

RANGE West Coast of United States. Zones 6–9.

POINT OF FACT Crowned the state flower of Washington, its big, showy clusters of pink, trumpet-shaped flowers bloom in the spring.

I SPOTTED IT!

WHEN I SAW IT
DATE

WHERE I SAW IT
SPECIFIC LOCATION,
INCLUDE STATE

NOTES

Cabbage Palmetto
(Sabal palmetto)

VASE   PALM

REGIONAL NAMES Cabbage Palm, Sabal Palm, Carolina Palmetto

HEIGHT 30–65 feet (9–20 m)

SHAPE Small to medium with a stout, straight trunk and rounded crown.

LEAVES 5–6 feet (1.5–2 m) long; evergreen, fan-shaped with stiff leaflets; intermediate palmate and pinnate compound.

BARK Young trees have dead leaves or leaf scars, while older trees are smooth and gray.

FRUIT 0.25 inch (0.5 cm) long; black berries in clusters on a long stalk.

HABITAT Marshes, sandy coasts, and yards.

RANGE North Carolina to Florida. Zones 8–10.

POINT OF FACT Its name comes from its edible bud, which has a cabbage-like flavor.

I SPOTTED IT!

WHEN I SAW IT
DATE

WHERE I SAW IT
SPECIFIC LOCATION,
INCLUDE STATE

NOTES

....

....

American Witch Hazel
(Hamamelis virginiana)

VASE   OVAL

REGIONAL NAMES Winterbloom

HEIGHT 10–30 feet (3–9 m)

SHAPE Shrub or small tree with one or more trunks and an irregularly shaped crown.

LEAVES 3–6 inches (7.5–15 cm) long; shallow, rounded teeth; pale underneath; alternate, simple.

BARK Blotchy, dark gray, smooth, and thin.

FRUIT 0.5 inch (1.5 cm) long; brown woody capsules that eject seeds.

HABITAT Shady understories of woods and swamps.

RANGE Eastern United States. Zones 3–8.

POINT OF FACT Its spindle-like yellow flowers bloom after its leaves drop in late autumn.

I SPOTTED IT!

WHEN I SAW IT
DATE

WHERE I SAW IT
SPECIFIC LOCATION,
INCLUDE STATE

NOTES

California Laurel
(Umbellularia californica)

OVAL   OVAL

REGIONAL NAMES Oregon Myrtle, Pepperwood, California Bay

HEIGHT 20–70 feet (6–21.5 m)

SHAPE Small to large, often with many trunks and upright branches and a rounded crown.

LEAVES 2–4 inches (5–10 cm) long and narrow; shiny, evergreen, and leatherlike; dark green with a pale underside; alternate, simple.

BARK Gray and smooth with low ridges.

FRUIT 1 inch (2.5 cm) long; green to purple and olive-shaped.

HABITAT Mixed moist forests, along streams, and in yards and parks.

RANGE West Coast of United States. Zones 8–10.

POINT OF FACT Its leaves have a strong pepper or spicy scent similar to that of bay leaves used in cooking.

I SPOTTED IT!

WHEN I SAW IT
DATE

WHERE I SAW IT
SPECIFIC LOCATION, INCLUDE STATE

NOTES

....

....

Ohio Buckeye
(Aesculus glabra)

OVAL   COMPOUND

REGIONAL NAMES American Horse Chestnut

HEIGHT 30–50 feet (9–15 m)

SHAPE Shrub or small to medium tree.

LEAVES 8–10 inches (20.5–25.5 cm) long; 5 fine-toothed, pointed-tip leaflets, each 3–6 inches (7.5–15 cm); opposite, palmately compound.

BARK Thick and gray-brown with furrows and irregular ridges.

FRUIT 2 inches (5 cm) long; leathery, spiked capsules with large, glossy brown nuts inside.

HABITAT Moist woods and hillsides and along streams.

RANGE Eastern and Central United States. Zones 4–7.

POINT OF FACT The state tree of Ohio; a personified buckeye seed named Brutus is the official mascot of The Ohio State University.

I SPOTTED IT!

WHEN I SAW IT
DATE

WHERE I SAW IT
SPECIFIC LOCATION, INCLUDE STATE

NOTES

BROADLEAF SHRUBS

Prairie Rose
(Rosa setigera)

IRREGULAR COMPOUND

REGIONAL NAMES Climbing Rose

HEIGHT 4–10 feet (1–3 m)

SHAPE Shrub or woody vine with arching or climbing branches.

LEAVES 3 toothed leaflets, each 2–4 inches (5–10 cm) long; alternate, compound.

BARK Green and smooth with large thorns on its branches and twigs.

FRUIT 0.5 inch (1.5 cm) long, red ball.

HABITAT Prairies, fields, and woodland thickets.

RANGE Eastern and Central United States. Zones 5–8.

POINT OF FACT Its pink and fragrant rose fruits are called hips.

I SPOTTED IT!

WHEN I SAW IT
DATE

WHERE I SAW IT
SPECIFIC LOCATION,
INCLUDE STATE

NOTES

Red Osier Dogwood

(Cornus sericea / stolonifera)

IRREGULAR   OVAL

REGIONAL NAMES Red Dogwood, Red-Stem Dogwood, Red Willow

HEIGHT 7–12 feet (2–3.5 m)

SHAPE Shrub or small tree.

LEAVES 2–4 inches (5–10 cm) long; smooth-edged with pointed tips and sunken veins; opposite, simple.

BARK Brown to bright red and smooth with light-colored lenticels.

FRUIT Clusters of 0.3-inch (1 cm), pea-size white berries.

HABITAT Moist woods, along streams, and yards.

RANGE Canada, Western and Northern United States. Zones 2–7.

POINT OF FACT Native dogwoods grow in the wild, but many are planted on lawns as ornamentals because of their pretty red twigs.

I SPOTTED IT!

WHEN I SAW IT
DATE

WHERE I SAW IT
SPECIFIC LOCATION,
INCLUDE STATE

NOTES

Southern Bayberry

(Morella / Myrica cerifera)

IRREGULAR OVAL

REGIONAL NAMES Common Wax Myrtle, Candleberry

HEIGHT 10–20 feet (3–6 m)

SHAPE Shrub or small tree with multiple trunks.

LEAVES 2–4 inches (5–10 cm) long and narrow; evergreen with a spicy scent; tapered at the stalk; pale yellow underneath; jagged-toothed tip; alternate, simple.

BARK Gray-green, thin, and smooth.

FRUIT 0.13 inch (0.5 cm) long; berries coated in pale blue wax.

HABITAT Open fields, swampy woods, and yards.

RANGE Southeastern United States. Zones 8–11.

POINT OF FACT Europeans that came to America made fragrant candles from the fruit's waxy covering.

I SPOTTED IT!

WHEN I SAW IT
DATE

WHERE I SAW IT
SPECIFIC LOCATION, INCLUDE STATE

NOTES

....

....

Blue Gum Eucalyptus

(Eucalyptus globulus)

OVAL   OVAL

REGIONAL NAMES Tasmanian Blue Gum, Fever Tree

HEIGHT 100–180 feet (30.5–55 m)

SHAPE Very tall with a straight trunk and narrow crown.

LEAVES 6–12 inches (15–30.5 cm) long; narrow and curved with a pointed tip; smooth and evergreen with minty smell; alternate, simple.

BARK Smooth and gray-brown; peels in long strips.

FRUIT 1 inch (2.5 cm) long; woody, urn-shaped blue-green capsule that turns brown as it ripens.

HABITAT Coastal areas, yards, and fields.

RANGE Coastal California. Zone 10.

POINT OF FACT Eucalyptus trees are native to Australia, but were introduced in California in the nineteenth century.

I SPOTTED IT!

WHEN I SAW IT
DATE

WHERE I SAW IT
SPECIFIC LOCATION, INCLUDE STATE

NOTES

....

....

Joshua Tree
(Yucca brevifolia)

IRREGULAR PALM

REGIONAL NAMES Yucca Palm

HEIGHT 15–40 feet (4.5–12 m)

SHAPE Shrub or small tree with a thick trunk and upward branches.

LEAVES 8–12 inches (20.5–30.5 cm) long; evergreen, stiff, and swordlike.

BARK Covered in shaggy remains of old leaves.

FRUIT 2–4 inches (5–10 cm) long; oblong, brown pod.

HABITAT Deserts.

RANGE Southwestern United States. Zones 7–10.

POINT OF FACT It's dependent on a single species of insect, the yucca moth, to pollinate its flowers.

I SPOTTED IT!

WHEN I SAW IT
DATE

WHERE I SAW IT
SPECIFIC LOCATION, INCLUDE STATE

NOTES

Saguaro
(Cereus giganteus)

IRREGULAR

REGIONAL NAMES Sahuaro, Carnegiea Gigantea

HEIGHT 25–50 feet (7.5–15 m)

SHAPE Column-like with thick, upward-branching arms.

SPINES 0.5–2 inches (1.5–5 cm) long; clusters in vertical rows that grow on the trunk and arm ridges.

FRUIT Red, oval, fleshy, spine-covered fruit, 2–3 inches (5–7.5 cm) long.

HABITAT Deserts.

RANGE Southwestern United States. Zones 9–11.

POINT OF FACT Its height and single trunk qualify this giant cactus as a tree, but it has no bark or leaves like most other trees.

I SPOTTED IT!

WHEN I SAW IT
DATE

WHERE I SAW IT
SPECIFIC LOCATION, INCLUDE STATE

NOTES

....

....

Eastern White Pine
(Pinus strobus)

IRREGULAR

NEEDLELEAF

REGIONAL NAMES Northern White Pine, Weymouth Pine

HEIGHT 50–150 feet (15–45.5 m)

SHAPE Tall with long, widely spaced, horizontal branches and an irregular crown.

LEAVES 3–5 inches (7.5–12.5 cm) long; thin needles in bundles of 5.

BARK Dark gray rectangular blocks with furrows.

CONE 5–6 inches (12.5–15 cm) long; slender and brown.

HABITAT Cool upland forests, yards, and parks.

RANGE Eastern United States. Zones 3–7.

POINT OF FACT It's named for its light-colored heartwood (the wood at the center of a tree's trunk).

I SPOTTED IT!

WHEN I SAW IT
DATE

WHERE I SAW IT
SPECIFIC LOCATION,
INCLUDE STATE

NOTES

....

....

Loblolly Pine
(Pinus taeda)

TRIANGLE

NEEDLELEAF

REGIONAL NAMES Oldfield Pine

HEIGHT 60–90 feet (18.5–27.5 m)

SHAPE Large with a straight trunk and cone–shaped crown.

LEAVES 6–8 inches (15–20.5 cm) long; thin and stiff yellow-green needles in bundles of 2 or 3.

BARK Red-brown with scaly, rectangular plates.

CONE 2–5 inches (5–12.5 cm) long; stout oval shape with prickles on scales.

HABITAT Fields, forests, and swamps.

RANGE Southeastern United States. Zones 6–9.

POINT OF FACT *Loblolly* is a Southern word for bog or swamp.

I SPOTTED IT!

WHEN I SAW IT
DATE

WHERE I SAW IT
SPECIFIC LOCATION,
INCLUDE STATE

NOTES

Ponderosa Pine
(Pinus ponderosa)

TRIANGLE

NEEDLELEAF

REGIONAL NAMES Yellow Pine, Rock Pine, Western Red Pine

HEIGHT 80–120 feet (24.5–36.5 m)

SHAPE Large with a long, straight trunk with open branches and a cone-shaped crown.

LEAVES 6–11 inches (15–28 cm) long; flexible, yellow-green needles in bundles of 2 or 3.

BARK Red with large, smooth, and flat plates that are broken into rectangles; vanilla or butterscotch scent.

CONE 3–6 inches (7.5–15 cm) long; prickly; red-brown; oval or egg shape.

HABITAT Forests from coasts to mountains.

RANGE Western United States. Zones 3–6.

POINT OF FACT This Western-abundant tree's iconic fallen bark chunks are shaped like jigsaw puzzle pieces.

I SPOTTED IT!

WHEN I SAW IT
DATE

WHERE I SAW IT
SPECIFIC LOCATION, INCLUDE STATE

NOTES

....

....

Lodgepole Pine
(Pinus contorta)

OVAL   NEEDLELEAF

REGIONAL NAMES Tamarack Pine, Scrub Pine

HEIGHT 30–80 feet (9–24.5 m)

SHAPE Medium to large with a slender and straight trunk that becomes shrub-like and twisted along coasts.

LEAVES 1–3 inches (2.5–7.5 cm) long; thick, curved, yellow-green needles in bundles of 2.

BARK Gray to pale orange with thin scales.

CONE 1–2 inches (2.5–5 cm) long; prickly; oval shape.

HABITAT Mountains and along coasts.

RANGE Western United States and Canada. Zones 5–8.

POINT OF FACT Trees only 5–7 years old produce cones, making it one of the first trees to grow back after a wildfire.

I SPOTTED IT!

WHEN I SAW IT
DATE

WHERE I SAW IT
SPECIFIC LOCATION,
INCLUDE STATE

NOTES

....

....

Scotch Pine
(Pinus sylvestris)

IRREGULAR
NEEDLELEAF

REGIONAL NAMES Scots Pine, Northern Pine

HEIGHT 25–50 feet (7.5–15 m)

SHAPE Small to medium with a curved trunk and irregular crown.

LEAVES 1.5–3 inches (4–7.5 cm) long; stiff, twisted needles in bundles of 2.

BARK Gray with thin, scaly ridges below, with a rusty-orange and smooth upper trunk and branches.

CONE 2 inches (5 cm) long; teardrop shape.

HABITAT Woods, fencerows, old fields, and yards.

RANGE Northeastern United States. Zones 3–7.

POINT OF FACT It was brought from Europe and grown for timber, paper pulp, and Christmas trees. It's considered invasive in some areas of North America.

I SPOTTED IT!

WHEN I SAW IT
DATE

WHERE I SAW IT
SPECIFIC LOCATION,
INCLUDE STATE

NOTES

Norway Spruce
(Picea abies)

TRIANGLE

NEEDLELEAF

REGIONAL NAMES European Spruce

HEIGHT 50–80 feet (15–24.5 m)

SHAPE Medium to large with upward branches and drooping branchlets.

LEAVES 0.5–0.8 inch (1.5–2 cm) long; stiff, sharp, dark green, single needles.

BARK Red–brown and scaly.

CONE 4–7 inches (10–18 cm) long; narrow; pointed and slightly toothed scales.

HABITAT Forests and yards.

RANGE Eastern United States. Zones 3–7.

POINT OF FACT It's mainly grown for lumber and Christmas trees.

I SPOTTED IT!

WHEN I SAW IT
DATE

WHERE I SAW IT
SPECIFIC LOCATION,
INCLUDE STATE

NOTES

....

....

White Spruce

(Picea glauca)

TRIANGLE

NEEDLELEAF

REGIONAL NAMES Skunk Spruce, Canada Spruce

HEIGHT 50–90 feet (5–27.5 m)

SHAPE Medium to large and tall; narrow with a pointed crown.

LEAVES 0.5 inch (1.5 cm) long; stiff, blue-green single needles with a diamond-shaped cross section.

BARK Gray-brown and scaly.

CONE 1.5–2 inches (4–5 cm) long; egg shape with smooth-edged scales.

HABITAT Northern forests, bogs, riverbanks, and mountain slopes.

RANGE Alaska, Canada, the Great Lakes, and New England. Zones 2–6.

POINT OF FACT Its crushed needles have a stinky smell, which is why some call it "skunk spruce."

I SPOTTED IT!

WHEN I SAW IT
DATE

WHERE I SAW IT
SPECIFIC LOCATION, INCLUDE STATE

NOTES

....

....

Engelmann Spruce
(Picea engelmannii)

TRIANGLE

NEEDLELEAF

REGIONAL NAMES Mountain Spruce

HEIGHT 80–125 feet (24.5–38 m)

SHAPE Medium to large with a tall, pointed crown.

LEAVES 1 inch (2.5 cm) long; stiff, sharp, gray-green single needles with a square cross section.

BARK Gray to red-brown, thin, and scaly.

CONE 1.5–2.5 inches (4–6.5 cm) long; yellow to red-brown; oval shape with ragged-edged scales.

HABITAT High mountain forests and slopes.

RANGE United States and Canada. Zones 3–5.

POINT OF FACT The crushed foliage is often said to be fetid, but after the first sniff, the scent is sweet and like menthol or camphor.

I SPOTTED IT!

WHEN I SAW IT
DATE

WHERE I SAW IT
SPECIFIC LOCATION, INCLUDE STATE

NOTES

Eastern Hemlock
(Tsuga canadensis)

TRIANGLE

NEEDLELEAF

REGIONAL NAMES Canada Hemlock, Hemlock Spruce

HEIGHT 60–75 feet (18.5–23 m)

SHAPE Medium to large with slightly drooping branches and a cone-shaped crown.

LEAVES 0.5 inch (1.5 cm) long; soft, flat, and dark green single needles that have pale, visible lines underneath.

BARK Dark brown and scaly with furrows.

CONE 0.5–0.75 inch (1.5–2 cm) long; light brown and rounded.

HABITAT Shady, cool, and moist forests.

RANGE Eastern United States. Zones 3–7.

POINT OF FACT It's currently threatened by an introduced aphid-like insect pest, called the hemlock woolly adelgid, that kills hemlock trees.

○ I SPOTTED IT!

WHEN I SAW IT
DATE

WHERE I SAW IT
SPECIFIC LOCATION,
INCLUDE STATE

NOTES

....

....

White Fir

(Abies concolor)

TRIANGLE

NEEDLELEAF

REGIONAL NAMES Colorado Fir, Colorado White Fir

HEIGHT 60–90 feet (18–27.5 m)

SHAPE Medium to large with drooping branches and a flat-topped crown.

LEAVES 2–3 inches (5–7.5 cm) long; flat and round-tipped; blue-green single needles.

BARK Dark gray and thick with rough ridges.

CONE 3–5 inches (7.5–12.5 cm) long; olive-green or purple; smooth, oblong shape; sits upright on branch.

HABITAT Conifer forests and mountains.

RANGE Western United States. Zones 4–7.

POINT OF FACT Young trees have a triangular shape, sturdy branches, and needles that stay well after the tree is cut, making it a favorite for Christmas tree farms.

I SPOTTED IT!

WHEN I SAW IT
DATE

WHERE I SAW IT
SPECIFIC LOCATION,
INCLUDE STATE

NOTES

....

....

Redwood
(Sequoia sempervirens)

OVAL   NEEDLELEAF

REGIONAL NAMES California Redwood, Coast Redwood

HEIGHT 150–300 feet (45.5 91.5 m)

SHAPE Tall with a narrow, pointed crown.

LEAVES 0.5–1 inch (1.5–2.5 cm) long; flat, single needles.

BARK Red-brown, fibrous, and ridged with furrows; up to 12 inches (30.5 cm) thick.

CONE 0.75–1 inch (2–2.5 cm) long; brown and oval-shaped, with flat, thick, woody scales.

HABITAT Coastal fog forests.

RANGE West Coast of United States. Zones 7–9.

POINT OF FACT It's the tallest tree in the world, with a record height of 379 feet (115.5 m).

I SPOTTED IT!

WHEN I SAW IT
DATE

WHERE I SAW IT
SPECIFIC LOCATION, INCLUDE STATE

NOTES

....

....

Douglas Fir
(Pseudotsuga menziesii)

TRIANGLE

NEEDLELEAF

REGIONAL NAMES Common Douglas Fir, Douglas Spruce

HEIGHT 80–200 feet (24.5–61 m)

SHAPE Medium to very large with a long trunk and bushy crown.

LEAVES 1–1.5 inches (2.5–4 cm) long; soft, single needles.

BARK Dark and thick with deep furrows.

CONE 2–3 inches (5–7.5 cm) long; light brown and egg-shaped with shaggy, 3-pointed bracts between its scales.

HABITAT Moist and shady coastal and mountain forests.

RANGE Western United States. Zones 4–6.

POINT OF FACT Unlike true firs, its cones don't stand up on branches—they hang down instead.

I SPOTTED IT!

WHEN I SAW IT
DATE

WHERE I SAW IT
SPECIFIC LOCATION,
INCLUDE STATE

NOTES

....

....

Bald Cypress
(Taxodium distichum)

IRREGULAR
NEEDLELEAF

REGIONAL NAMES Deciduous Cypress, Swamp Cypress

HEIGHT 80–100 feet (24.5–30.5 m)

SHAPE Medium to large with a wide trunk base that's surrounded by cone-shaped stumps called *knees.*

LEAVES 0.75 inch (2 cm) long; pale green, soft, single needles.

BARK Red to gray with fibrous ridges.

CONE 1 inch (2.5 cm) long; round, wrinkled balls.

HABITAT Swamps and wet areas.

RANGE Southeastern United States. Zones 4–11.

POINT OF FACT While considered a conifer, the tree is actually deciduous—its feathery needles turn red-brown in autumn, then drop off.

I SPOTTED IT!

WHEN I SAW IT
DATE

WHERE I SAW IT
SPECIFIC LOCATION,
INCLUDE STATE

NOTES

....

....

Eastern Red Cedar

(Juniperus virginiana)

TRIANGLE

NEEDLELEAF

REGIONAL NAMES ▸ Pencil Cedar, Red Juniper

HEIGHT ▸ 20–50 feet (6–15 m)

SHAPE ▸ Small to medium with a narrow, pointed crown or more bush-like.

LEAVES ▸ 0.06–0.25 inch (1.5–6.5 mm) long; overlapping, dark green scales that are longer and pointier on new growth.

BARK ▸ Gray to red-brown and fibrous with thin, peeling strips.

CONE ▸ 0.125 inch (0.5 cm) long; blue to purple and berrylike round shape.

HABITAT ▸ Old fields and pastures, roadsides, fencerows, and rocky hillsides.

RANGE ▸ Eastern and Central United States. Zones 3–9.

POINT OF FACT ▸ It's the source of the red-and-yellow-streaked wood that's used to build "cedar" chests and linen closets, but it's actually a juniper.

◖ I SPOTTED IT! ▸

WHEN I SAW IT
DATE

WHERE I SAW IT
SPECIFIC LOCATION,
INCLUDE STATE

NOTES ▸

....

....

CONIFER TREES

Common Juniper

(Juniperus communis)

WIDE
SPREADING

NEEDLELEAF

REGIONAL NAMES Dwarf Juniper

HEIGHT 1–20 feet (0.5–6 m)

SHAPE Ground-hugging shrub to small tree with many trunks and twisting branches.

LEAVES 0.3–0.5 inch (1–1.5 cm) long; concave needles that grow in whorls of 3.

BARK Gray-brown, thin, and fibrous; shreds in thin strips.

CONE 0.2 inch (0.5 cm) long; round, blue, and berrylike.

HABITAT Rocky slopes, old fields and pastures, and mountains.

RANGE Canada and Northern and Western United States. Zones 2–6.

POINT OF FACT It's native to North America, Europe, and Asia, making it the most widespread conifer in the world.

◉ I SPOTTED IT!

WHEN I SAW IT
DATE

WHERE I SAW IT
SPECIFIC LOCATION,
INCLUDE STATE

NOTES

....

....

PART III

WILDFLOWERS

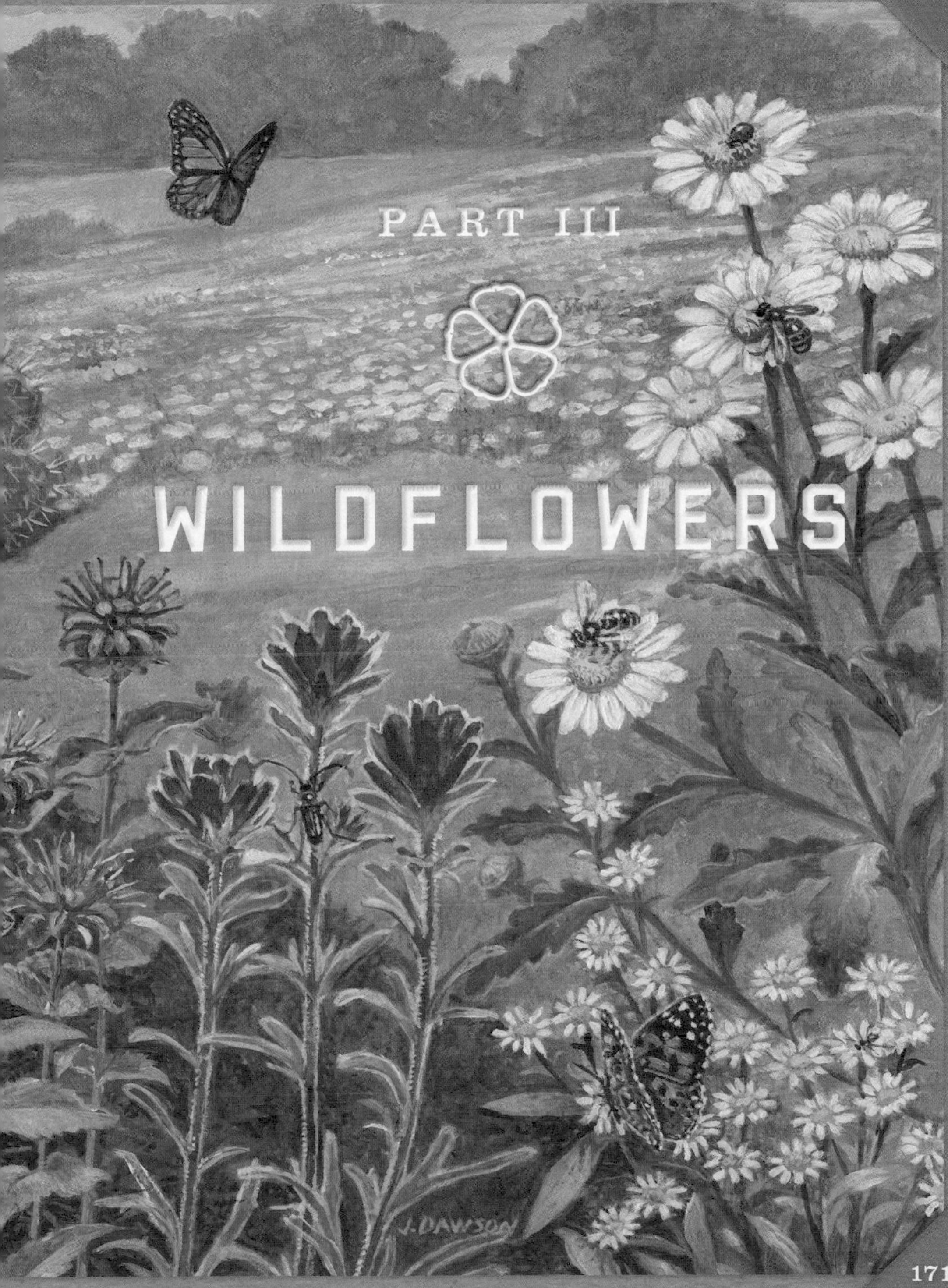

J. DAWSON

What would YOU do?

You're mountain biking at your local

park—pedaling along a dirt track, weaving around trees, and . . . yikes! Your front tire slams into a rock, and in less than an instant, you're on the ground. Ouch! Unhurt, you pick your bike up out of the weeds. Suddenly your shins are on fire! Oh, no— you walked through a patch of stinging nettle! Washing your legs would help, but the water bottle is empty. Wow, it stings!

Then you remember—jewelweed stems are full of skin-soothing sap. You look around for plants with orange flowers. There's some! But how can you know for sure they're jewelweed flowers? Should you crush up a stem and smear it on your shins? Could the sap hurt you if it's not jewelweed? *What would you do?*

CHAPTER 1

Spotting Wildflowers

What sort of scenery pops into your head when someone says *wildflower*? A prairie of swaying yellow sunflowers? A mountain meadow dotted with clumps of purple and blue blossoms? Perhaps a sun-dappled forest with fragile white flowers? Or the desert in spring with papery cacti blooms?

YELLOW PAINTBRUSH

Those are all fantastic examples of wildflowers. But how about a highway median covered in clover and goldenrod, or a fence covered in thorny vines? What about a "weedy" lot of dandelions, cockleburs, and tall grass? Are these wildflower-filled scenes, too? Absolutely!

A wildflower is any flowering plant that grows freely. Unlike crops or garden plants, wildflowers aren't planted by people. They grow wild on their own. Many wildflowers are native plants that have lived in North America for thousands of years. Others are non-native plants, which were imported plants, stowaway weeds, and garden escapees that naturalized into wildflowers over time. Dandelions are a good example of a non-native wildflower. European colonists brought dandelion with them to America to grow for food and medicine. The plants eventually naturalized, spreading from gardens into the wild.

PAINTED CUP

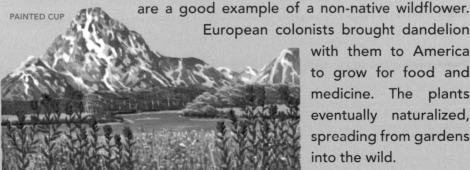

What a Wildflower Is—and Isn't

Wildflowers are seed-making flowering plants, or angiosperms. This is the most diverse plant group on earth. About four out of every five plant species are angiosperms. What kinds of plants are not angiosperms? Pines, spruces, and other cone-making trees are gymnosperms (page 89). They make seeds, but not flowers. Other kinds of nonflowering plants like ferns, mosses, horsetails, and liverworts (page 310) don't make seeds at all.

While all wildflowers are angiosperms, not all angiosperms are wildflowers. Broadleaf trees, deciduous trees, and shrubs all produce flowers, but they aren't *wild*flowers. If it has bark, it isn't a wildflower. But neither are all wildflowers *herbaceous*, or plants whose leaves and stems die back in winter. The stems of some vine wildflowers like trumpet creeper are thick and tough, and the thorny branches of wild roses also continue growing over the years. Cacti are another wildflower that aren't herbaceous. They grow too slow to have to restart every spring.

And don't be fooled by the *flower* part of wildflower. Not all flowers are big and colorful like roses or daisies. Grasses have flowers, but most are small, brown, and have plain petals. Some wildflowers have green flowers that blend in with leaves. For the purposes of this book, a wildflower is any wild-growing, flowering plant that isn't a tree or shrub.

Only one of these is NOT a wildflower.

WOODY WILD VINE

PRICKLY PEAR CACTI

WILD GRASS

FLOWERING TREE

Flowers Are for Seeds

More than fifteen thousand species of wildflowers live in the United States and Canada. They live in nearly every habitat and come in a dizzying assortment of sizes, scents, shapes, textures, and colors. But they all have one thing in common: flowers.

SUNFLOWERS

Flowers are part of a plant's reproductive system because they make seeds. A seed contains an embryo plant that starts out as a fertilized egg with a mix of genes from a male and a female, just like what grows in a mother's womb or a wasp's nest. In flowering plants, male flower parts fertilize the female parts through pollination.

Flower Parts

A flower's job is to make seeds through pollination. Each kind of flower, whether a huge lily or a nearly invisible grass flower, is trying to solve the same problem: how to get pollinated.

TRUMPET CREEPER

A flower's shape, size, color, scent, and bloom time is all about pollination. Tube-shaped flowers pollinated by needle-beaked hummingbirds are often sweet-smelling and a red or orange color. The shade and scent attract the tiny birds, which transfer sticky pollen grains from one plant to another as they sip nectar. Wildflowers pollinated by spring bees and flies bloom early when those insects are most active. Bumblebee-pollinated flowers often have a wide shape for easy landings. And wildflowers pollinated by the wind don't need to attract pollinators at all, so their flowers are often plain and petalless.

THISTLE

The wide variety of flowers is linked to the many sorts of pollinators they depend on. Just a glance around a yard proves that not all flowers have the same shape and structures—but most have some variation of a few basic parts.

GOLDENROD

The female part of a flower is the pistil, which is usually in the center of the flower. A pistil has three parts: the *stigma* (the sticky pollen-trapping opening) which sits atop a tube called the *style*, that leads down to the *ovary*.

The male parts of a flower are called the stamens. The number of stamens a flower has varies by species, but each stamen has two parts: a stalk called a *filament* that's topped with a pollen-making *anther*.

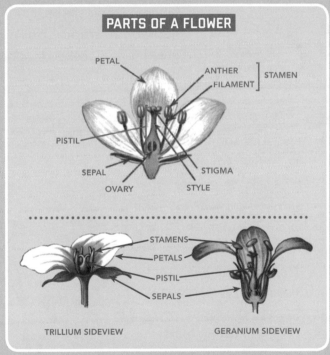

PARTS OF A FLOWER

PETAL

ANTHER
FILAMENT } STAMEN

PISTIL

SEPAL

OVARY

STIGMA

STYLE

STAMENS
PETALS
PISTIL
SEPALS

TRILLIUM SIDEVIEW

GERANIUM SIDEVIEW

Most of the flowers found on wildflowers have both male and female parts, but a few species have separate male flowers with just stamens, and separate female flowers with just pistils. Orchid flowers have a combined pistil and stamen structure called a *column*.

ORCHID

A composite wildflower, such as a daisy or sunflower, looks like a single flower but is actually numerous flowers tightly packed together. Many composites have hundreds of small, tube-shaped reproductive flowers, called *disk flowers*, that are surrounded by single-petaled sterile flowers, called *ray flowers*, that have no pistils or stamens.

SUNFLOWER

DISK FLOWER

RAY FLOWER

Petals are the outer parts of flowers. Their shape, color, and configuration attract pollinators and give them places to land. *Sepals* are the leaflike structures underneath the flower. They're usually green but can sometimes look like petals. All the sepals together on a flower are called a *calyx*. And some flowers have *bracts*, which are leaflike structures farther down the flower stalk, or *pedicel*. Bracts are usually green and protect a budding flower from harsh weather and hungry pests, but some fully grown flowers have bracts that act as petals and attract pollinators. The wide array and combinations of flower parts and structures are what make them endlessly fascinating. Plus, they give valuable clues when it comes time for identification.

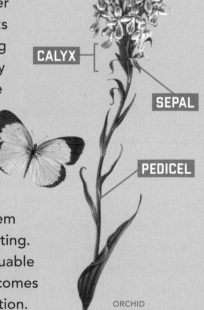

CALYX

SEPAL

PEDICEL

ORCHID

BRACT

THISTLE

How Pollination Makes Seeds

STEP 1 The male part of the flower, the *stamen*, produces pollen. Inside the pollen grains arc sperm cells.

STEP 2 A pollinator (wind, insect, etc.) carries the pollen to the female part, the *pistil*, of another flower of the same species. This transfer is called *pollination*.

STEP 3 Once the pollen lands on the *stigma*, the sperm cells travel down its tubelike structure to the egg cells in the *ovary*.

STEP 4 Egg and sperm cells unite to create fertilized eggs that grow into seeds. The surrounding ovary becomes a fruit.

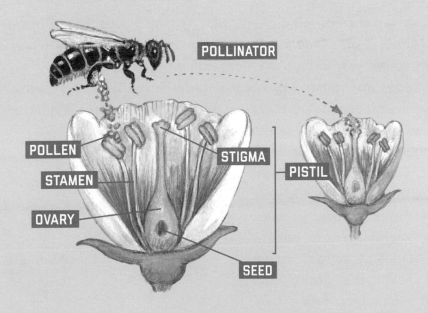

POLLINATOR

POLLEN

STAMEN

OVARY

STIGMA

PISTIL

SEED

Is Grass a Wildflower?

Look around anywhere outside and you're likely to spot grass of some kind. Ball fields, lawns, pastures, roadsides, and weedy lots are all home to grasses. Some grasses are planted, but many grow wild. Grasses dominate habitats like prairies and meadows. Much of central North America between the Rocky Mountains and the Mississippi River was once a vast prairie with many grass types.

UMBRELLA SEDGE

WILD OATS

CRABGRASS

Grasses are flowering plants with narrow leaves, called *blades*, and fibrous roots. Their stems are hollow, and each of their leaves is wrapped partway around the stem with a sheath.

Sedges are wetland plants that grow in marshes and swamps. They have blades for leaves, like grasses, but the stems are different. Sedge stems are often triangular with three flattened sides, which you can remember with the phrase, "Sedges have edges." Unlike grasses, their stems aren't hollow. The blades of sedges attach with sheaths that encircle the stem completely, rather than partway.

STEM CROSS SECTIONS

GRASS

SEDGE

Wild grasses and sedges have tiny flowers that develop numerous seeds within seed heads. Grass seed heads, or *spikelets*, come in various shapes—from fluffy, feathery plumes to densely packed clusters. Grasses and sedges are mostly pollinated by the wind. They don't need extravagant flowers to attract pollinating insects or animals. The tiny flowers, or *florets*, are hard to see and are covered in protective bracts, not petals. Each flower's stamen makes many tiny pollen grains that travel easily through the air. (And to your nose—achoo!) The pollen is caught by the feathery stigmas of other grass plants, which triggers fertilization and seed development.

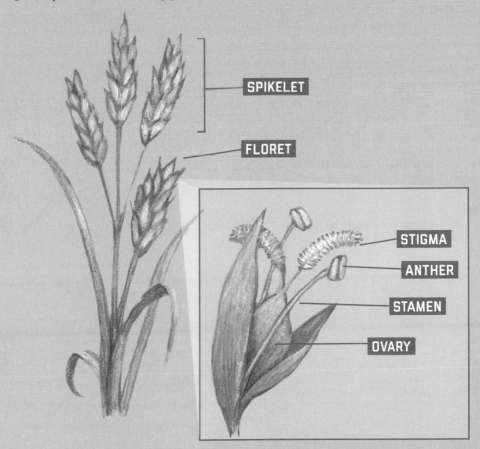

SPIKELET

FLORET

STIGMA

ANTHER

STAMEN

OVARY

TRY IT → Investigate a Flower

Put your new knowledge of seed-creating flower parts to the test. Tell sepals apart from stigmas by getting in close with a flower.

WHAT YOU'LL NEED

➢ A pencil or pen, a ruler, a hand lens or magnifying glass (optional).

STEP 1 Go outside and find a wildflower blossom to observe. Choose a common wildflower so you don't risk interfering with a rare plant's chance at reproduction.

STEP 2 Write some information about the wildflower here.

DATE

LOCATION

Describe the habitat where it's growing.

Can you identify the wildflower yet?

STEP 3 Take a close look at the flower, then check off all the parts you see:

☐ petals   ☐ sepals   ☐ stamen

☐ pistil   ☐ bracts   ☐ pedicel

I DID IT!   DATE:

TRACK IT → Identify Flower Parts

Dive deeper into wildflowers by drawing the blossom you observed.

> **WHAT YOU'LL NEED**
>
> ➣ A pencil or pen, a ruler, a hand lens or magnifying glass (optional).

STEP 1 Draw the wildflower you observed. Label the drawing with as many of these parts as you can:

PETALS   SEPALS   BRACTS   PEDICEL   STAMEN   ANTHER
FILAMENT   PISTIL   STIGMA   STYLE   OVARY

STEP 2 Count and record the numbers for each part. Use 0 if the answer is none.

petals ....   sepals ....   bracts ....

stamens.......................   pistils ....

Composite flower? ☐ yes ☐ no

If yes: ☐ disk flowers ☐ ray flowers

STEP 3 Measure and record the width or length (whichever is more) of the wildflower.

Flower width or length:

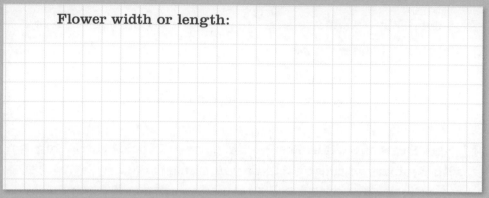

STEP 4 Can you identify the wildflower now? If so, check off its I SPOTTED IT! box in the identification section (pages 202–303) and fill in the blanks. Wonderful work, wildflower observer!

I DID IT! DATE:

TAKE IT TO THE NEXT LEVEL ↗

From Flower to Seed, the Documentary

A wildflower's purpose is reproduction through seed creation. Document the reproductive journey of a particular wildflower. Choose a nearby blooming plant that's easy to observe over time. Select a flower bud to observe. (Tie a colorful string around its stem if you need help finding it.) Visit the bud every few days, noting when it blooms, when it loses its petals, and when seeds develop. Depending on the species, these growth milestones can take days, weeks, or even months to occur. Patience is a plant-spotting virtue!

I DID IT! DATE:

The Identifying Power of Flowers

Has this ever happened to you? You're hiking in the woods or out in a natural area someplace when you spot a bit of color in the greenery. It's a wildflower! It almost feels like finding treasure. Later on, when you start telling someone about your find, the details get fuzzy. Was it blue or more purple? Did it have sepals and lots of stamens? It would be easier to remember and report your discovery if you'd known the plant's name.

That's what this chapter is all about. When wildflowers are in bloom, their flowers are almost always the best clue for identification. Many are lovely to look at, and all wildflower blossoms are interesting—especially up close. That's because each species of wildflower has its own unique flower. Some are surrounded by fragile petals, while others have little bells or cups. There are flowers with a single large blossom at the end of a stem, clusters of tiny blooms up and down a long spike, or a puffy, dangling, round ball.

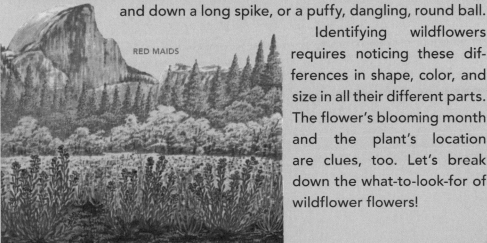

RED MAIDS

Identifying wildflowers requires noticing these differences in shape, color, and size in all their different parts. The flower's blooming month and the plant's location are clues, too. Let's break down the what-to-look-for of wildflower flowers!

Flower Shapes

When wildflower experts talk about a flower's shape, they're describing more than the shape of an individual flower. While some flowers like buttercups and violets grow in one blossom at the end of a stem, many flowers do not. Lots of flowers instead grow flower heads that include many small flowers arranged in clusters (such as butterfly weed or Queen Anne's lace), or up and down the end of a stalk (like lupine). And then there are composite flowers, like sunflowers, that can hold dozens of ray and disk flowers. The arrangement of a plant's flowers is called *inflorescence*.

INFLORESCENCE EXAMPLES

QUEEN ANNE'S LACE

UMBEL

LUPINE

DAISY

SPIKE

COMPOSITE

Wildflower field guides also often categorize flower shapes by different terms of symmetry. The most common symmetry is *radial symmetry*, which means it can be divided into identical sections by slicing anywhere through the center. To get identical sections of something with *bilateral symmetry*, there's only one way to slice—down the middle to get a left and a right side. Sea stars, pizzas, and buttercups are radially symmetrical. Butterflies, burritos, and violets are bilaterally symmetrical.

FLOWER SYMMETRY EXAMPLES

RADIAL SYMMETRY

BILATERAL SYMMETRY

In this book's Wildflower Identification section, the flowers are divided into six general shapes:

CALIFORNIA POPPY

 SIMPLE flowers have radial symmetry and usually have a single blossom on the end of a pedicel. Examples: poppies, buttercups, cacti, geraniums

 COMPOSITE flower heads are radially symmetrical and made up of numerous small ray and disk flowers that may look like a single flower. Examples: daisies, asters, dandelions, sunflowers

ASTER

 IRREGULAR flowers are bilaterally symmetrical and have a single blossom on the end of a pedicel. Examples: violets, orchids, irises, jewelweed

VIOLET

 BELL OR TRUMPET flowers are radially symmetrical and often have petals that are at least partially fused into a tube or cup at the flower's base. Examples: lilies, morning glory, bluebells, honeysuckle

MORNING GLORY

 ROUND CLUSTER flower heads are made up of multiple flowers on individual pedicels that form a round or umbrella-shaped cluster. Examples: butterfly weed, clovers, milkweed, cow parsnip

CLOVER

 LONG CLUSTER flower heads are made up of multiple flowers usually without pedicels along an upright, tall, spikelike stem. Examples: mullein, lizard's tail, foxgloves, pokeweed

POKEWEED

Flower Colors and Parts

Flower color is another identification clue for wildflowers. Most field guides give a flower's color when it's in peak bloom, not the color of a new bud or a *senescing* (aging) bloom. Color can be difficult to describe because everyone sees colors a bit differently. So a color you see as blue-purple may be seen by someone else as purple-blue, violet, or lavender. That's why color is just one characteristic among many that help to identify wildflowers.

Flower parts are less subjective identifiers. The flowers of most wildflowers have a specific number of petals, sepals, pistils, and stamens. Counting them can make a big difference for identifying wildflower species.

What colors are these flowers? Count their petals, sepals, stamens, and pistils.

TRILLIUM

GERANIUM

Talk Like a Wildflower Watcher

Here are some terms to know for wildflowers and their identification.

ANTHER ▸ the pollen grain-producing tip of a flower's stamen

BRACTS ▸ leaflike structures at the base of some flowers

CALYX ▸ all the sepals combined

COMPOSITE FLOWER ▸ a flower, such as a daisy, made up of many tiny flowers in a dense head

DISK FLOWER ▸ a small, tube-shaped flower in the center of a composite flower

FILAMENT ▸ the thin stalk of a stamen that supports the anther

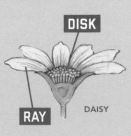

DISK

RAY

DAISY

FLORET a single flower of a flower head cluster; the small, petalless flower of a grass plant ————————

FRUIT the ripened ovary with seeds inside

INFLORESCENCE the arrangement of flowers on a plant

OVARY the chamber at the base of the pistil that contains eggs that develop into seeds

GILIA

PEDICEL the stem on a flower

PETALS leaflike structures surrounding the stamens and pistil, often nongreen in color and forming a cup, bell, or tube shape

PISTIL the female part of the flower; combination of stigma, style, and ovary

POLLEN the part of the male flower that contains sperm cells and is carried to other flowers for fertilization

RAY FLOWER a single petal flower, often sterile, that surrounds a head of disk flowers

SEPAL an often green, leaflike structure under the flower

SPIKELET a grass plant's flowering cluster, usually made up of florets and bracts

STAMEN the male flower part, including a filament and anther

STIGMA the tip of the pistil that receives pollen

QUEEN ANNE'S LACE

STYLE the tubelike structure between the pistil and ovary

UMBEL a flower cluster with all pedicels growing from a common center that form a flattish top

TRY IT →

Wildflower Shape Survey

How are your flower shape-recognition skills *shaping* up? Go outside to spot all six flower shapes. (Remember to review Plant Spotting Skills and Thrills on page 4 before heading out.)

WHAT YOU'LL NEED

➢ A pencil or pen, a hand lens or magnifying glass (optional).

STEP 1 Head outside to an area with a variety of flowering plants. Check off any of the six flower shapes from page 187 you see:

☐ simple

☐ composite

☐ irregular

☐ bell or trumpet

☐ round cluster

☐ long cluster

STEP 2 Choose three different found flower shapes to describe and draw. Write the flower's shape in the top line after the number.

SHAPE 1 ....

DRAW THE FLOWER.

Describe the flower's symmetry and color.

Can you name the wildflower?

SHAPE 2 ....

DRAW THE FLOWER.

Describe the flower's symmetry and color.

Can you name the wildflower?

SHAPE 3 ....

DRAW THE FLOWER.

Describe the flower's symmotry and color.

Can you name the wildflower?

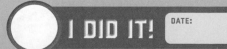

I DID IT!   DATE:

TRACK IT ↘ See Symmetrically

Practice seeing radial and bilateral symmetries by noting the symmetry of everyday objects.

WHAT YOU'LL NEED

➢ A pencil or pen, a small square or rectangular mirror (optional).

STEP 1 Review bilateral versus radial symmetry on page 186, and by looking at the examples on the chart below.

STEP 2 List any objects you see around you by their symmetry.

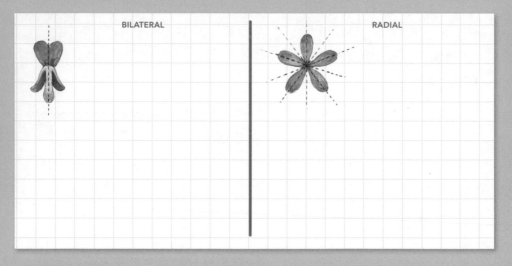

BILATERAL

RADIAL

TIP If you're unsure of an object's symmetry, use a mirror to check. Bilateral things have a single line of symmetry. Only by placing the mirror on that line will the reflection look like a complete object. Radially symmetrical objects have multiple lines of symmetry. The mirror can be placed along any of the lines to reflect a complete object.

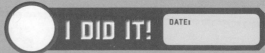

I DID IT! DATE:

Press and Preserve Wildflowers

Collected wildflowers will last longer if you press them. Try it yourself! Collect only wildflowers where you're allowed to do so, and then choose flowers that are abundant and common. Flat flowers like buttercups, phlox, and violets work best. Bulky flowers like sunflowers or thistle are more difficult to press.

→ Fold some newspaper into four layers (or stack four thin pieces of cardboard). Set a paper towel on top of the newspaper, then arrange the flowers on top of the paper towel.

→ Cover the flowers with another sheet of paper towel. Fold up more newspaper or use cardboard in four layers on top of the paper towel. Keep adding more layers of paper towel, flowers, and newspaper if you'd like.

→ Once your stack is finished, place four or five heavy books on top. Check the flowers after two weeks by lifting the newspaper and gently peeling back the paper towel. If they don't feel dry yet, leave them stacked up for another week.

→ Make labeled identification cards with the pressed flowers using index cards and laminating sheets. Or display them by carefully gluing the pressed flowers to a picture frame mat and then covering with glass in a frame.

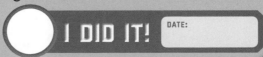
I DID IT! DATE:

CHAPTER 3

Looking at Leaves

Many people think that flowers are always the best way to identify wildflowers. After all, the flowers are often what grab a viewer's attention. However, grasses and many other wild flowering plants don't always have showy blossoms. And even those with stunning flowers don't bloom all year round. This is why learning to recognize the rest of the plant is important, especially the leaves.

Like all plants, wildflowers depend on leaves for food. Leaves are sugar factories fueled by carbon dioxide and water and then powered by the sun. (See page 18 for more information on photo-synthesis.) Leaves also offer superb clues to wildflower identification. Their shape and arrangement on a plant vary from species to species. And leaves are usually on a wild-flower plant both before and after it blooms!

Looking at a weed patch or thicket from a distance, perhaps all you see is a bunch of green leaves. But as you get up close and begin to look at the leaves that grow from specific stems, you'll soon notice lots of distinctions that help in wild-flower identification.

PARTS OF A LEAF

BEE BALM

BLADE

PETIOLE

STEM

Leaf Learning

Wildflower plants don't have bark, like trees or shrubs, and most sprout and grow new stems every year. Their leaves bud off the stems in arrangements that differ among species. As with trees (page 66), wildflower leaves can be simple or compound.

Simple leaves are arranged on stems in four main ways. Alternate leaves grow one per node. Opposite leaves grow two per node. Whorled leaves grow three or more per node. Basal leaves grow at the base of the stem.

(page 66),

ALTERNATE

WHORLED

OPPOSITE

BASAL

COMPOUND LEAF ARRANGEMENTS

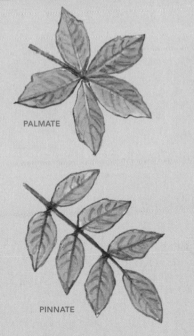

PALMATE

PINNATE

A leaf made up of more than one leaflet that attaches to a single petiole is a compound leaf. Compound leaves come in different arrangements, too. The leaflets of palmately compound leaves grow out from one center point, like fingers from a palm. Pinnately compound leaves have leaflets along both sides of a stalk and often on the end, too. The three-leaflet leaf of poison ivy is pinnately compound, and so are the frond-like, feathery leaves of common garden poppies.

Leaves and leaflets come in an abundance of shapes, including heart-shaped, oval, ribbonlike, and lance-shaped. As in trees, the margins (edges) of wildflower leaves are also great identifiers. Leaf margins can be lobed, toothed, or smooth.

Leaf Shapes

HEART-SHAPED   OVAL   RIBBONLIKE   LANCE-SHAPED

Leaf Margins

LOBED   TOOTHED   SMOOTH

Texture is another trait of wildflower leaves that varies by species. Some leaves are smooth and waxy, while others are thin and papery, fuzzy and thick, or rough and hairy. There are even wildflower leaves with prickles, such as stinging nettle.

STINGING NETTLE

TRY IT →

Wildflower Leaf Look-About

Put all you've learned about wildflower leaves to work!

WHAT YOU'LL NEED
➤ A pencil or pen.

STEP 1 Go to a nature area with lots of wildflower plants. It doesn't matter if they're blooming—they just need to be leafy plants that aren't trees, shrubs, ferns, or mosses.

STEP 2 Find and check off as many leaf characteristics as possible.

SIMPLE LEAF ARRANGEMENTS
- [ ] opposite
- [ ] alternate
- [ ] whorled
- [ ] basal

COMPOUND LEAF ARRANGEMENTS
- [ ] palmate
- [ ] pinnate

LEAF SHAPES
- [ ] heart-shaped
- [ ] oval
- [ ] ribbonlike
- [ ] lance-shaped
- [ ] other ....

LEAF MARGINS
- [ ] smooth
- [ ] toothed
- [ ] lobed
- [ ] lobed & toothed
- [ ] lobed & smooth

OTHER TRAITS ....

STEP 3 Did you see any leaves that have characteristics not mentioned? Note them in the "Other Traits" section above.

I DID IT! DATE:

197

TRACK IT ↘ Compare Two Wildflower Leaves

Record an in-depth examination of leaves from two different wildflower plants.

> ### WHAT YOU'LL NEED
> ➤ A pencil or pen, a ruler, a hand lens or magnifying glass (optional).

CANADA VIOLET

STEP 1 Find two safe wildflower plant leaves to collect. Before collecting, notice how the leaves are arranged on the stems. Are the leaves single, opposite, alternate, whorled, or basal? Or is it compound palmate or compound pinnate? Record the leaf arrangements on the chart and then collect the leaves.

STEP 2 Record each leaf's shape and margin type. If either leaf has any extra noteworthy characteristics, include them under Other.

STEP 3 Draw each leaf. Pay attention to the midrib and vein pattern.

STEP 4 Can you identify the wildflower plants that either leaf came from, using the Wildflower Identification section on pages 202–303? Awesome IDing! Fill in the blanks and check off the I SPOTTED IT! boxes.

DUTCHMAN'S-BREECHES

WILDFLOWER LEAF #1   DATE .... LOCATION ....

Leaf Arrangement:

Shape: Margin:

Other:

Draw the leaf:

What wildflower is it?

WILDFLOWER LEAF #2   DATE .... LOCATION ....

Leaf Arrangement:

Shape: Margin:

Other:

Draw the leaf:

What wildflower is it?

I DID IT!   DATE:

199

Make a Quadrat

When botanists want to know the number and kinds of plants that live in a particular place, they don't count every single plant. Instead, they sample the area. Line transects (page 12) are one sampling method. Quadrats, or two-dimensional frames or grids that outline a sampling area, are another method. You can make a simple quadrat from a wire clothes hanger.

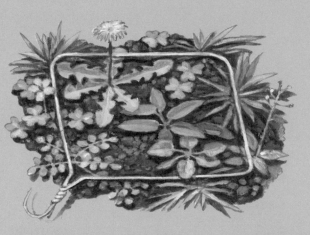

Stretch and bend the hanger until it forms a square. Then go to an area where you'd like to take a sample of wildflowers. Close your eyes and toss the quadrat like a flying disc to select a random sample area. Find the fallen quadrat, and identify what's growing within it. Consider visiting one or two different habitats and doing the same. How different are the mixes of plants growing in the various places?

I DID IT! DATE:

TAKE IT TO THE NEXT LEVEL ↗

Plant Spotter Deep Dive: Profile a Wildflower

Profile and draw a a favorite blooming wildflower!

DATE

LOCATION

Is it a ☐ wildflower ☐ grass ☐ cactus ☐ vine
☐ other flowering plant ....

Plant's Habitat: ....

Plant Height (with units): ....

Leaf Arrangement: ....

Leaf Shape and Margin: ....

Draw the full plant: Draw a leaf:

Flower Shape: ....

Flower Symmetry: ☐ radial ☐ bilateral

Draw the flower and label its parts.

What kind of wildflower is it? ....

Check off the I SPOTTED IT! box in the identification section and fill in the blanks. Superior effort, wildflower spotter!

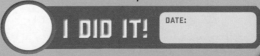

I DID IT!   DATE:

WILDFLOWER IDENTIFICATION

Welcome to your Wildflower Identification guide!

Here are some tips to get started, and where in the book you'll find more information:

In this book, a wildflower is any wild-growing, nongarden, flowering plant that's not a tree or shrub. These identification pages have two groups: Wildflowers, which includes flowering plants, vines, and cacti, and Grasses and Sedges, which are in their own group for easier identification.

PARTS OF A WILDFLOWER

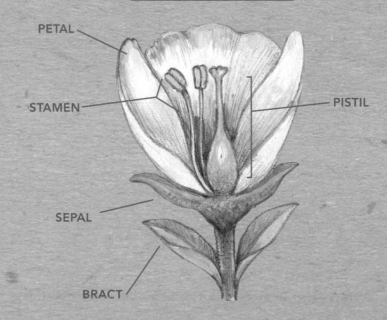

PETAL

STAMEN

PISTIL

SEPAL

BRACT

SHAPE is shown as an icon next to the name. There are six shape icons (page 187):

SIMPLE   COMPOSITE   ROUND CLUSTER   LONG CLUSTER   BELL OR TRUMPET   IRREGULAR

COLOR is represented by the color of the shape icon. This color shows the flower's peak bloom color, not the color of a new bud or a senescing (aging) bloom. Color can vary, so if you're looking for a blue flower and don't find it, try purple—and it's the same for orange and yellow, pink and red, etc.

IN BLOOM seasons depend on geography and weather, not the calendar. For example, an "early spring" wild-flower might bloom in February in Georgia and not until May in Vermont.

FLOWER HEADS for grasses and sedges can be packed loosely or densely, and are represented by icons on the Grasses and Sedges pages.

LOOSE   DENSE

PLANT HEIGHT given is an average. Soil, rainfall, sun exposure, and other local growing conditions affect a plant's exact height.

RANGE refers to the USDA Hardiness Zones in which the wildflower, grass, or sedge grows (page 47).

Bloodroot

(Sanguinaria canadensis)

SIMPLE

FLOWER 1.5 inches (4 cm) across; 8–10 white petals around yellow stamens.

IN BLOOM Early spring.

PLANT HEIGHT 6–10 inches (15–25.5 cm)

LEAVES Single, large, round, blue-green, multilobed leaf that wraps around flower stalk.

HABITAT Moist deciduous forests and sides of streams.

RANGE Southeastern Canada and Eastern and Central United States. Zones 3–8.

POINT OF FACT Its name comes from the poisonous, bloodred sap that oozes from the roots when they're cut.

I SPOTTED IT!

WHEN I SAW IT
DATE

WHERE I SAW IT
SPECIFIC LOCATION, INCLUDE STATE

NOTES

....
....

Bearberry

(Arctostaphylos uva–ursi)

BELL

REGIONAL NAME Kinnikinnick

FLOWER 0.25 inch (6.5 mm) across; white, bell-shaped clusters with pink tips.

IN BLOOM Late spring.

PLANT HEIGHT 4–8 inches (10–20.5 cm)

LEAVES Leathery, evergreen, dark green, and oblong-shaped; alternate, simple.

HABITAT Rocky and sandy areas, often in mountains or near coasts.

RANGE Canada, Northern United States to Virginia, and California. Zones 2–6.

POINT OF FACT This low, creeping evergreen shrub grows up to 10 feet (3 m) wide, and its red to purple berries last through the winter.

◖ I SPOTTED IT! ◗

WHEN I SAW IT
DATE

WHERE I SAW IT
SPECIFIC LOCATION,
INCLUDE STATE

NOTES

....

....

Ghost Plant

(Monotropa uniflora)

BELL

REGIONAL NAME Indian Pipe

FLOWER 0.5–1 inch (1.5–2.5 cm) across; floppy, nodding, white, and waxy; made of 4–5 petals.

IN BLOOM Late spring to summer.

PLANT HEIGHT 3–9 inches (7.5–23 cm)

LEAVES White with small scales; simple, alternate.

HABITAT Shaded woods.

RANGE Southern Canada and throughout the United States. Zones 4–8.

POINT OF FACT This nongreen plant is a fungal parasite that absorbs nutrients from fungi that grow on tree roots, rather than making its food through photosynthesis.

I SPOTTED IT!

WHEN I SAW IT
DATE

WHERE I SAW IT
SPECIFIC LOCATION, INCLUDE STATE

NOTES

....

....

Broadleaf Plantain

(Plantago major)

LONG
CLUSTER

REGIONAL NAME Common Plantain

FLOWER Spikes of tiny, green-white flowers.

IN BLOOM Early to late summer.

PLANT HEIGHT 6–18 inches (15–45.5 cm)

LEAVES Wide, large ovals with thick ribs and long stalks; whorled, basal.

HABITAT Lawns, roadsides, fields, and weedy empty lots.

RANGE Throughout North America. Zones 3–9.

POINT OF FACT Brought from Europe and now a common lawn and garden weed, its young leaves are richer in iron and vitamins A and C than spinach leaves.

I SPOTTED IT!

WHEN I SAW IT
DATE

WHERE I SAW IT
SPECIFIC LOCATION,
INCLUDE STATE

NOTES

....

....

WILDFLOWERS
Cleavers
(Galium aparine)

ROUND CLUSTER

REGIONAL NAMES Goosegrass, Catchweed

FLOWER 0.125 inch (3 mm) across; clusters of 1–3 small white flowers.

IN BLOOM Late spring to summer.

PLANT HEIGHT 8–36 inches (20.5–91.5 cm) long

LEAVES 6–8 long, slender, and bristly leaves arranged in whorls.

HABITAT Woods, fields, weedy lots, and thickets.

RANGE Throughout North America. Zones 3–9.

POINT OF FACT Nearly every part of this plant "cleaves" or clings to passersby, thanks to backward-hooked bristles on its seeds, stems, and leaves.

I SPOTTED IT!

WHEN I SAW IT
DATE

WHERE I SAW IT
SPECIFIC LOCATION, INCLUDE STATE

NOTES

Common Chickweed
(Stellaria media)

ROUND CLUSTER

REGIONAL NAMES > Winterweed, Starwort

FLOWER > 0.25 inch (6.5 mm) across; white flowers with 5 divided petals that look like 10 separate ones, with 5 green sepals larger than its petals.

IN BLOOM > Late winter to late autumn.

PLANT HEIGHT > 3–8 inches (7.5–20.5 cm) with trailing stems to 16 inches (40.5 cm) long

LEAVES > Smooth and oval-shaped with pointed tips; simple, opposite.

HABITAT > Lawns, weedy and empty lots, and pastures.

RANGE > Throughout North America. Zones 4–11.

POINT OF FACT > This hardy plant was introduced from Eurasia and is food for ranging chickens and wild birds.

I SPOTTED IT!

WHEN I SAW IT
DATE

WHERE I SAW IT
SPECIFIC LOCATION, INCLUDE STATE

NOTES

....

....

Cow Parsnip
(Heracleum maximum)

ROUND CLUSTER

FLOWER 4–8 inches (10–20.5 cm) across; flat–topped cluster of many 5-petaled tiny, white flowers.

IN BLOOM Late spring to summer.

PLANT HEIGHT 4–9 feet (1–2.5 m)

LEAVES 3 large, wide, toothed, lobed leaflets; petiole becomes a sheath where it attaches to stalk; compound, alternate.

HABITAT Meadows; marshes; and moist, open woods.

RANGE Throughout North America. Zones 4–8.

POINT OF FACT As its name hints, cow parsnip is a pasture plant that goats, sheep, and cows like to eat.

I SPOTTED IT!

WHEN I SAW IT
DATE

WHERE I SAW IT
SPECIFIC LOCATION, INCLUDE STATE

NOTES

....

....

Daisy Fleabane
(Erigeron annuus)

COMPOSITE

FLOWER At least 40 white to pale pink, feathery ray flowers that are tightly packed around a yellow center disk about 0.5 inch (1.5 cm) across.

IN BLOOM Late spring to autumn.

PLANT HEIGHT 1–5 feet (0.5–1.5 m)

LEAVES Long, toothed, and hairy; simple, alternate.

HABITAT Fields, roadsides, and weedy empty lots.

RANGE Throughout North America. Zones 3–8.

POINT OF FACT This wildflower was used as a bug repellent in homes because of its toxic qualities, bestowing its old-fashioned name for poison, "bane."

I SPOTTED IT!

WHEN I SAW IT
DATE

WHERE I SAW IT
SPECIFIC LOCATION, INCLUDE STATE

NOTES

....
....
....

Dutchman's Breeches
(Dicentra cucullaria)

LONG CLUSTER

FLOWER 0.75 inch (2 cm) across; drooping, white, pantaloon-shaped, and hanging from leafless stalk.

IN BLOOM Early spring.

PLANT HEIGHT 4–12 inches (10–30.5 cm)

LEAVES Feathery, gray-green leaflets; compound, basal.

HABITAT Moist woods, hillsides, and valleys.

RANGE Southeastern Canada and Eastern and Pacific Northwest United States. Zones 3–7.

POINT OF FACT Early spring bumblebees with long, nectar-sipping mouths pollinate these flowers, named for their pantaloon shape.

I SPOTTED IT!

WHEN I SAW IT
DATE

WHERE I SAW IT
SPECIFIC LOCATION, INCLUDE STATE

NOTES

....

....

Round–Lobed Hepatica

(Anemone americana [syn. *Hepatica nobilis*])

SIMPLE

REGIONAL NAME Liverwort

FLOWER 0.5–1 inch (1.5–2.5 cm) across; white to pale lavender flowers with 5–9 petallike sepals.

IN BLOOM Early spring.

PLANT HEIGHT 4–6 inches (10–15 cm)

LEAVES Wide and leathery with 3 rounded lobes at the base of the plant.

HABITAT Rocky or moist woods.

RANGE Eastern Canada and Eastern and Central United States. Zones 3–8.

POINT OF FACT The old leaves you see with its newly bloomed flowers are from last year. Once the flowers are gone, the plant sprouts new leaves.

I SPOTTED IT!

WHEN I SAW IT
DATE

WHERE I SAW IT
SPECIFIC LOCATION,
INCLUDE STATE

NOTES

....

....

213

Japanese Honeysuckle
(Lonicera japonica)

BELL

FLOWER 1–1.5 inches (2.5–4 cm) long; white, tubular, fragrant flowers that yellow with age; backswept, lobed petals and long stamens.

IN BLOOM Spring to summer.

PLANT HEIGHT Vine up to 60 feet (18.5 m) long

LEAVES Smooth, untoothed, evergreen, and oval-shaped; simple, opposite.

HABITAT Roadsides, thickets, fencerows, empty lots, and woods.

RANGE Throughout the United States and Southern Canada. Zones 4–9.

POINT OF FACT Honeysuckle vines with clusters of bright red, tubelike flowers are the less common trumpet honeysuckle native to North America (*Lonicera sempervirens*).

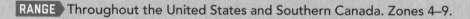

I SPOTTED IT!

WHEN I SAW IT
DATE

WHERE I SAW IT
SPECIFIC LOCATION, INCLUDE STATE

NOTES

....

....

Large–Flowered Trillium
(Trillium grandiflorum)

SIMPLE

FLOWER 1–3 inches (2.5–7.5 cm) across; white flowers that turn pink with age; 3 ruffled petals and 3 green sepals.

IN BLOOM Spring.

PLANT HEIGHT 8–18 inches (20.5–45.5 cm)

LEAVES 3 large, oval-shaped leaves with pointy tips whorled around single stem.

HABITAT Mixed, moist forests.

RANGE Southeastern Canada and Eastern United States. Zones 4–8.

POINT OF FACT This plant showcases the power of 3 its name describes— *trillium* means triplet—with its leaves, sepals, and petals growing in sets of 3.

I SPOTTED IT!

WHEN I SAW IT
DATE

WHERE I SAW IT
SPECIFIC LOCATION, INCLUDE STATE

NOTES

....

....

Lizardtail
(Saururus cernuus)

LONG
CLUSTER

FLOWER White to cream tiny, fragrant flowers that are stacked tightly on a 3–6 inch (7.5–15 cm) tapering plume with a drooping tip.

IN BLOOM Summer.

PLANT HEIGHT 2–5 feet (0.5–1.5m)

LEAVES Heart-shaped and leathery; simple, alternate.

HABITAT Pond edges, shallow swamps, sides of streams, and wet ditches.

RANGE Eastern United States and Canada. Zones 4–11.

POINT OF FACT Named for its taillike, drooping tip, this water-loving plant spreads from underground stems called *rhizomes*.

I SPOTTED IT!

WHEN I SAW IT
DATE

WHERE I SAW IT
SPECIFIC LOCATION,
INCLUDE STATE

NOTES

Mayapple
(Podophyllum peltatum)

SIMPLE

FLOWER 1 inch (2.5 cm) across; white single flower with 6–9 waxy petals that hangs from a stalk.

IN BLOOM Spring.

PLANT HEIGHT 1–1.5 feet (0.5 m)

LEAVES Pairs of large, wide, deeply lobed leaves; simple, opposite.

HABITAT Mixed deciduous forests, shady fields, and riverbanks.

RANGE Southeastern Canada and Central and Eastern United States. Zones 3–8.

POINT OF FACT The fruit, or "apple," doesn't arrive in May—instead, the blossom arrives and is often hidden under the umbrella-like leaves.

I SPOTTED IT!

WHEN I SAW IT
DATE

WHERE I SAW IT
SPECIFIC LOCATION, INCLUDE STATE

NOTES

....

....

Oxeye Daisy
(Leucanthemum vulgare)

COMPOSITE

FLOWER 1–2 inches (2.5–5 cm) across; white, petallike ray flowers that surround a yellow and dented center disk.

IN BLOOM Spring to summer.

PLANT HEIGHT 8–31 inches (20.5–78.5 cm)

LEAVES Dark green with many rounded lobes; simple, alternate.

HABITAT Fields, roadsides, and prairies.

RANGE Throughout North America. Zones 3–8.

POINT OF FACT A single mature plant can produce more than 25,000 seeds.

I SPOTTED IT!

WHEN I SAW IT
DATE

WHERE I SAW IT
SPECIFIC LOCATION, INCLUDE STATE

NOTES

Poison Hemlock
(Conium maculatum)

ROUND
CLUSTER

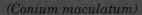

FLOWER 1.5–2 inches (4–5 cm) across; white, rounded, flat-topped clusters of tiny, 5-petaled flowers.

IN BLOOM Late spring to summer.

PLANT HEIGHT 2–10 feet (0.5–3 m)

LEAVES Frond-like, deeply lobed leaflets that are attached to stems with purple spots; compound, alternate.

HABITAT Edges of woods, ditches, and fields.

RANGE Throughout the United States and Southern Canada. Zones 4–8.

POINT OF FACT This plant contains coniine, a poison that, when consumed, halts breathing in mammals, including humans. It is not related in any way to conifer hemlock trees.

I SPOTTED IT!

WHEN I SAW IT
DATE

WHERE I SAW IT
SPECIFIC LOCATION,
INCLUDE STATE

NOTES

....

....

Pokeweed

(Phytolacca americana)

**LONG
CLUSTER**

FLOWER 0.25 inch (6.5 mm) across; small green-white flowers on upright spikes with red stems.

IN BLOOM Summer.

PLANT HEIGHT 1–10 feet (0.3–3 m)

LEAVES Smooth and oval-shaped with pointed tips.

HABITAT Open woods, roadsides, fields, and weedy empty lots.

RANGE Throughout most of the United States and Southern Canada. Zones 4–8.

POINT OF FACT Its flowers turn into dark purple, poisonous berries, whose juice was used as ink and dye by early colonists.

I SPOTTED IT!

WHEN I SAW IT
DATE

WHERE I SAW IT
SPECIFIC LOCATION,
INCLUDE STATE

NOTES

....

....

Queen Anne's Lace
(Daucus carota)

ROUND
CLUSTER

FLOWER 3–5 inches (7.5–12.5 cm) across; flat-topped clusters of tiny, cream-white flowers with a single red flower in the center; 3-forked, leaflike bracts.

IN BLOOM Late spring to early autumn.

PLANT HEIGHT 1–3.5 feet (0.3–1 m)

LEAVES Fernlike fronds with feathery leaflets; compound, alternate.

HABITAT Fields, roadsides, open woods, and weedy empty lots.

RANGE Throughout North America except in the Arctic. Zones 3–9.

POINT OF FACT Its leaves smell like carrots when they are crushed, which gives away its carrot ancestry.

I SPOTTED IT!

WHEN I SAW IT
DATE

WHERE I SAW IT
SPECIFIC LOCATION,
INCLUDE STATE

NOTES

....

....

Red Baneberry
(Actaea rubra)

ROUND
CLUSTER

FLOWER 0.125 inch (3 mm) across; white flowers in round clusters with 4–10 petals at the ends of stems.

IN BLOOM Late spring to early summer.

PLANT HEIGHT 1–3 feet (0.3–0.9 m)

LEAVES Pinnately compound, opposite.

HABITAT Moist woods and sides of streams.

RANGE Canada and Western and Northern United States. Zones 3–9.

POINT OF FACT When eaten, its bright red, toxic berries cause severe mouth burning and throat pain to humans.

I SPOTTED IT!

WHEN I SAW IT
DATE

WHERE I SAW IT
SPECIFIC LOCATION,
INCLUDE STATE

NOTES

....

....

Shepherd's Purse

(Capsella bursa–pastoris)

ROUND
CLUSTER

FLOWER Clusters of tiny, white flowers on the ends of its stem.

IN BLOOM Early spring to late autumn.

PLANT HEIGHT 6–18 inches (15–45.5 cm)

LEAVES Long and deeply lobed; simple, alternate.

HABITAT Lawns, fields, and weedy empty lots.

RANGE Throughout North America except in the Arctic. Zones 4–10.

POINT OF FACT The seedpods look like upside-down puffed hearts, which is the shape of a medieval shepherd's purse, and is how the plant got its name.

I SPOTTED IT!

WHEN I SAW IT
DATE

WHERE I SAW IT
SPECIFIC LOCATION,
INCLUDE STATE

NOTES

....

....

Shooting Star
(Dodecatheon meadia)

FLOWER ▸ 1 inch (2.5 cm) across; white to pink flowers in a loose cluster with 5 backward-pointing petals and 5 yellow stamens.

IN BLOOM ▸ Spring.

PLANT HEIGHT ▸ 8–20 inches (20.5–51 cm)

LEAVES ▸ Dark green and lance-shaped with rounded tips at the base of the plant; simple basal, whorled.

HABITAT ▸ Open woods, prairies, and meadows.

RANGE ▸ Southern Canada and Eastern and Central United States. Zones 4–8.

POINT OF FACT ▸ Bees must poke their tongues hard between the stuck-together stamens to reach the flower's nectar.

◖ **I SPOTTED IT!** ▸

WHEN I SAW IT ▸
DATE

WHERE I SAW IT ▸
SPECIFIC LOCATION,
INCLUDE STATE

NOTES ▸

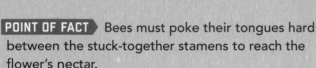

Soapweed
(Yucca glauca)

LONG CLUSTER

REGIONAL NAME ▸ Plains Yucca

FLOWER ▸ 1.5–2.25 inches (4–5.5 cm) across; bell-shaped, green-white flowers that are densely packed along a 4-foot (1.2 m) tall stalk.

IN BLOOM ▸ Late spring to early summer.

PLANT HEIGHT ▸ 2–6 feet (0.5–2 m)

LEAVES ▸ Stiff, evergreen, and dusty-green in color with hairy edges and sharp tips; simple, whorled.

HABITAT ▸ Dry plains, dunes, and hillsides.

RANGE ▸ South Central Canada and Central and Mountain West United States. Zones 4–8.

POINT OF FACT ▸ Yucca moths are the only pollinators of yucca flowers, and yucca fruits are the only food that larval yucca moths eat—they depend on each other!

◖ **I SPOTTED IT!** ▸

WHEN I SAW IT ▸
DATE

WHERE I SAW IT ▸
SPECIFIC LOCATION,
INCLUDE STATE

NOTES ▸

....

....

Solomon's Plume
(Smilacina racemosa)

LONG
CLUSTER

REGIONAL NAMES False Solomon's Seal, Solomon's Zigzag

FLOWER 0.125 inch (3 mm) across; tiny, white, starlike flowers in branching clusters at end of stem; 3 petallike sepals, 3 petals, and 6 stamens.

IN BLOOM Late spring to early summer.

PLANT HEIGHT 1–3 feet (0.3–0.9 m)

LEAVES Long and oval-shaped with parallel veins and pointed tips; simple, alternate.

HABITAT Woods, edges, and clearings.

RANGE Throughout North America except in the Arctic. Zones 3–8.

POINT OF FACT Its stem gently zigzags back and forth between its alternate leaves.

I SPOTTED IT!

WHEN I SAW IT
DATE

WHERE I SAW IT
SPECIFIC LOCATION, INCLUDE STATE

NOTES

....

....

Virgin's Bower
(Clematis virginiana)

ROUND
CLUSTER

FLOWER 1 inch (2.5 cm) across; white flowers in clusters on branches, with 4–5 petallike sepals.

IN BLOOM Summer.

PLANT HEIGHT Vine is 6–10 feet (2–3 m)

LEAVES 3 toothed leaflets; compound, opposite.

HABITAT Edges of woods, thickets, and roadsides.

RANGE Southern Canada and Eastern and Central United States. Zones 3–9.

POINT OF FACT This vine has no tendrils of its own, so it wraps its petioles around other plants or fences for stability.

I SPOTTED IT!

WHEN I SAW IT
DATE

WHERE I SAW IT
SPECIFIC LOCATION,
INCLUDE STATE

NOTES

....

....

Calico Aster

(Symphyotrichum lateriflorum [syn. *Aster lateriflorus*])

COMPOSITE

FLOWER 0.5 inch (1.5 cm) across; 9–15 white ray flowers that surround a yellow or red disk.

IN BLOOM Late summer to early autumn.

PLANT HEIGHT 1–5 feet (0.5–1.5 m)

LEAVES Narrow, lance-shaped, and coarsely toothed; simple, alternate.

HABITAT Fields and thickets.

RANGE Southeastern Canada and Central and Eastern United States. Zones 3–8.

POINT OF FACT Its center disks start off yellow, then turn into a purple-red as they senesce—and some plants will have both colors at once, like the coat of a calico cat.

I SPOTTED IT!

WHEN I SAW IT
DATE

WHERE I SAW IT
SPECIFIC LOCATION,
INCLUDE STATE

NOTES

White Snakeroot

(Eupatorium rugosum)

ROUND
CLUSTER

FLOWER 0.25 inch (6.5 mm) across; small, fuzzy, and white flower heads that are in flat-topped clusters.

IN BLOOM Summer to autumn.

PLANT HEIGHT 1–5 feet (0.5–1.5 m)

LEAVES Oval-shaped and sharp-toothed with pointed tips; simple, opposite.

HABITAT Woods, thickets, and pastures.

RANGE Southeastern Canada and Central and Eastern United States. Zones 4–8.

POINT OF FACT Because all parts of the plant are toxic,
even milk from cows who've eaten it can make humans sick.

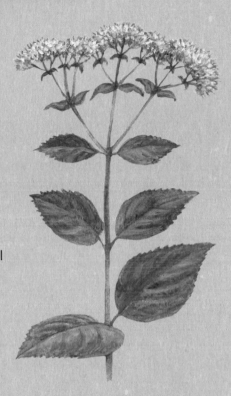

I SPOTTED IT!

WHEN I SAW IT
DATE

WHERE I SAW IT
SPECIFIC LOCATION,
INCLUDE STATE

NOTES

....

....

229

Fragrant Water Lily

(Nymphaea odorata)

SIMPLE

REGIONAL NAME ▸ White Water Lily

FLOWER ▸ 3–5 inches (7.5–12.5 cm) across; white flowers with many petals, yellow stamens, and 4 green sepals.

IN BLOOM ▸ Summer.

PLANT HEIGHT ▸ Above water, about an inch (2.5 cm); underwater stalks, 2–4 feet (0.5–1.2 m)

LEAVES ▸ Large and round with shiny green on top and purple underneath; float on water.

HABITAT ▸ Aquatic places like ponds, canals, and still waters.

RANGE ▸ Throughout much of Canada and the United States. Zones 4–9.

POINT OF FACT ▸ The fragrant flowers open in the early morning and close again after midday.

◑ I SPOTTED IT!

WHEN I SAW IT
DATE

WHERE I SAW IT
SPECIFIC LOCATION,
INCLUDE STATE

NOTES

....

....

Wild Leek
(Allium tricoccum)

ROUND
CLUSTER

REGIONAL NAME Ramps

FLOWER 0.25 inch (6.5 mm) long; creamy-white flowers in dome-shaped clusters with 3 petals and 3 petallike sepals.

IN BLOOM Early summer.

PLANT HEIGHT 6–20 inches (15–51 cm)

LEAVES Large, wide, lance-shaped, and clustered at the base of the plant.

HABITAT Woods.

RANGE Southeastern Canada and Central and Eastern United States. Zones 4–8.

POINT OF FACT By the time it flowers, the plant's leaves wither and die, leaving a naked stem topped with a dome of blooms.

I SPOTTED IT!

WHEN I SAW IT
DATE

WHERE I SAW IT
SPECIFIC LOCATION, INCLUDE STATE

NOTES

....

....

Wild Sarsaparilla
(Aralia nudicaulis)

**ROUND
CLUSTER**

FLOWER 1.5–2 inches (4–5 cm) across; tiny, green-white flowers in a round cluster with 5 petals and 5 stamens.

IN BLOOM Summer.

PLANT HEIGHT 8–20 inches (20.5–51 cm)

LEAVES Single stems that branch into 3 petioles, each with 3–5 toothed, oval leaflets; compound, opposite.

HABITAT Woods.

RANGE Throughout North America except the West Coast and the Arctic. Zones 3–8.

POINT OF FACT Early colonists from Europe brewed root beer from the strong-smelling roots.

I SPOTTED IT!

WHEN I SAW IT
DATE

WHERE I SAW IT
SPECIFIC LOCATION, INCLUDE STATE

NOTES

....

....

Wild Strawberry

(Fragaria virginiana)

SIMPLE

REGIONAL NAME Common Strawberry

FLOWER 0.75 inch (2 cm) across; white flowers with 5 rounded petals, 5 sepals; has a dome of many stamens and pistils.

IN BLOOM Spring and early summer.

PLANT HEIGHT Creeping flower stalks, 3–6 inches (7.5–15 cm) tall

LEAVES 3 leaflets with hairy petioles; compound, alternate.

HABITAT Fields, edges of woods, and prairies.

RANGE Throughout North America except in the Arctic. Zones 5–9.

POINT OF FACT The bigger, sweeter strawberries found in grocery stores and gardens were made by crossing this plant with another species from South America.

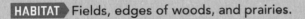

I SPOTTED IT!

WHEN I SAW IT
DATE

WHERE I SAW IT
SPECIFIC LOCATION,
INCLUDE STATE

NOTES

....

....

Canada Violet
(Viola canadensis)

IRREGULAR

FLOWER 0.75–1 inch (2–2.5 cm) across; white, fragrant, 5-petal flowers with a yellow center and purple vertical lines.

IN BLOOM Spring.

PLANT HEIGHT 8–16 inches (20.5–40.5 cm)

LEAVES Heart-shaped with toothed edges; simple, alternate.

HABITAT Woods.

RANGE Canada and Northern and mountainous United States. Zones 3–8.

POINT OF FACT North America is home to dozens of species of violets that all vary in color—some are purple, and others are yellow, white, and even green!

I SPOTTED IT!

WHEN I SAW IT
DATE

WHERE I SAW IT
SPECIFIC LOCATION, INCLUDE STATE

NOTES

....

....

Black-Eyed Susan
(Rudbeckia hirta)

COMPOSITE

FLOWER 2–3 inches (5–7 cm); up to 20 bright-yellow rays surrounding a cone-shaped, dark brown central disk.

IN BLOOM Summer to early autumn.

PLANT HEIGHT 1–3 feet (0.3–0.9 m)

LEAVES Large, oval-shaped, and hairy; simple, alternate.

HABITAT Prairies and roadsides.

RANGE Throughout North America. Zones 3-9.

POINT OF FACT Each of its stiff, hairy stems holds up one single flower.

I SPOTTED IT!

WHEN I SAW IT
DATE

WHERE I SAW IT
SPECIFIC LOCATION, INCLUDE STATE

NOTES

....

....

Common Dandelion

(Taraxacum officinale)

COMPOSITE

FLOWER 1.5 inches (4 cm) across; yellow flower made up of many ray florets.

IN BLOOM Early spring to late summer.

PLANT HEIGHT 2–18 inches (5–45.5 cm)

LEAVES Long, toothed, and clustered at the base of the plant; simple basal, whorled.

HABITAT Lawns, fields, roadsides, and weedy empty lots.

RANGE Throughout North America. Zones 3–8.

POINT OF FACT Each yellow "petal" is a tiny, individual ray flower that becomes a parachute-topped seed.

I SPOTTED IT!

WHEN I SAW IT
DATE

WHERE I SAW IT
SPECIFIC LOCATION,
INCLUDE STATE

NOTES

Evening Primrose
(Oenothera biennis)

SIMPLE

FLOWER 1–2 inches (2.5–5 cm) across; yellow flowers in loose clusters, with 4 petals, an X-shaped sigma, and 4 sepals.

IN BLOOM Early summer to early autumn.

PLANT HEIGHT 2–5 feet (0.5–1.5 m)

LEAVES Hairy, slightly toothed, slender, and pointy; simple, opposite.

HABITAT Roadsides and fields.

RANGE Southern Canada and the United States except Northwest. Zones 4–9.

POINT OF FACT Its flowers only open at night and are visited by pollinating moths attracted to their lemon scent.

I SPOTTED IT!

WHEN I SAW IT
DATE

WHERE I SAW IT
SPECIFIC LOCATION, INCLUDE STATE

NOTES

....

....

Common Mullein

(Verbascum thapsus)

LONG
CLUSTER

FLOWER 1 inch (2.5 cm) across; yellow, 5-petaled flowers on a spike.

IN BLOOM Early summer to early autumn.

PLANT HEIGHT 2–7 feet (0.5–2.1 m)

LEAVES Gray-green, velvety, long, and oval-shaped at the base; also arranged along a single woolly stalk; simple basal at base, alternate on stalk.

HABITAT Fields, roadsides, lawns, weedy empty lots, and old pastures.

RANGE Throughout North America. Zones 3–9.

POINT OF FACT Mulleins are also called velvet plants or flannel leaf plants because of the white, woolly texture of its leaves and stems.

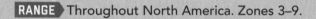

O I SPOTTED IT!

WHEN I SAW IT
DATE

WHERE I SAW IT
SPECIFIC LOCATION,
INCLUDE STATE

NOTES

....

....

Common Purslane

(Portulaca oleracea)

SIMPLE

FLOWER 0.25 inch (6.5 mm) across; yellow, simple, 5-petaled flowers.

IN BLOOM Early summer to autumn.

PLANT HEIGHT 12 inches (30.5 cm) long, along the ground

LEAVES Thick, fleshy, and oval-shaped on red stems; simple, alternate or opposite.

HABITAT Lawns, weedy empty lots, and fields.

RANGE Throughout North America except in the Arctic. Zones 2–11.

POINT OF FACT Though considered a weed by many gardeners, it's an excellent iron-rich salad plant or cooking herb.

◖ I SPOTTED IT! ⟩

WHEN I SAW IT
DATE

WHERE I SAW IT
SPECIFIC LOCATION, INCLUDE STATE

NOTES

....

....

Common Sunflower

(Helianthus annuus)

COMPOSITE

FLOWER 3–6 inches (7.5–15 cm) across; brown disk surrounded by yellow ray flowers.

IN BLOOM Summer to autumn.

PLANT HEIGHT 3–10 feet (0.9–3 m)

LEAVES Large, rough, stiff-haired, toothed, and heart-shaped with pointy tips; simple, alternate.

HABITAT Prairies, roadsides, and weedy empty lots.

RANGE Throughout North America. Zones 2–11.

POINT OF FACT Its flower heads turn to follow the sun throughout the day.

I SPOTTED IT!

WHEN I SAW IT
DATE

WHERE I SAW IT
SPECIFIC LOCATION, INCLUDE STATE

NOTES

Yellow Trout Lily
(Erythronium americanum)

BELL

REGIONAL NAMES Dogtooth Violet, Adder's Tongue

FLOWER 1 inch (2.5 cm) across; yellow nodding flower with 6 similar-looking petals and sepals that curve backward with 6 long stamens.

IN BLOOM Early spring.

PLANT HEIGHT 4–10 inches (10–25.5 cm)

LEAVES Leathery and long from the base of the stalk, with brown-purple splotches on their green color; simple, opposite.

HABITAT Moist woods and meadows.

RANGE Southeastern Canada and Eastern United States. Zones 3–8.

POINT OF FACT The trout part of this lily's name comes from its mottled leaves that look somewhat like a brown or brook trout.

I SPOTTED IT!

WHEN I SAW IT
DATE

WHERE I SAW IT
SPECIFIC LOCATION,
INCLUDE STATE

NOTES

Yellow Wood Sorrel
(Oxalis stricta)

SIMPLE

REGIONAL NAME Lemon Clover

FLOWER 0.5 inch (1.5 cm) across; yellow, 5-petaled flowers with 10 stamens.

IN BLOOM Spring and sometimes again in autumn.

PLANT HEIGHT 6–10 inches (15–25.5 cm)

LEAVES 3 heart-shaped leaflets; compound, alternate.

HABITAT Lawns, roadsides, open woods, and weedy empty lots.

RANGE Southern Canada and throughout the United States. Zones 3–10.

POINT OF FACT *Sorrel* is an old German word that means sour, which hearkens back to its leaves' sour taste.

◉ I SPOTTED IT!

WHEN I SAW IT
DATE

WHERE I SAW IT
SPECIFIC LOCATION,
INCLUDE STATE

NOTES

....

....

Tall Goldenrod

(Solidago canadensis)

REGIONAL NAMES Meadow Goldenrod, Canada Goldenrod

FLOWER Arrowhead-shaped clusters of tiny yellow flowers on the ends of arching stalks.

IN BLOOM Late summer to autumn.

PLANT HEIGHT 1–5 feet (0.3–1.5 m)

LEAVES Long, rough, and toothed.

HABITAT Fields, open woods, and roadsides.

RANGE Throughout most of North America. Zones 3–8.

POINT OF FACT This plant is often thought to trigger allergies for hay fever sufferers—but the allergies actually start from the windblown pollen from ragweed (*Ambrosia spp.*).

I SPOTTED IT!

WHEN I SAW IT
DATE

WHERE I SAW IT
SPECIFIC LOCATION,
INCLUDE STATE

NOTES

....

....

Rubber Rabbitbrush

(Ericameria nauseosa)

FLOWER 0.25–0.5 inch (0.5–1.5 cm) across; small, yellow, starlike flowers in clusters.

IN BLOOM Late summer to autumn.

PLANT HEIGHT 2–7 feet (0.5–2.1 m)

LEAVES Narrow, long, and covered in white hairs; foul-scented; simple, alternate.

HABITAT Deserts, grasslands, and open woods.

RANGE Western Canada and Western United States. Zones 4–9.

POINT OF FACT Deer, rabbits, and other mammals graze on this shrub, whose flowers many Navajo made into yellow dye.

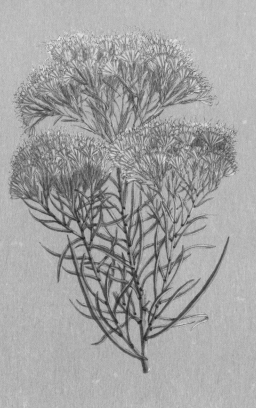

I SPOTTED IT!

WHEN I SAW IT
DATE

WHERE I SAW IT
SPECIFIC LOCATION,
INCLUDE STATE

NOTES

....

....

Common Saint-John's-Wort

(Hypericum perforatum)

SIMPLE

REGIONAL NAME Klamath Weed

FLOWER 0.75–1 inch (2–2.5 cm) across; bright-yellow, 5-petaled flowers with black dots on margins.

IN BLOOM Early summer to early autumn.

PLANT HEIGHT 1–2.5 feet (0.3–0.8 m)

LEAVES Slender and oval-shaped with see-through dots that look like holes; simple, opposite, or whorled.

HABITAT Fields, roadsides, and weedy empty lots.

RANGE Southern Canada and throughout the United States. Zones 3–8.

POINT OF FACT It's a super-spreading invasive species—a single plant over its lifetime can make 23,000 seeds that can survive underground for a decade.

◊ I SPOTTED IT!

WHEN I SAW IT
DATE

WHERE I SAW IT
SPECIFIC LOCATION, INCLUDE STATE

NOTES

....

....

Common Buttercup

(Ranunculus acris)

SIMPLE

REGIONAL NAMES Meadow Buttercup, Tall Buttercup

FLOWER 1 inch (2.5 cm) across; waxy, shiny bright-yellow flowers with 5 sepals, 5 petals, and numerous stamens and pistils.

IN BLOOM Spring to late summer.

PLANT HEIGHT 2–3 feet (0.5–0.9 m)

LEAVES Palmate and deeply lobed into 5–7 toothed, leaflet-like sections; simple, alternate.

HABITAT Fields, meadows, and roadsides.

RANGE Throughout North America except Southwestern United States. Zones 4–8.

POINT OF FACT The wide-open cup shape of this flower makes it accessible to pollinating beetles, wasps, flies—and bees.

I SPOTTED IT!

WHEN I SAW IT
DATE

WHERE I SAW IT
SPECIFIC LOCATION,
INCLUDE STATE

NOTES

....

....

Mossy Stonecrop
(Sedum acre)

**ROUND
CLUSTER**

REGIONAL NAME Wallpepper

FLOWER 0.3 inch (7.6 mm) across; yellow, star-shaped flowers in small clusters.

IN BLOOM Late spring to summer.

PLANT HEIGHT 1–3 inches (2.5–7.5 cm)

LEAVES Fleshy, succulent, and evergreen on creeping stems; simple, alternate.

HABITAT Rock walls and dry clearings.

RANGE Throughout North America except the Deep South, Southwest, and Arctic. Zones 4–9.

POINT OF FACT It's not moss, but it does grow in a mosslike way—it covers the ground with low, evergreen, creeping stems that form mats of succulent leaves.

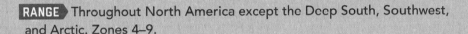

I SPOTTED IT!

WHEN I SAW IT
DATE

WHERE I SAW IT
SPECIFIC LOCATION,
INCLUDE STATE

NOTES

....

....

247

Yellow Lady's Slipper

(Cypripedium calceolus)

IRREGULAR

FLOWER 2 inches (5 cm) across; yellow, pouch-like petals with 2 green-brown and twisted side petals; 2 sepals above and below.

IN BLOOM Spring to midsummer.

PLANT HEIGHT 8–28 inches (20.5–71 cm)

LEAVES Large, wide, and oval-shaped with parallel veins; simple, opposite.

HABITAT Bogs, swamps, and woods.

RANGE Throughout North America except in the Arctic. Zones 3–7.

POINT OF FACT Insects that enter the slipper-like pouch formed by its lower petal can only exit by squeezing past a pollen-filled area, which helps to pollinate the orchids.

I SPOTTED IT!

WHEN I SAW IT
DATE

WHERE I SAW IT
SPECIFIC LOCATION, INCLUDE STATE

NOTES

....
....

Plains Prickly Pear
(Opuntia polyacantha)

SIMPLE

FLOWER 2–3 inches (5–7.5 cm) across; bright-yellow flowers with many petals.

IN BLOOM Late spring to early summer.

PLANT HEIGHT 3–6 inches (7.5–15 cm); stems are shaped like stacked flat oval pads

SPINES 2 inches (5 cm) long; clusters of 6–10.

HABITAT Plains, deserts, and dry mountain slopes.

RANGE Southwestern, Western, and Central United States, and South Central Canada. Zones 3–9.

POINT OF FACT The popular Mexican dish nopales is made from the pads of *Opuntia spp.* cacti. Candies, jelly, beverages, and other sweet treats are made from the deep pink fruits.

◖ I SPOTTED IT! ▷

WHEN I SAW IT
DATE

WHERE I SAW IT
SPECIFIC LOCATION, INCLUDE STATE

NOTES

....

....

Teddy Bear Cholla
(Cylindropuntia (Opuntia) bigelovii)

SIMPLE

FLOWER 1–1.5 inches (2.5–4 cm) across; green-yellow flowers with lavender-streaked petals.

IN BLOOM Spring.

PLANT HEIGHT 2–5 feet (0.5–1.5 m)

SPINES 0.5–1 inch (1.5–2.5 cm); white to yellow spines tipped with tiny, backward-pointing barbs.

HABITAT Rocky desert slopes and scrublands.

RANGE Southeastern California, Arizona, and Northwestern Mexico. Zones 8–10.

POINT OF FACT From a distance, its branches look like the arms or legs of a fuzzy, stuffed-toy animal.

I SPOTTED IT!

WHEN I SAW IT
DATE

WHERE I SAW IT
SPECIFIC LOCATION, INCLUDE STATE

NOTES

Butterfly Weed

(Asclepias tuberosa)

ROUND CLUSTER

REGIONAL NAME Orange Milkweed

FLOWER 2 inches (5 cm) across; orange, tiny, star-shaped, 5-petaled flowers in clusters.

IN BLOOM Early summer to early autumn.

PLANT HEIGHT 1–2.5 feet (0.3–0.8 m)

LEAVES Dark green, long, and narrow; simple, alternate.

HABITAT Prairies, hillsides, open woods, fields, and roadsides.

RANGE Eastern and Southern United States. Zones 3–9.

POINT OF FACT Butterflies and hummingbirds love the flowers' nectar, as its name hints.

I SPOTTED IT!

WHEN I SAW IT
DATE

WHERE I SAW IT
SPECIFIC LOCATION, INCLUDE STATE

NOTES

....

....

California Poppy

(Eschscholzia californica)

SIMPLE

FLOWER 1–2 inches (2.5–5 cm) across; cup formed by 4 fan-shaped, silky, dark orange petals.

IN BLOOM Early spring to early autumn.

PLANT HEIGHT 8–24 inches (20.5–61 cm)

LEAVES Blue-green and feathery on long stalks; compound, opposite.

HABITAT Grassy areas, hillsides, and roadsides.

RANGE West Coast and Southwestern United States. Zones 6–10.

POINT OF FACT The flowers close at night and when clouds cover the sun.

I SPOTTED IT!

WHEN I SAW IT
DATE

WHERE I SAW IT
SPECIFIC LOCATION, INCLUDE STATE

NOTES

....

....

Jewelweed
(Impatiens capensis)

IRREGULAR

REGIONAL NAME Spotted Touch-Me-Not

FLOWER 1 inch (2.5 cm) across; orange, cornucopia-shaped flower with dark spots.

IN BLOOM Midsummer to autumn.

PLANT HEIGHT 2–5 feet (0.5–1.5 m)

LEAVES Oval-shaped and pale-bottomed on weak, water-filled stems; simple, alternate.

HABITAT Shady woods and wetlands.

RANGE Most of North America (except the Southwest and Southern California) and Northeast Canada. Zones 2–11.

POINT OF FACT It's also called "touch-me-not" because its swollen fruits burst open when touched, which disperses the seeds inside.

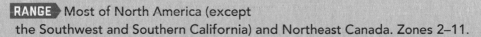

◗ I SPOTTED IT!

WHEN I SAW IT
DATE

WHERE I SAW IT
SPECIFIC LOCATION,
INCLUDE STATE

NOTES

....

....

Wild Columbine
(Aquilegia canadensis)

BELL

REGIONAL NAME ▶ Red Columbine

FLOWER ▶ 1–2 inches (2.5–5 cm) across; drooping, bell-like, red and yellow flowers.

IN BLOOM ▶ Spring to early summer.

PLANT HEIGHT ▶ 1–2 feet (0.3–0.5 m)

LEAVES ▶ Many 3-lobed leaflets on long stalks; compound, alternate.

HABITAT ▶ Rocky woods, shaded cliffs, and ledges.

RANGE ▶ Southeastern Canada and Central and Eastern United States. Zones 3–8.

POINT OF FACT ▶ Inside each hollow, tubelike spur is nectar sippable only by long-tongued hummingbirds and insects.

◖ I SPOTTED IT! ▶

WHEN I SAW IT
DATE

WHERE I SAW IT
SPECIFIC LOCATION,
INCLUDE STATE

NOTES ▶

....

....

Cardinal Flower
(Lobelia cardinalis)

LONG CLUSTER

REGIONAL NAME Scarlet Lobelia

FLOWER 8–12 inches (20.5–30.5 cm) across; spire made of bright-red, tubular flowers with 2 upper and 3 lower petals.

IN BLOOM Summer.

PLANT HEIGHT 2–4 feet (0.5–1.2 m)

LEAVES Spear-shaped, toothed, and long; simple, alternate.

HABITAT Moist woods, meadows, and streamsides.

RANGE Eastern Canada and Eastern, Midwestern, and Southwestern United States. Zones 3–9.

POINT OF FACT It was named after the red robes of Catholic cardinals.

I SPOTTED IT!

WHEN I SAW IT
DATE

WHERE I SAW IT
SPECIFIC LOCATION, INCLUDE STATE

NOTES

Painted Cup

(Castilleja coccinea)

ROUND
CLUSTER

REGIONAL NAMES Indian Paintbrush, Scarlet Paintbrush

FLOWER 1 inch (2.5 cm) across; small, green-yellow flowers inside a dense cluster of red-tipped, fanlike bracts.

IN BLOOM Spring to summer.

PLANT HEIGHT 1–2 feet (0.3–0.5 m)

LEAVES Long-lobed segments; simple, opposite.

HABITAT Meadows, fields, and prairies.

RANGE East and Central North America. Zones 4–8.

POINT OF FACT Its bracts are upright and look as if they've been dipped in red paint, giving this flower its name.

I SPOTTED IT!

WHEN I SAW IT
DATE

WHERE I SAW IT
SPECIFIC LOCATION,
INCLUDE STATE

NOTES

....

....

Trumpet Creeper
(Campsis radicans)

BELL

REGIONAL NAME ▸ Trumpet Vine

FLOWER ▸ 2.5 inches (6.5 cm) across; orange-red, 5-lobed, trumpet-shaped flowers in clusters.

IN BLOOM ▸ Summer.

PLANT HEIGHT ▸ Vine grows to 50 feet (15 m) long.

LEAVES ▸ Pinnately compound with 7–11 toothed leaflets; compound, opposite.

HABITAT ▸ Fencerows, thickets, and old fields.

RANGE ▸ Southern Canada and Eastern and Central United States. Zones 4–10.

POINT OF FACT ▸ This woody vine climbs fences, wooden posts, and trees by sending out rootlets that grow from its stems.

I SPOTTED IT!

WHEN I SAW IT
DATE

WHERE I SAW IT
SPECIFIC LOCATION, INCLUDE STATE

NOTES

....

....

Wood Lily
(Lilium philadelphicum)

BELL

FLOWER 2 inches (5 cm) across; orange-red, funnel-shaped flower with dark purple spots toward its center; 6 total petals and petallike sepals, and 6 stamens.

IN BLOOM Summer.

PLANT HEIGHT 1–3 feet (0.3–0.9 m)

LEAVES Whorls of 3–8 slender, lance-shaped leaves; simple, alternate.

HABITAT Prairies, meadows, and open woods.

RANGE Southwestern Canada and throughout the United States except the Southwest. Zones 4–7.

POINT OF FACT If you're lucky enough to see one of these beauties, enjoy the view but leave it be—picking the flowers has made them rare in many places.

I SPOTTED IT!

WHEN I SAW IT
DATE

WHERE I SAW IT
SPECIFIC LOCATION,
INCLUDE STATE

NOTES

....

....

Red Clover

(Trifolium pratense)

ROUND
CLUSTER

FLOWER 1 inch (2.5 cm) across; tiny, pealike deep pink flowers in a rounded head.

IN BLOOM Spring to summer.

PLANT HEIGHT 6–24 inches (15–61 cm)

LEAVES Pointed, oval-shaped leaflets in groups of 3 with a pale white V; compound, alternate.

HABITAT Meadows, fields, lawns, roadsides, and valleys.

RANGE Throughout the United States and Canada. Zones 3–8.

POINT OF FACT Like all members of the pea family, it fertilizes the soil with nitrogen taken from the air and stored in its roots.

I SPOTTED IT!

WHEN I SAW IT
DATE

WHERE I SAW IT
SPECIFIC LOCATION,
INCLUDE STATE

NOTES

....

....

259

Common Foxglove
(Digitalis purpurea)

LONG
CLUSTER

FLOWER 1.5–2.5 inches (4–6.5 cm) across; deep-pink to purple, thimble-shaped flowers stacked in a drooping cluster with pale insides speckled with red dots.

IN BLOOM Summer.

PLANT HEIGHT 2–7 feet (0.5–2.1 m)

LEAVES Narrow and oval-shaped; simple, opposite.

HABITAT Roadsides, stream banks, and fields.

RANGE Throughout North America except Central and farthest Northern regions. Zones 4–8.

POINT OF FACT Though it's a poisonous plant introduced from Europe, this plant's toxin creates a greatly beneficial heart drug, called digitalis.

I SPOTTED IT!

WHEN I SAW IT
DATE

WHERE I SAW IT
SPECIFIC LOCATION,
INCLUDE STATE

NOTES

....

....

Common Milkweed
(Asclepias syriaca)

ROUND
CLUSTER

FLOWER 0.5 inch (1.5 cm) across; deep-pink, star-shaped, 5-petal flowers in drooping clusters.

IN BLOOM Summer.

PLANT HEIGHT 2–6 feet (0.5–1.8 m)

LEAVES Wide, oval-shaped, and sap-filled; light-green above and downy-gray underneath; simple, opposite.

HABITAT Fields, roadsides, and weedy empty lots.

RANGE Southeastern Canada and Eastern and Central United States. Zones 3–9.

POINT OF FACT The caterpillars of Monarch butterflies eat only milkweed leaves.

I SPOTTED IT!

WHEN I SAW IT
DATE

WHERE I SAW IT
SPECIFIC LOCATION,
INCLUDE STATE

NOTES

....

....

Common Morning Glory

(Ipomoea purpurea)

BELL

FLOWER 2–3 inches (5–7.5 cm) across; pink, blue, purple, or white trumpet-shaped flowers.

IN BLOOM Midsummer to early autumn.

PLANT HEIGHT Vine that climbs to 10 feet (3 m) in length.

LEAVES Wide and heart-shaped; simple, alternate.

HABITAT Fields, roadsides, and weedy empty lots.

RANGE Southern Canada and throughout United States. Zones 2–11.

POINT OF FACT The flowers on this climbing vine earn their name by opening at dawn and then closing a few hours later.

I SPOTTED IT!

WHEN I SAW IT
DATE

WHERE I SAW IT
SPECIFIC LOCATION, INCLUDE STATE

NOTES

....

....

Field Thistle

(Cirsium discolor)

COMPOSITE

REGIONAL NAME Pasture Thistle

FLOWER 1 inch (2.5 cm) across; deep-pink heads of feathery disk flowers enclosed in spiny, cup-shaped bracts.

IN BLOOM Midsummer to early autumn.

PLANT HEIGHT 3–9 feet (0.9–2.7 m)

LEAVES Long, deeply lobed, pointy-tipped, and bristly; simple, alternate.

HABITAT Fields, pastures, and meadows.

RANGE Eastern and Central Canada and Eastern and Midwestern United States. Zones 2–8.

POINT OF FACT Its large flowers full of nectar attract butterflies, hummingbirds, bees, and moths, while its late-summer seeds attract seed-eating birds like goldfinches.

◖ I SPOTTED IT! ▸

WHEN I SAW IT
DATE

WHERE I SAW IT
SPECIFIC LOCATION,
INCLUDE STATE

NOTES

....

....

Field Mint
(Mentha arvensis)

ROUND CLUSTER

REGIONAL NAME Wild Mint

FLOWER 0.25 inch (6.5 mm) across; pale pink, bell-shaped flowers in clusters.

IN BLOOM Midsummer to early autumn.

PLANT HEIGHT 6–24 inches (15–61 cm)

LEAVES Long, pointed, oval-shaped, and toothed; mint-scented with a square stem; simple, opposite.

HABITAT Moist woods, wet fields, ditches, and stream banks.

RANGE Throughout North America except the Deep South. Zones 4–8.

POINT OF FACT Its fragrant leaves are used as mint flavoring in household goods and toiletries.

I SPOTTED IT!

WHEN I SAW IT
DATE

WHERE I SAW IT
SPECIFIC LOCATION,
INCLUDE STATE

NOTES

....

....

Halberdleaf Rose Mallow
(Hibiscus laevis)

SIMPLE

FLOWER 4–6 inches (10–15 cm) across; pale pink to white flower with a deep-pink center, 5 overlapping petals, a thick column of combined stamens, and a pistil in the center.

IN BLOOM Summer to early autumn.

PLANT HEIGHT 3–6 feet (0.9–1.8 m)

LEAVES 3 toothed lobes with a longer center; simple, alternate.

HABITAT Marshes, swamps, ditches, and wet soil along streams, rivers, and ponds.

RANGE Ontario, Canada, and Eastern and Central United States. Zones 4–9.

POINT OF FACT This mallow's leaves have the shape of halberd's blade, which was a mean-looking medieval weapon.

I SPOTTED IT!

WHEN I SAW IT
DATE

WHERE I SAW IT
SPECIFIC LOCATION, INCLUDE STATE

NOTES

....

....

265

Pinkweed

(Polygonum pensylvanicum)

LONG
CLUSTER

REGIONAL NAMES > Pink Knotweed,
Pennsylvania Smartweed

FLOWER > 0.125 inch (3 mm) across; pink
flowers in dense, spiky clusters on the
ends of stems.

IN BLOOM > Late spring to autumn.

PLANT HEIGHT > 1–4 feet (0.3–1.2 m)

LEAVES > Long, lancelike, and pointy-tipped on
branching, jointed stems; simple, alternate.

HABITAT > Fields, weedy empty lots, roadsides, and lawns.

RANGE > Throughout the United States except Mountain
West and Southern Canada. Zones 3–10.

POINT OF FACT > Members of this genus (*Polygonum*) are often called
knotweeds, named for the knotty stem joints, as well as smartweeds,
because their sharp taste smarts the mouth.

I SPOTTED IT!

WHEN I SAW IT
DATE

WHERE I SAW IT
SPECIFIC LOCATION,
INCLUDE STATE

NOTES

....

....

Rocky Mountain Bee Plant
(Cleome serrulata)

REGIONAL NAME Stinkweed

FLOWER 0.5 inch (1.5 cm) across; violet-pink flowers in a cluster on a long stalk with 4 petals and 6 long stamens.

IN BLOOM Summer.

PLANT HEIGHT 6–60 inches (15–152.5 cm)

LEAVES 3 long, lance-shaped leaflets; compound, alternate.

HABITAT Plains, mountain foothills, and open woods.

RANGE Southwestern Canada and Western and Central United States. Zones 3–10.

POINT OF FACT While the plant's leaves smell like a skunk's spray, its flowers make lots of sweet nectar that attracts butterflies, hummingbirds, and bees.

I SPOTTED IT!

WHEN I SAW IT
DATE

WHERE I SAW IT
SPECIFIC LOCATION, INCLUDE STATE

NOTES

....

....

267

Spring Beauty
(Claytonia virginica)

SIMPLE

FLOWER 0.5–0.75 inch (1.5–2 cm) across; pale pink or white flower with a dark pink stripe, 5 petals, 5 stamens, and 2 sepals.

IN BLOOM Early spring.

PLANT HEIGHT 2–10 inches (5–25.5 cm)

LEAVES Single, bladelike pair on a thin stem; simple, opposite.

HABITAT Moist woods, thickets, clearings, and lawns.

RANGE Southeastern Canada and Eastern and Central United States. Zones 4–9.

POINT OF FACT The roots, called corms, are edible and can be cooked like small potatoes.

I SPOTTED IT!

WHEN I SAW IT
DATE

WHERE I SAW IT
SPECIFIC LOCATION,
INCLUDE STATE

NOTES

....

....

Swamp Smartweed
(Polygonum amphibium)

LONG CLUSTER

FLOWER 2–7 inches (5–18 cm) across; spike made of clusters of tiny, dark pink flowers.

IN BLOOM Midsummer to early autumn.

PLANT HEIGHT 2–3 feet (0.5–0.9 m)

LEAVES Long and lance-shaped with base encircling the stem; simple, alternate.

HABITAT Swamps, ponds, slow streams, wet prairies, and shorelines.

RANGE Throughout North America except the Deep South and Arctic. Zones 3–8.

POINT OF FACT It can grow on land as a terrestrial plant and in the water as an aquatic plant.

I SPOTTED IT!

WHEN I SAW IT
DATE

WHERE I SAW IT
SPECIFIC LOCATION, INCLUDE STATE

NOTES

....

....

Wild Bergamot

(Monarda fistulosa)

ROUND CLUSTER

FLOWER 1 inch (2.5 cm) across; lavender to pink, tubular flowers in a round cluster with long stamens; has bracts that are often pink along the midrib.

IN BLOOM Summer to early autumn.

PLANT HEIGHT 2–4 feet (0.5–1.2 m)

LEAVES Gray-green, spearhead-shaped, and toothed; simple, opposite.

HABITAT Dry fields, thickets, and prairies.

RANGE Eastern and Central North America. Zones 3–8.

POINT OF FACT After the Boston Tea Party occurred, many American colonists boycotted imported tea—instead, they brewed their own tea from native plants, including wild bergamot.

I SPOTTED IT!

WHEN I SAW IT
DATE

WHERE I SAW IT
SPECIFIC LOCATION, INCLUDE STATE

NOTES

....

....

Wild Geranium
(Geranium maculatum)

SIMPLE

FLOWER 1–1.5 inch (2.5–4 cm) across; pink flowers in loose clusters with 5 rounded petals, 5 pointed sepals, and 10 stamens.

IN BLOOM Spring.

PLANT HEIGHT 1–2 feet (0.3–0.5 m)

LEAVES 5 deep lobes and palmately toothed; simple, opposite.

HABITAT Woods, thickets, and meadows.

RANGE Central and Eastern North America. Zones 3–9.

POINT OF FACT As the seedpod dries, it shrinks until it bursts to catapult the seeds away from the parent plant.

I SPOTTED IT!

WHEN I SAW IT
DATE

WHERE I SAW IT
SPECIFIC LOCATION, INCLUDE STATE

NOTES

....

....

Pincushion Cactus

(Coryphantha vivipara [syn. *Escobaria vivipara])*

SIMPLE

REGIONAL NAME ▷ Cushion Cactus

FLOWER ▷ 1–2 inches (2.5–5 cm) across; red, lavender, or pink flowers with many pointy-tipped petals.

IN BLOOM ▷ Late spring.

PLANT HEIGHT ▷ 1.5–6 inches (4–15 cm)

SPINES ▷ 0.5–0.75 inch (1.5–2 cm) long, with red, pink, or black tips; arranged in radiating clusters of 3–10 and ringed by dozens of shorter white spines.

HABITAT ▷ Rocky slopes, deserts, arid plains, and dry conifer forests.

RANGE ▷ Central Canada, Central and Western United States, and Northern Mexico. Zones 5–9.

POINT OF FACT ▷ These miniature cacti with pretty, papery flowers are often poached from public lands and sold to collectors, which threatens their slow-growing populations.

I SPOTTED IT!

WHEN I SAW IT
DATE

WHERE I SAW IT
SPECIFIC LOCATION,
INCLUDE STATE

NOTES

....
....

Blue Flag Iris

(Iris versicolor)

IRREGULAR

FLOWER 2.5–4 inches (6.5–10 cm) across; blue-purple flower with 3 upright petals surrounded by 3 veined, bent-over sepals with yellow patches.

IN BLOOM Spring to summer.

PLANT HEIGHT 2–3 feet (0.5–0.9 m)

LEAVES Long, narrow, pale green, and swordlike blades; simple, alternate.

HABITAT Swamps, marshes, and wet meadows.

RANGE Southern Canada, the Great Lakes, and Northeastern and Midwestern United States. Zones 3–9.

POINT OF FACT In Greek mythology, Iris is the goddess of the rainbow—which is why flowers that come in many colors are named irises.

I SPOTTED IT!

WHEN I SAW IT
DATE

WHERE I SAW IT
SPECIFIC LOCATION,
INCLUDE STATE

NOTES

....

....

Common Blue Violet
(Viola sororia)

IRREGULAR

REGIONAL NAME Wood Violet

FLOWER 0.75 inch (2 cm) wide; blue-violet to purple flowers with 5 petals, a white center, and purple veins.

IN BLOOM Early spring to early summer.

PLANT HEIGHT 3–8 inches (7.5–20.5 cm)

LEAVES Heart-shaped, toothed, and located at the base of the plant on separate stalks; simple, alternate.

HABITAT Moist woods and meadows, lawns, and roadsides.

RANGE Southeastern and Central Canada and Eastern and Central United States. Zones 3–7.

POINT OF FACT Wisconsin, New Jersey, Rhode Island, and Illinois all chose this pretty flower as their official state flower.

I SPOTTED IT!

WHEN I SAW IT
DATE

WHERE I SAW IT
SPECIFIC LOCATION,
INCLUDE STATE

NOTES

....

....

Cow Vetch
(Vicia cracca)

LONG
CLUSTER

REGIONAL NAME Blue Vetch

FLOWER 0.5 inch (1.5 cm) across; purple, tubular flowers lined along one side on top of the stalk.

IN BLOOM Late spring to summer.

PLANT HEIGHT Vine grows to 4 feet (1.2 m)

LEAVES 14–24 small, pointy leaflets that end in tendrils; pinnately compound, alternate.

HABITAT Fields, grasslands, and roadsides.

RANGE North America except the Southwest and Southern California. Zones 4–6.

POINT OF FACT It often escapes from farm fields and grows wild because it's commonly planted to feed animals or to cover spaces between crops.

I SPOTTED IT!

WHEN I SAW IT
DATE

WHERE I SAW IT
SPECIFIC LOCATION,
INCLUDE STATE

NOTES

....

....

Flowering Raspberry
(Rubus ordoratus)

SIMPLE

FLOWER 1–2 inches (2.5–5 cm) across; red-purple flowers with 5 overlapping petals around many stamens and pistils.

IN BLOOM Summer.

PLANT HEIGHT 3–6 feet (0.9–1.8 m)

LEAVES Large, wide, toothed, and maple-shaped with 3–5 lobes; simple, alternate.

HABITAT Thickets, roadsides, rocky woods, and slopes.

RANGE Eastern Canada and Eastern and Southern United States. Zones 3–8.

POINT OF FACT The genus *Rubus* includes blackberries, dewberries, raspberries, and other kinds of berry-producing brambles with thorny branches.

I SPOTTED IT!

WHEN I SAW IT
DATE

WHERE I SAW IT
SPECIFIC LOCATION, INCLUDE STATE

NOTES

....

....

Purple Passionflower

(Passiflora incarnata)

IRREGULAR

REGIONAL NAME ▸ Maypop Vine

FLOWER ▸ 1.5–2.5 inches (4–6.5 cm) across; large, purple, fringed flower with 5 drooping stamens and a 3-part pistil.

IN BLOOM ▸ Summer.

PLANT HEIGHT ▸ Vine grows to 7 feet (2 m).

LEAVES ▸ 3-lobed and pointy–tipped with curly tendrils; simple, alternate.

HABITAT ▸ Sunny, open areas, thickets, and roadsides.

RANGE ▸ Central and Eastern United States. Zones 5–10.

POINT OF FACT ▸ Its fruit, often called maypop, has sour, edible pulp inside its lime-size hull.

◖ I SPOTTED IT! ▸

WHEN I SAW IT
DATE

WHERE I SAW IT
SPECIFIC LOCATION,
INCLUDE STATE

NOTES

....

....

New England Aster

(Aster novae–angliae)

COMPOSITE

FLOWER 1–2 inches (2.5–5 cm) across; flower head of 35–45 pink-purple ray flowers that surround a yellow disk flower.

IN BLOOM Late summer to autumn.

PLANT HEIGHT 3–7 feet (0.9–2.1 m)

LEAVES Long and lance-shaped; clasp the hairy, sticky stem; simple, alternate.

HABITAT Meadows, moist fields, and roadsides.

RANGE Southern Canada and Central and Eastern United States. Zones 3–8.

POINT OF FACT Aster comes from the Greek word for star, which describes the starburst shape of the flower heads.

I SPOTTED IT!

WHEN I SAW IT
DATE

WHERE I SAW IT
SPECIFIC LOCATION, INCLUDE STATE

NOTES

....

....

Purple Coneflower
(Echinacea purpurea)

COMPOSITE

FLOWER 2.5–4 inches (6.5–10 cm) across; flower head with a bristly, brown, cone-shaped center surrounded by pink-purple, drooping ray flowers.

IN BLOOM Midsummer to autumn.

PLANT HEIGHT 1–5 feet (0.3–1.5 m)

LEAVES Lance-shaped with rounded tips and a rough texture; simple, opposite.

HABITAT Prairies and dry, open woods.

RANGE Southeastern Canada and Eastern and Central United States. Zones 3–9.

POINT OF FACT Its flowers are made into herbal supplements that boost your immune system.

◖ I SPOTTED IT! ▷

WHEN I SAW IT
DATE

WHERE I SAW IT
SPECIFIC LOCATION,
INCLUDE STATE

NOTES

....

....

Periwinkle
(Vinca minor)

SIMPLE

REGIONAL NAME Running Myrtle

FLOWER 1 inch (2.5 cm) across; five blue-purple petals surrounding a faint, white star.

IN BLOOM Spring.

PLANT HEIGHT 6–8 inches (15–20.5 cm)

LEAVES Evergreen, shiny, and oval-shaped on trailing stems; simple, opposite.

HABITAT Roadsides, woods, weedy empty lots, and shady backyards.

RANGE Throughout North America. Zones 4–9.

POINT OF FACT Colonists from Europe brought and grew this hardy plant for medicinal uses and its pretty flowers, and it later escaped and naturalized into the wild.

I SPOTTED IT!

WHEN I SAW IT
DATE

WHERE I SAW IT
SPECIFIC LOCATION, INCLUDE STATE

NOTES

....

....

Purple Loosestrife
(Lythrum salicaria)

LONG
CLUSTER

FLOWER 0.5–0.75 inch (1.5–2 cm) across; pink-purple flowers with 4–6 wrinkly petals in a long spike.

IN BLOOM Summer.

PLANT HEIGHT 2–4 feet (0.5–1.2 m)

LEAVES Narrow, long, and spear-shaped; simple, opposite.

HABITAT Wet meadows, pond and stream edges, and roadside ditches.

RANGE Southern Canada and throughout most of the United States. Zones 4–9.

POINT OF FACT This fast-spreading non-native plant is on the World Conservation Union's list of 100 of the World's Worst Invasive Alien Species—it crowds out native plants that wildlife depends on for survival.

◉ I SPOTTED IT!

WHEN I SAW IT
DATE

WHERE I SAW IT
SPECIFIC LOCATION,
INCLUDE STATE

NOTES

....

....

Dwarf Larkspur

(Delphinium tricorne)

LONG CLUSTER

REGIONAL NAME Spring Larkspur

FLOWER 1–1.5 inches (2.5–4 cm) across; deep-purple, spurred flowers along the top of a thick stem; 5 petallike sepals and 4 small inner petals.

IN BLOOM Spring.

PLANT HEIGHT 4–24 inches (10–61 cm)

LEAVES Deep, palmate lobes divided into thin sections; simple, alternate.

HABITAT Moist woods.

RANGE Eastern and Central United States. Zones 4–8.

POINT OF FACT Its seedpods are in the shape of three horns, like the species name *tricorne* suggests.

I SPOTTED IT!

WHEN I SAW IT
DATE

WHERE I SAW IT
SPECIFIC LOCATION, INCLUDE STATE

NOTES

Eastern Waterleaf
(Hydrophyllum virginianum)

ROUND CLUSTER

REGIONAL NAME Virginia Waterleaf

FLOWER Clusters of white or purple, bell-shaped flowers on long stalks with 5 lobes and 5 long, hairy stamens that stick out beyond its petals.

IN BLOOM Spring to summer.

PLANT HEIGHT 1–2.5 feet (0.3–0.8 m)

LEAVES Sharply toothed and oval-shaped with 5–7 leaflets; compound, alternate.

HABITAT Moist woods, stream valleys, and clearings.

RANGE Southeastern Canada. Zones 3–8.

POINT OF FACT Its first leaves of early spring are covered in light splotches that look a bit like water stains.

I SPOTTED IT!

WHEN I SAW IT
DATE

WHERE I SAW IT
SPECIFIC LOCATION,
INCLUDE STATE

NOTES

....

....

Pickerelweed
(Pontederia cordata)

LONG
CLUSTER

FLOWER 0.38 inch (9.5 mm) across; blue-purple, funnel-shaped flowers on a spike.

IN BLOOM Summer to autumn.

PLANT HEIGHT Stalks are 1–2 feet (0.3–0.5 m) above water

LEAVES Single, long, and heart-shaped with a pointed tip; no arrangement, aquatic.

HABITAT Marshes, ponds, lakes, and streams.

RANGE Southeastern Canada and Central and Eastern United States. Zones 3–10.

POINT OF FACT It's named after the pickerel fish that shares its aquatic home.

I SPOTTED IT!

WHEN I SAW IT
DATE

WHERE I SAW IT
SPECIFIC LOCATION,
INCLUDE STATE

NOTES

....

....

Wild Lupine
(Lupinus perennis)

LONG
CLUSTER

FLOWER 0.5 inch (1.5 cm) across;
purplish-blue flowers in a spire.

IN BLOOM Spring to midsummer.

PLANT HEIGHT 8–24 inches (20.5–61 cm)

LEAVES Palmately compound with
7–11 leaflets; compound, alternate.

HABITAT Open woods and fields.

RANGE Southeastern Canada and
Eastern United States. Zones 3–8.

POINT OF FACT It's the sole host plant
of the endangered Karner blue butterfly,
whose larvae only feed on wild lupine leaves.

I SPOTTED IT!

WHEN I SAW IT
DATE

WHERE I SAW IT
SPECIFIC LOCATION,
INCLUDE STATE

NOTES

....

....

Blue Phlox
(Phlox divaricata)

SIMPLE

REGIONAL NAME Wild Sweetwilliam

FLOWER 1 inch (2.5 cm) across; 5-petal pinwheel flowers often in loose clusters.

IN BLOOM Spring.

PLANT HEIGHT 10–20 inches (25.5–51 cm)

LEAVES Slender and oval-shaped with pointy tips; simple, opposite.

HABITAT Woods and fields.

RANGE Eastern Canada and Eastern and Midwestern United States. Zones 3–8.

POINT OF FACT The petals of this phlox in the East are notched, while those in the West are smooth and rounded.

I SPOTTED IT!

WHEN I SAW IT
DATE

WHERE I SAW IT
SPECIFIC LOCATION,
INCLUDE STATE

NOTES

....

....

Virginia Bluebells
(Mertensia virginica)

BELL

FLOWER 1 inch (2.5 cm) across; light blue, trumpet-shaped flowers with 5 lobes in nodding clusters.

IN BLOOM Early spring.

PLANT HEIGHT 8–24 inches (20.5–61 cm)

LEAVES Large, light green, oval-shaped, and floppy on a single stem; simple, alternate.

HABITAT Moist woods and floodplains.

RANGE Southeastern Canada and Central and Eastern United States. Zones 3–8.

POINT OF FACT Bluebells don't start blue—they bloom as clusters of drooping pink buds that change color as they open and age over three weeks.

I SPOTTED IT!

WHEN I SAW IT
DATE

WHERE I SAW IT
SPECIFIC LOCATION, INCLUDE STATE

NOTES

Jack–in–the–Pulpit

(Arisaema triphyllum)

IRREGULAR

FLOWER 2–3 inches (5–7.5 cm) across; club-like spike with tiny flowers at its base, surrounded by a purple-and-green-striped hood.

IN BLOOM Spring.

PLANT HEIGHT 1–3 feet (0.3–0.9 m)

LEAVES 3 long, oval-shaped leaflets with pointy tips; compound, opposite.

HABITAT Moist and shady woods and swamps.

RANGE Southeastern Canada and Central and Eastern United States. Zones 4–9.

POINT OF FACT "Jack" is the club-like flower that's giving a talk inside the hooded, tube-shaped "pulpit."

I SPOTTED IT!

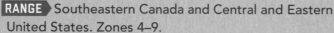

WHEN I SAW IT
DATE

WHERE I SAW IT
SPECIFIC LOCATION,
INCLUDE STATE

NOTES

....

....

Lamb's Quarter
(Chenopodium album)

LONG CLUSTER

REGIONAL NAME ▶ White Goosefoot

FLOWER ▶ Dense clusters of minute flowers on the ends of branching spikes.

IN BLOOM ▶ Summer to autumn.

PLANT HEIGHT ▶ 1–6 feet (0.3–1.8 m)

LEAVES ▶ Diamond-shaped and toothed with mealy-white undersides attached to red-streaked stems; simple, alternate.

HABITAT ▶ Fields, yards, weedy empty lots, and roadsides.

RANGE ▶ Throughout North America except the Arctic. Zones 2–9.

POINT OF FACT ▶ Though many consider this plant a weed, it's rich in vitamins and related to beets, spinach, and Swiss chard.

◉ **I SPOTTED IT!** ▶

WHEN I SAW IT
DATE

WHERE I SAW IT
SPECIFIC LOCATION,
INCLUDE STATE

NOTES ▶

....

....

Virginia Creeper
(Parthenocissus quinquefolia)

LONG
CLUSTER

FLOWER Clusters of tiny, white-green flowers on branching reddish stalks.

IN BLOOM Summer.

PLANT HEIGHT Vine grows to 150 feet (45.5 m)

LEAVES Palmate and toothed with 5 leaflets; compound.

HABITAT Woods, riverbanks, thickets, field edges, and weedy empty lots.

RANGE Southeastern Canada and Central and Eastern United States. Zones 3–9.

POINT OF FACT Don't confuse it with poison ivy just because it climbs up trees and poles and turns brilliant red in autumn. This plant has 5 leaflets, not 3.

◖ I SPOTTED IT! ▷

WHEN I SAW IT
DATE

WHERE I SAW IT
SPECIFIC LOCATION,
INCLUDE STATE

NOTES

....

....

Cocklebur
(Xanthium strumarium)

ROUND
CLUSTER

FLOWER Green and tiny, with separate male and female flowers.

IN BLOOM Summer to autumn.

PLANT HEIGHT 1–6 feet (0.3–1.8 m)

LEAVES Large, lobed, and toothed with a long stalk; simple, alternate.

HABITAT Roadsides, fields, weedy empty lots, and open woods.

RANGE Throughout North America. Zones 6–9.

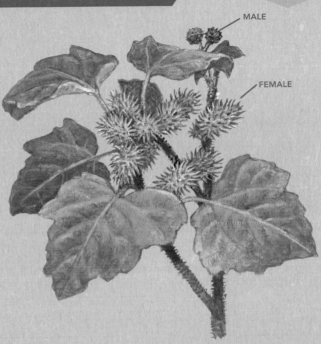

MALE

FEMALE

POINT OF FACT The female flowers grow in clusters at the base of the leaves and become egg-shaped fruits covered in hooked prickles.

I SPOTTED IT!

WHEN I SAW IT
DATE

WHERE I SAW IT
SPECIFIC LOCATION,
INCLUDE STATE

NOTES

....

....

Wild Ginger
(Asarum canadense)

SIMPLE

FLOWER 1.5 inches (4 cm) across; dark red-brown, cup-shaped flower with 3 pointed lobes.

IN BLOOM Spring.

PLANT HEIGHT 6–12 inches (15–30.5 cm)

LEAVES Large, wide, hairy, and heart-shaped; simple, opposite.

HABITAT Woods.

RANGE Southeastern Canada and Central and Eastern United States. Zones 3–8.

POINT OF FACT Its flowers bloom near the ground and have a rotting smell that attracts pollinating flies.

I SPOTTED IT!

WHEN I SAW IT
DATE

WHERE I SAW IT
SPECIFIC LOCATION, INCLUDE STATE

NOTES

....
....

Common Cattail

(Typha latifolia)

LONG
CLUSTER

FLOWER Green-to-brown tiny female flowers in a dense, long, cylindrical cluster that's topped with a thin spike of yellow male flowers.

IN BLOOM Late spring to midsummer.

PLANT HEIGHT 3–9 feet (0.9–2.7 m)

LEAVES Long, stiff, and sword-shaped; no arrangement visible, aquatic.

HABITAT Marshes, ponds, ditches, and freshwater shorelines.

RANGE Throughout North America except in the Arctic. Zones 2–10.

POINT OF FACT The brown, sausage-shaped part of a cattail is its fruit. Inside are seeds with long, thin hairs that catch the wind as the fruit crumbles in winter.

I SPOTTED IT!

WHEN I SAW IT
DATE

WHERE I SAW IT
SPECIFIC LOCATION,
INCLUDE STATE

NOTES

....

....

Side Oats Grama
(Bouteloua curtipendula)

DENSE

FLOWER 0.25 inch (6.5 mm) across; green spikelets on short, densely packed spikes that hang from a single side of a stem.

IN BLOOM Summer.

PLANT HEIGHT 1.5–2.6 feet (0.5–1 m)

LEAVES Long, ribbonlike, and rough blades along the stem; simple, alternate.

HABITAT Dry plains and desert grasslands.

RANGE Southern Canada and throughout the United States except the Northwest. Zones 3–9.

POINT OF FACT Protein-rich grama grasses fed the huge herds of bison that once roamed the Western prairies.

I SPOTTED IT!

WHEN I SAW IT
DATE

WHERE I SAW IT
SPECIFIC LOCATION, INCLUDE STATE

NOTES

Big Bluestem
(Andropogon gerardii)

LOOSE

REGIONAL NAME Turkeyfoot Grass

FLOWER 0.25–0.5 inch (0.5–1.5 cm) across; purple-bronze spikelets that are forked into clusters of slim spikes.

IN BLOOM Summer.

PLANT HEIGHT 2–8 feet (0.5–2.4 m)

LEAVES Long, ribbonlike blades with drooping tips along the slender stem; simple, alternate.

HABITAT Fields, prairies, wetlands, and cliffs.

RANGE Southern Canada and throughout the United States except the Northwest. Zones 4–9.

POINT OF FACT It's also called "turkeyfoot grass" because its 3-flower head clusters look a bit like the 3-toed foot of a wild turkey.

▶ I SPOTTED IT!

WHEN I SAW IT
DATE

WHERE I SAW IT
SPECIFIC LOCATION,
INCLUDE STATE

NOTES

....

....

Indian Grass

(Sorghastrum nutans)

LOOSE

FLOWER 10 inches (25.5 cm) across; plume-like clusters of shiny, golden-brown, tufted spikelets tipped with long bristles.

IN BLOOM Late summer.

PLANT HEIGHT 3–8 feet (0.9–2.4 m)

LEAVES Long, thin blades that lean away from the stem at a 45-degree angle; simple, alternate.

HABITAT Prairies, fields, and roadsides.

RANGE Throughout North America except the West Coast and the Arctic. Zones 4–9.

POINT OF FACT It was once an important plant of the tall-grass prairie that swayed and shone across thousands of square miles.

◎ I SPOTTED IT!

WHEN I SAW IT
DATE

WHERE I SAW IT
SPECIFIC LOCATION,
INCLUDE STATE

NOTES

....

....

Bottlebrush Grass
(Elymus hystrix)

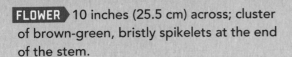

DENSE

FLOWER 10 inches (25.5 cm) across; cluster of brown-green, bristly spikelets at the end of the stem.

IN BLOOM Summer.

PLANT HEIGHT 2–5 feet (0.5–1.5 m)

LEAVES Long, rough blades with smooth sheaths; simple, alternate.

HABITAT Woods.

RANGE Eastern Canada and Central and Eastern United States. Zones 5–9.

POINT OF FACT The bristly spikelets all along the ends of the flower head stems look like bottlebrushes, which is how the grass got its name.

I SPOTTED IT!

WHEN I SAW IT
DATE

WHERE I SAW IT
SPECIFIC LOCATION, INCLUDE STATE

NOTES

....
....

Common Reed

(Phragmites australis)

REGIONAL NAME Giant Reed

FLOWER Plume of red-brown, downy clusters of hairy spikelets on the end of the stem.

IN BLOOM Late summer.

PLANT HEIGHT 5–15 feet (1.5–4.5 m)

LEAVES Long, wide, stiff, blue-green blades with rough edges that are scattered along the thick stem; simple, alternate.

HABITAT Marshes, ditches, and shorelines.

RANGE Throughout North America except in the Arctic. Zones 4–10.

POINT OF FACT This grass filters pollutants out of the water where it grows, but it can also spread and overtake wetlands in both fresh and salt water.

I SPOTTED IT!

WHEN I SAW IT
DATE

WHERE I SAW IT
SPECIFIC LOCATION,
INCLUDE STATE

NOTES

Common Rye
(Secale cereale)

DENSE

FLOWER 0.5 inch (1.5 cm) across; spikelets with stiff bristles that form a dense spike at the end of an upright stem.

IN BLOOM Summer.

PLANT HEIGHT 1.5–3 feet (0.5–1 m)

LEAVES Soft, long, and ribbonlike blades along the stem; simple, alternate.

HABITAT Fields, roadsides, and empty lots.

RANGE Throughout North America except in the Arctic. Zones 3–8.

POINT OF FACT Rye is a cereal grass like wheat, oats, corn, millet, and rice, and is a crop that's depended on to feed the world's population.

I SPOTTED IT!

WHEN I SAW IT
DATE

WHERE I SAW IT
SPECIFIC LOCATION, INCLUDE STATE

NOTES

....

....

Little Bluestem
(Andropogon scoparius)

DENSE

FLOWER 0.25 inch (6.5 mm) across; spikelets with hairy tufts in zigzag clusters.

IN BLOOM Late summer to autumn.

PLANT HEIGHT 1.5–4.5 feet (0.5–1.4 m)

LEAVES Long, ribbonlike, and drooping blades; simple, alternate.

HABITAT Old fields, prairies, and open woods.

RANGE Throughout North America except in the Northwestern United States and Arctic. Zones 3–9.

POINT OF FACT Its bluestem name comes from the new growth part of the stem that has a bluish tint in spring.

I SPOTTED IT!

WHEN I SAW IT
DATE

WHERE I SAW IT
SPECIFIC LOCATION, INCLUDE STATE

NOTES

....

....

Kentucky Bluegrass
(Poa pratensis)

LOOSE

FLOWER Loose, branching cluster at the end of a wiry stem with very small spikelets.

IN BLOOM Late spring to summer.

PLANT HEIGHT 1–3 feet (0.3–0.9 m)

LEAVES 8 inches (20.5 cm); narrow leaves with pointed tips in tufts; simple, alternate.

HABITAT Lawns, fields, and meadows.

RANGE Throughout North America. Zones 3–9.

POINT OF FACT Kentucky's nickname, the Bluegrass State, comes from this sod-forming grass that's grown in horse country.

I SPOTTED IT!

WHEN I SAW IT
DATE

WHERE I SAW IT
SPECIFIC LOCATION, INCLUDE STATE

NOTES

....

....

Umbrella Sedge
(Cyperus esculentus)

LOOSE

REGIONAL NAMES Chufa, Yellow Nutgrass

FLOWER 0.25–1 inch (6.5–25.5 mm) across; red-brown, densely packed spikelets in a loose cluster.

IN BLOOM Late summer to autumn.

PLANT HEIGHT 6–30 inches (15–76 cm)

LEAVES Stiff blades on triangular 3-sided stems; flower head stems topped in whorls of leaves; simple, alternate.

HABITAT Pastures, meadows, and wet fields.

RANGE Southern Canada and throughout the United States. Zones 8–10.

POINT OF FACT Tiger nuts are the dried tubers from this sedge and are also the original ingredient in the milky drink horchata.

I SPOTTED IT!

WHEN I SAW IT
DATE

WHERE I SAW IT
SPECIFIC LOCATION, INCLUDE STATE

NOTES

....

....

Great Bulrush

(Schoenoplectus tabernaemontani [syn. *Scirpus validus*])

LOOSE

FLOWER 0.25–0.5 inch (0.5–1.5 cm) across; red-brown, spearhead-shaped spikelets in loose hanging clusters.

IN BLOOM Summer.

PLANT HEIGHT 2–10 feet (0.5–3 m)

LEAVES Often leafless with tubular, straight stems; simple, alternate.

HABITAT Bogs, marshes, and wetlands.

RANGE Throughout North America except in the Arctic. Zones 4–9.

POINT OF FACT Bulrushes are important wetland plants—songbirds nest in them, waterfowl eat their seeds and stems, and otters and muskrats use them for cover.

I SPOTTED IT!

WHEN I SAW IT
DATE

WHERE I SAW IT
SPECIFIC LOCATION,
INCLUDE STATE

NOTES

PART IV

FERNS AND MOSSES

J. DAWSON

What would
YOU do?

The trickiest part of geocaching is actually finding the logbook once you've reached the GPS coordinates, especially in a thick forest. You check your app for a hint: *Look in a cliffy nook above a patch of ferns and moss.*

But which cliff should you scramble up? It'll be dark long before you could climb them all. Wandering under the cliff line, you spot a fern patch. You kneel down to look for moss, too. Soft, green clubmoss that looks like miniature pine trees sprouts from the moist soil. Hmm.

Clubmoss isn't a true moss. So, is this the "patch of ferns and moss" from the hint? Should you climb the cliff and look for the logbook? Or should you keep searching until you find real moss growing with ferns? *What would you do?*

CHAPTER 1

Spotting Nonflowering Plants

A towering redwood tree or a field of sunflowers are awesome sights. But both trees and flowers are relative newcomers to earth's plant kingdom. Moss, on the other hand, has been around for 450 million years. That's right—that soft green stuff that grows on rocks was the first ever plant to live on land. Today's mosses, liverworts, clubmosses, horsetails, and ferns are the descendants of the earliest land plants on earth. All of these are nonflowering, seedless plants.

Mosses and Liverworts

Mosses and their liverwort relatives are nonflowering plants. They don't make flowers, seeds, or fruits. They're also *nonvascular*. That means they can't move water from the soil out to their leaves, like trees and flowering plants can. Moss plants aren't equipped with water-carrying structures, like true roots or tissue in their stems. Not having water-shuttling plumbing limits the size of mosses—most are no more than a couple of inches in height.

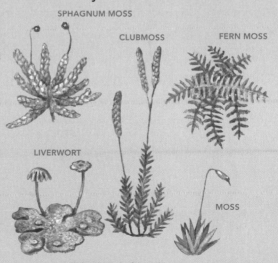

SPHAGNUM MOSS

CLUBMOSS

FERN MOSS

LIVERWORT

MOSS

Liverworts have larger, flatter leaves than mosses.

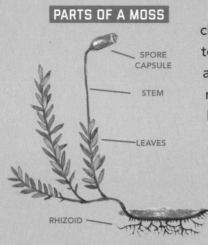

SPORE CAPSULE

STEM

LEAVES

RHIZOID

A benefit of the mosses' nonvascular characteristic is that they don't need to live in soil. The leaves absorb water and nutrients from rain, dew, or other moisture the moss directly encounters. Mosses usually grow low to the damp ground and in large groups called mats or carpets, which also helps them hold in moisture. These mats or carpets of moss are actually a colony of thousands of individual plants.

Each moss plant has a short stem with threadlike *rhizoids* that grow out from the bottom and anchor it to a surface. Tiny leaves sprout from all around the stem and make the plant's food through photosynthesis. A spore capsule or case grows on the end of its own stalk.

Fabulous Ferns

Ferns are also nonflowering, seedless plants. However, ferns differ from mosses because they are vascular plants with structures for transporting water. Their well-developed roots, stems, and leaves allow them to grow much larger (and older) than mosses. Some ferns are tree-size, and some live to be one hundred years old.

COMMON NORTH AMERICAN FERNS

MAIDENHAIR FERN

WALKING FERN

BRACKEN FERN

CHRISTMAS FERN

POLYPODY

The fern plant's core is a mostly underground, horizontal stem called a *rhizome*. Roots sprout from the rhizome down into the soil to anchor the fern and soak up water and minerals. A fern rhizome might live for decades or longer, but new leaves grow from the rhizome each year. A young fern leaf is called a *fiddlehead* because its curled-up shape looks like the top of a violin. The tight bundle unrolls and opens into a frond as it grows. A stiff stalk or stipe attaches the frond to the rhizome and holds up the frond.

PARTS OF A FERN

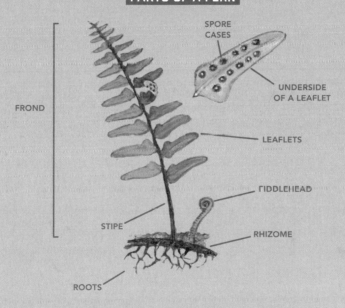

SPORE CASES

UNDERSIDE OF A LEAFLET

FROND

LEAFLETS

FIDDLEHEAD

STIPE

RHIZOME

ROOTS

Photosynthesis happens in the leaves of ferns. Many fern fronds are made up of leaflets, like a compound leaf. Some delicate, feathery ferns have leaflets that are divided into smaller sets of sub-leaflets. Other kinds of ferns have fronds that are a single, long leaf. A fern's spore cases are on the undersides of their fronds or on a stalk. Some ferns have separate fertile fronds that develop spore cases, as well as sterile nonspore-producing fronds.

Fern Friends

Like ferns, horsetails and clubmosses are nonflowering, seedless, vascular plants with structures for shuttling water.

Horsetails are pretty easy to recognize. They look very different from other plants. Horsetails have segmented or jointed hollow, ridged stems. Some horsetails have plain stems, while others have whorls of long, needlelike, green branches that grow from the stem joints. The spores of horsetails are in small, cone-shaped structures at the tips of stems and branches, or sometimes on a separate stalk.

Clubmosses are plants with small leaves that are often spiky. Many clubmosses are creeping evergreens that look a bit like miniature conifers sprouting from the ground. Some even have names like running-cedar or ground pine. Small club- or cone-shaped structures in clubmosses produce spores, though most spread by sending out new, creeping stems.

COMMON NORTH AMERICAN HORSETAILS AND CLUBMOSSES

CLUBMOSS

HORSETAIL

Spores, Not Seeds

Ferns, mosses, and their relatives don't make flowers or seeds—they reproduce with spores. Fern and moss spores are single cells that can grow into new plants. That may sound similar to seeds, but moss and fern spores are only one microscopic cell (that's too tiny to see), surrounded by a protective coating. Unlike an apple or maple seed, a spore doesn't hold an embryo or store food for that plant.

Another way spores are different from seeds is how they are created. Seeds are the result of fertilization, the combination of separate male and female genetic material after pollination. Spores are created by a single fern or moss. They only contain the genetic information of one plant, not two, as in flowering plants. Nor does a spore grow into a plant like the one that created it.

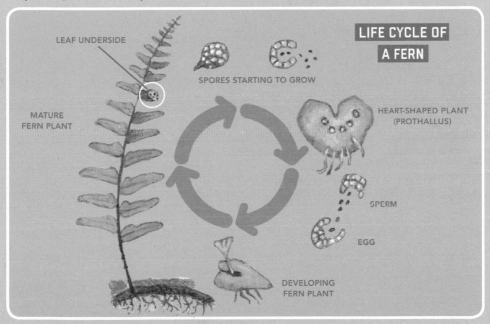

LIFE CYCLE OF A FERN

LEAF UNDERSIDE

SPORES STARTING TO GROW

MATURE FERN PLANT

HEART-SHAPED PLANT (PROTHALLUS)

SPERM

EGG

DEVELOPING FERN PLANT

A grass seed grows into a grass that can make its own seeds. But a fern spore doesn't grow into a plant like the one it came from. Instead, it germinates into a small, heart-shaped plant called a *prothallus*. The prothallus is where fertilization happens—an embryo is created, which then grows into a fern with fronds. A germinating moss spore grows into a microscopic chain of cells called a *protonema*. A bud then sprouts on the protonema and becomes a leafy male or female plant, or grows as a plant with male and female branches. When water washes sperm into the egg-carrying structure, fertilization happens. Then the embryo grows on the female plant or branch, becoming a stalk and spore capsule.

Finding Ferns, Mosses, and Their Kin

For being such ancient, simple plants, mosses and ferns sure have complicated reproduction. The process involves multiple stages, different forms of the plant, and fertilization that's dependent on water. But that last fact is a clue to where you're most likely to find these non-flowering plants. They usually live in places where water is abundant for at least some part of the year. Their complex life cycles can't be completed without water, after all.

In North America, some of the environments with the greatest diversity of nonflowering plants are wet ones—swampy forests, temperate rain forests, bogs, lakeshores, and soggy fields. Anywhere damp enough for moss to cover logs, ferns to grow under trees, and ditches to sprout horsetails are great places to spot these unusual plants. Where it's extra wet and warm, ferns sprout on living tree limbs and moss takes over roofs.

HORSETAIL

If you're searching for ferns and mosses in drier areas, seek the shade and shelter of rocky cliffs and ledges, where they'll usually hug the ground without needing a lot of space to thrive. Many brown, dead-looking mosses are actually just dormant. When rain arrives, they green up and grow again. And fern rhizomes can endure cold spells and drought that kill the fronds. Even the space between mountain boulders or a damp roadside ditch can reveal green treasures. Seek them out!

PURPLE MOSS

SWORD FERN

Talk Like a Pteridologist/Bryologist

Here are some terms to know when identifying nonflowering, seedless plants.

BLADE
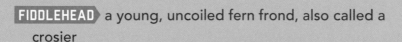

BLADE the leafy part of a fern frond

BRYOLOGIST a scientist who studies mosses, liverworts, and hornworts

CHLOROPHYLL a green pigment in plants that absorbs energy from sunlight to power photosynthesis

CLUBMOSS a nonflowering, vascular, green plant with club-shaped spore-producing cones related to ferns

FERN FROND

FERN a nonflowering, vascular green plant with roots and fronds that makes spores

FERTILE FROND a special spore-carrying structure of ferns with sterile fronds

SPORE

FIDDLEHEAD a young, uncoiled fern frond, also called a crosier

FROND an entire fern leaf with both blade and stipe

HORNWORT a leafy, nonflowering, nonvascular green plant related to mosses with a spikelike spore capsule

HORSETAIL

HORSETAIL a nonflowering, vascular green plant with hollow, jointed stems and scalelike leaves

LEAFLET one of the main leaflike parts of a fern blade, also called a pinna

LIVERWORT a flattened-leaf, nonflowering, nonvascular green plant related to mosses

MOSS a small, nonflowering, nonvascular green plant that often grows in mats and has small, narrow leaves

LIVERWORT

NONVASCULAR PLANTS green plants without a system and structures for transporting water from roots to leaves

NONFLOWERING PLANTS green plants that do not make seeds, flowers, or fruits and reproduce with spores instead

PHOTOSYNTHESIS a plant's food-making process that combines carbon dioxide and water in the presence of chlorophyll and light to create carbohydrate food and release oxygen

BONFIRE MOSS

PROTHALLUS a heart-shaped plant that grows from a spore and is part of a fern's life cycle

PROTONEMA a microscopic chain of cells that grows from a spore and is part of a moss's life cycle

PTERIDOLOGIST a scientist who studies ferns, horsetails, and clubmosses

RHIZOID rootlike anchoring structure of mosses and their relatives

RHIZOME long-lived, mostly underground, horizontal stem of a fern

SPORE a microscopic, reproductive, nonflowering plant cell capable of growing into a stage of the plant's life cycle

SPORE
CASE

SPORE

SPORE CASE a grouping of spores or a spore-containing structure in ferns and their relatives, also called sorus (plural is sori)

SPORE CAPSULE a spore-containing structure of mosses and their relatives

STERILE FROND a fern frond that doesn't produce spores

STIPE a stiff stalk or stem that holds up a fern frond

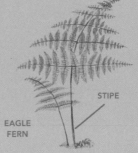

STIPE

EAGLE
FERN

SUB-LEAFLET one of the leaflike parts of a fern leaflet, also called a pinnule

VASCULAR PLANTS green plants with a system and structures for transporting water from roots to leaves

TRY IT →

Find Nonflowering Plants

Find out what you've been overlooking! Tour two damp and shady places with your low-and-green radar on, and see what nonflowering plants you find.

WHAT YOU'LL NEED

➢ A pencil or pen, a hand lens or magnifying glass.

STEP 1 Head outside to a moist, shady area or someplace near a creek or pond to spot some nonflowering plants. (Watch out for those Wild Plants to Avoid on page 37.)

STEP 2 Write short descriptions of the habitats and check off any nonflowering plants that you see. If you see more than one kind of the same thing, make an additional check mark or two. Try to find all these nonflowering plants!

HABITAT #1 ....
- [ ] moss [ ] liverwort [ ] fern [ ] horsetail
- [ ] clubmoss [ ] other

HABITAT #2 ....
- [ ] moss [ ] liverwort [ ] fern [ ] horsetail
- [ ] clubmoss [ ] other

STEP 3 Did you notice any patterns or connections between the habitats and the types of nonflowering plants seen?

I DID IT! DATE:

317

TRACK IT ↘ Draw and Compare Nonflowering Plants

Look closely and compare two of the nonflowering plants you found.

STEP 1 Choose two kinds of nonflowering plants to draw, such as a fern and a moss. If you're comparing two of the same type of nonflowering plant, such as two ferns, choose two that look as different as possible.

STEP 2 Write the names of the nonflowering plants on the chart. If you can't yet identify the species, just pick a few words to describe it, such as "brick moss" or "tall fern."

STEP 3 Fill in the Location sections with habitat hints, such as "roadside ditch near Elm and 12th Street" or "woods near Travers Creek."

STEP 4 Draw each plant. Label all the parts you can. (See page 309 for fern parts and page 308 for moss parts.)

STEP 5 Identify either nonflowering plant using the Ferns and Moss Identification section on pages 332–345, and then add the name to the chart. Don't forget to check off the I SPOTTED IT! boxes and fill in the blanks.

STAR MOSS

PLANT #1 DATE .... LOCATION ....

Name ....

Drawing:

PLANT #2 DATE .... LOCATION ....

Name ....

Drawing:

How are the two plants similar?

How are they different?

I DID IT! DATE:

Make a Fern Spore Print

Single fern spores are microscopic, but the patterns of spore cases on the undersides of fern leaves are visible and differ greatly between fern species. Spore arrangements can outline fern leaflets in dots or lines or grow in skin-like coverings. Pressing a fern frond between paper makes the pattern especially viewable. Get outside and make your own fern spore print!

→ Find and collect a frond with ripening spore cases on the undersides of its fronds. Late summer and autumn are best for finding ripening spore cases.

→ Place the frond so its underside is facedown onto a white sheet of paper. Cover the frond with a second sheet of paper and set it in a dry, still place indoors.

→ The spores should release within a few days. Carefully remove the top sheet and the frond to reveal the pattern of spore cases.

→ Immediately, before it smudges, photograph the spore print alongside its frond (as shown above). Label the print with the fern's name, if you know it.

→ Try growing the spores by sprinkling them into a small container filled with damp, sterile potting soil. Cover the container to keep in moisture, and add water as needed. Remember, each fern spore first grows into a tiny green prothallus. Good luck!

I DID IT! DATE:

CHAPTER 2

Identifying Ferns and Mosses

It's easy to tell a fern from an oak tree or a patch of moss from wild-flowers while walking around a park or hiking through a forest. But identifying which exact fern or moss you saw is not as simple. Nonflowering plants have no colorful flowers or fruit. They don't have fluffy or prickly seedpods, nor do they have distinctive bark. Many of the characteristics used to identify other kinds of plants simply don't work with ferns and mosses. Now find out what does!

The Hoh Rain Forest in Washington State is a nonflowering plant paradise.

Cluing into Ferns

Frond size and shape is the most important clue to fern identification. A few kinds of ferns, like hart's-tongue or walking fern, have simple, narrow fronds that are not divided into leaflets. But most fern fronds do have lobed fronds or compound fronds with leaflets.

HART'S-TONGUE

CLIFF FERN

Many, like cliff ferns, are even further divided into sub-leaflets, lobed sub-leaflets, and beyond. These frond configurations or blade divisions are often the most important identifying characteristic for these nonflowering plants.

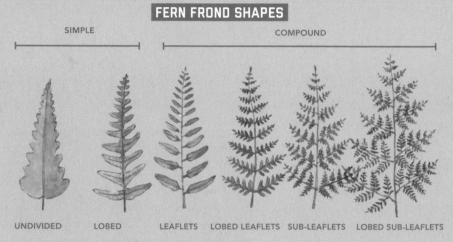

FERN FROND SHAPES

SIMPLE

COMPOUND

UNDIVIDED   LOBED   LEAFLETS   LOBED LEAFLETS   SUB-LEAFLETS   LOBED SUB-LEAFLETS

The texture and smells of fronds also differ among fern species. Christmas ferns, for example, are hardy with thick, waxy, or leathery fronds that stay green even in winter. Other ferns, such as maidenhairs, have lacy and delicate fronds. Stalk texture matters, too. Fern stalks vary from hairy to scaly to smooth or to sticky. And because ferns have no need to attract pollinating insects, they don't produce sweet nectar or scented flower petals. But there are some ferns known for their smell. Crush a bit of hay-scented fern fronds between your fingers and you'll smell its name.

The actual color of a frond isn't often a go-to characteristic for fern identification. Most are just variations

The fronds of the hay-scented fern have a fresh-mown hay smell.

on a green theme. However, stalk or stipe color is a fern trait that's useful in identification. For example, maidenhair ferns have shiny black stems, while lady fern stalks are more red.

Checking out a particular fern's spore cases, structures, and arrangements often helps determine its species. Some ferns, like cinnamon ferns and ostrich ferns, sprout special spore-carrying fronds that look totally different from the main fronds. These so-called *fertile fronds* are often brown and

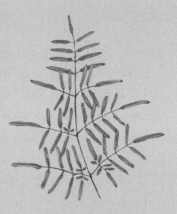

Purple cliff break is a fern with purplish stalks.

shriveled up, looking more like a dried plant seed head than part of a fern. Fertile fronds are fantastic clues for identification. Most ferns develop their spore cases on the undersides of their fronds. The pattern, shape, and size of these spore groupings differ greatly between species. Some look like dots outlining the leaflets, others' spore cases form little lines, while others grow on the leaflet edges or have skin-like coverings. All the variety in spore structures makes checking for them a must-do when identifying ferns.

FERTILE FRONDS

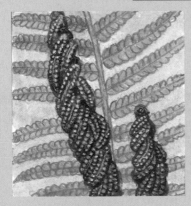

OSTRICH FERN

CINNAMON FERN

Get Up Close with Mosses

When looking around at moss-covered logs and rocks, it can seem a bit overwhelming to try to tell one species from another. That's because you're big and moss plants are small. It's like trying to identify the trees of a forest from an airplane. Moss identification calls for a hand lens and a willingness to get your knees damp. Moss experts have to get up close to see the individual moss plants within the green, fuzzy mat.

Both mosses and their liverwort cousins thrive in moist places.

Once you start looking at single moss plants, you'll see more and more things that will help you with identification. Those tiny leaves that stick out from the center stem aren't all the same. The leaves of haircap moss are long, skinny, and toothed. They're spread out along the stem, unlike cord moss leaves, which overlap. The shape of the spore capsules that grow on the ends of thin stalks can help identify mosses as well. Some spore capsules are round, like those of apple moss, while others are shaped like tiny jelly beans. It's amazing what you'll notice once you take the time to look.

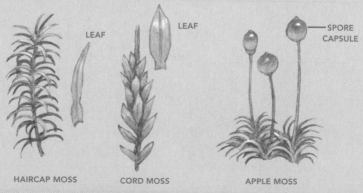

HAIRCAP MOSS   LEAF   CORD MOSS   LEAF   APPLE MOSS   SPORE CAPSULE

Identifying mosses is as much about noticing the habitat they're growing in as paying attention to the shape of their leaves and spore capsules. Many kinds of mosses grow on rocks or trees, but some are aquatic—which means you can take water pocket moss off your list if you've spotted a moss on a wall. Another example is feather moss, which prefers conifer forests, or rock moss, which is partial to limestone rock. This is why taking note of where exactly the plant is growing is so important. You can often eliminate possibilities just from the habitat. Good hunting!

MOSSES AND FERNS ARE SIMILAR AND DIFFERENT

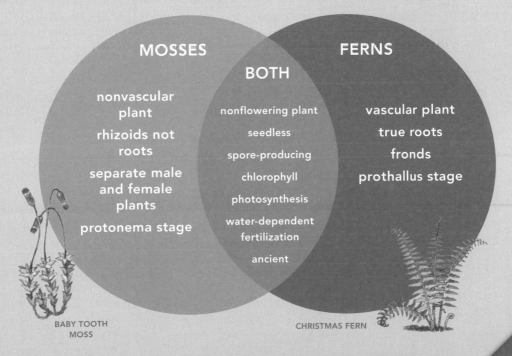

MOSSES

nonvascular plant

rhizoids not roots

separate male and female plants

protonema stage

BOTH

nonflowering plant

seedless

spore-producing

chlorophyll

photosynthesis

water-dependent fertilization

ancient

FERNS

vascular plant

true roots

fronds

prothallus stage

BABY TOOTH MOSS

CHRISTMAS FERN

TRY IT → Fern and Moss Scavenger Hunt

Use your fern and moss identification skills in the field.

WHAT YOU'LL NEED

➤ A pencil or pen, a hand lens.

STEP 1 Search anywhere outdoors for ferns and mosses. You'll likely have better luck someplace shady and damp, or someplace near a pond or stream.

STEP 2 Check off any of the characteristics that you see in the chart. If you see a characteristic more than once, add an extra check mark for each time. There's also a place to note down anything unknown, especially odd, or extra interesting.

DATE

LOCATION

Time of Day ....

FERNS

☐ fiddlehead ☐ rhizome ☐ roots

☐ simple, undivided frond ☐ lobed frond

☐ frond with leaflets

☐ frond with sub-leaflets

☐ frond with divided sub-leaflets

☐ lobed leaflets ☐ lacy leaflets

☐ waxy frond ☐ scented frond ☐ sticky frond

- [ ] black stipe or stalk   [ ] red stipe or stalk
- [ ] brown stipe or stalk
- [ ] hairy stipe or stalk   [ ] sticky stipe or stalk
- [ ] spore cases on underside of frond
- [ ] fertile frond
- [ ] something else interesting:

....

....

MOSSES

- [ ] moss on rock or pavement
- [ ] moss on wall or brick
- [ ] moss on tree or branch   [ ] aquatic moss
- [ ] spiky leaves [ ] toothed leaves [ ] oval leaves
- [ ] spore capsule on stalk   [ ] rhizoids
- [ ] round spore capsule [ ] oval spore capsule
- [ ] something else interesting:

....

....

I DID IT!   DATE:

327

TRACK IT ↘ Vertical Versus Horizontal Mosses

Are mosses that grow on vertical surfaces such as walls and tree trunks different from mosses growing on flat rocks, the ground, and other horizontal surfaces? Find out!

STEP 1 Find some moss growing on a horizontal surface. Fill in the left side of the chart, then draw its leaf, stem, and rhizoid and include measurements.

STEP 2 Find some moss growing on a vertical surface. Fill in the right side of the chart, then draw its leaf, stem, and rhizoid and include measurements.

HORIZONTAL MOSS	VERTICAL MOSS
DATE	DATE ....
LOCATION	LOCATION ....
Drawing & Measurements:	Drawing & Measurements:

STEP 3 Are there differences between the two mosses? What are they?

TAKE IT TO THE NEXT LEVEL ↗

Make a Moss Terrarium

Want to watch mosses grow? Create an environment that suits them—a moss terrarium!

→ Gather any kind of clean, transparent plastic or clear glass container, such as a fishbowl, large jar, glass canister, wide vase, etc.

→ Cover the bottom of the container with pebbles or small rocks, and then add a few inches of topsoil. Pour water over the soil until it's completely wet and draining into the pebble layer.

→ Collect some small chunks of moss and gently press them into the soil. Spray or drizzle water to moisten the moss. Set the terrarium someplace with indirect sunlight. Keep it watered and moist, then watch your moss grow over the weeks and months!

TAKE IT TO THE NEXT LEVEL ↗

Plant Spotter Deep Dive: Profile a Moss or Fern

Put all that nonflowering plant knowledge together and take a deeper dive. Choose a favorite fern or moss and profile it!

WHAT YOU'LL NEED

- **A pencil or pen, a ruler or measuring tape, a hand lens.**

DATE

LOCATION

Is it a ☐ fern or a ☐ moss?

What kind of habitat does it live in?

How tall is the plant (with units)?

Draw the entire plant and label its parts.

How is the plant anchored to its site?

What is its leaf arrangement?

What is the shape and the margin of its leaves?

Draw a single frond or leaf.

Describe the frond or leaf's color, texture, thickness, and shape.

Describe the fern or moss's spore-making structures.

List anything else unique about this plant.

Name the fern or moss, if possible.

Check off its I SPOTTED IT! box in the identification section and fill in the blanks. Fabulous effort, nonflowering plant spotter!

I DID IT! DATE:

FERN AND MOSS IDENTIFICATION

Welcome to your Fern and Moss Identification guide!

Here are some tips and information to get started:

These pages have three groups. Ferns, Clubmosses and Horsetails, and Mosses (which includes liverworts).

> **FRONDS** describes the leafy identification-essential parts to look for in the Fern group.
> ➤ This is called **PLANT SHAPE** in Clubmosses and Horsetails, and **PLANT SHAPE & LEAVES** in Mosses.

> **SPORES** gives the months when the spores of ferns and their relatives are mature and ready for release. That's when spore cases are often the most visible. In parentheses following the months is information about where the spore cases form.

> **SPORE CAPSULES** describes the stalk and capsule of the spore-producing structures of mosses and liverworts.

> **RANGE** explains general regions where you can find the fern or moss. Since USDA Hardiness Zones are very hard to find for the nonflowering plants, they're not included here.

PARTS OF A MOSS

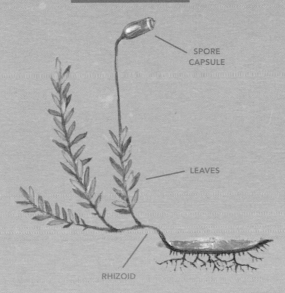

SPORE
CAPSULE

LEAVES

RHIZOID

PARTS OF A FERN

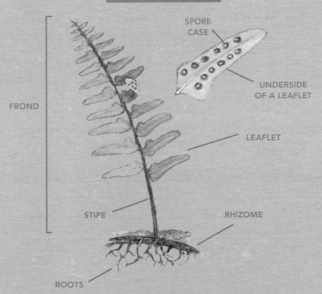

SPORE
CASE

UNDERSIDE
OF A LEAFLET

FROND

LEAFLET

STIPE

RHIZOME

ROOTS

Rattlesnake Fern

(Botrychium virginianum)

PLANT SIZE 8–20 inches (20.5–51 cm) tall

FRONDS Bright green, triangular, and horizontal fronds are divided into lacy leaflets held above the forest floor by a single thick stalk.

SPORES September to November (on separate fertile frond on long stalk).

HABITAT Rich woodlands and wet thickets.

RANGE Throughout Canada and the United States except the desert Southwest.

POINT OF FACT A spore-bearing cluster grows from the continuation of the stipe, and its opening cluster resembles a rattlesnake's tail tip.

I SPOTTED IT!

WHEN I SAW IT
DATE

WHERE I SAW IT
SPECIFIC LOCATION, INCLUDE STATE

NOTES

....

....

Northern Maidenhair

(Adiantum pedatum)

PLANT SIZE 1–2 feet (0.3–0.5 m) tall

FRONDS Fan-shaped, bright green sub-leaflets on shiny, black, wiry stems that branch off the stipe in graceful arcs.

SPORES August to October (on leaflets).

HABITAT Rich, deciduous woodlands and rocky slopes.

RANGE Eastern, Central, and Northwestern United States and Southern Canada.

POINT OF FACT Its spore cases grow on leaflets and are often covered by curled-over leaflet edges.

I SPOTTED IT!

WHEN I SAW IT
DATE

WHERE I SAW IT
SPECIFIC LOCATION,
INCLUDE STATE

NOTES

....

....

Bracken

(Pteridium aquilinum)

PLANT SIZE 2–3 feet (0.5–0.9 m) tall

FRONDS Broad, coarse, horizontal fronds usually divided into 3 triangular leaflets.

SPORES July to August (on leaflets).

HABITAT Old fields, burned areas, open woods, and thickets.

RANGE Throughout the United States and Southern Canada.

POINT OF FACT It's known to spread easily and quickly with rhizomes that can grow up to 6 feet (2 m) in the first year.

I SPOTTED IT!

WHEN I SAW IT
DATE

WHERE I SAW IT
SPECIFIC LOCATION, INCLUDE STATE

NOTES

....

....

Ostrich Fern
(Matteuccia struthiopteris)

PLANT SIZE 2–6 feet (0.5–2 m) tall

FRONDS Large and plumelike, with wide middles that grow in V-shaped clumps; deeply lobed, rich green leaflets.

SPORES April to June (separate fertile frond is smaller, stiffer, and turns brown).

HABITAT Damp woods, stream banks, and swamps.

RANGE Northeast and Upper-Midwestern United States and Southern Canada.

POINT OF FACT It's named for its ostrich-plume-like fronds.

I SPOTTED IT!

WHEN I SAW IT
DATE

WHERE I SAW IT
SPECIFIC LOCATION,
INCLUDE STATE

NOTES

....

....

Christmas Fern
(Polystichum acrostichoides)

PLANT SIZE 1–2.5 feet (0.5–1 m) tall

FRONDS Thick, waxy, minutely toothed leaflets with earlike lobes that are moderately spaced and tapered.

SPORES June to October (on small leaflets near frond tip).

HABITAT Woods, stream banks, and rocky slopes.

RANGE Eastern and Central United States and Southern Canada.

POINT OF FACT The evergreen fronds are green even in snow and are sometimes used for winter holiday decorations, like holly or pine boughs.

I SPOTTED IT!

WHEN I SAW IT
DATE

WHERE I SAW IT
SPECIFIC LOCATION, INCLUDE STATE

NOTES

....
....

Western Sword Fern

(Polystichum munitum)

PLANT SIZE 1.6–4.1 feet (0.5–1.5 m) tall

FRONDS Long, bladelike, dark evergreen, and erect with tapering ends; has a thick stipe and long, toothed leaflets.

SPORES May to August (on leaflets).

HABITAT Shady conifer forests and rocky slopes.

RANGE Western United States and Canada.

POINT OF FACT It's one of the most abundant and hardy ferns along the Pacific Coast from Alaska to California.

I SPOTTED IT!

WHEN I SAW IT
DATE

WHERE I SAW IT
SPECIFIC LOCATION, INCLUDE STATE

NOTES

....

....

Fragile Fern
(Cystopteris fragilis)

REGIONAL NAME Brittle Fern

PLANT SIZE 6–12 inches (15–30.5 cm) tall

FRONDS Bright green and short with a wide center and thin, spaced leaflets that grow upward and arch over or along rocks.

SPORES May to August (on leaflets).

HABITAT Rocky areas, cliff faces, and between boulders.

RANGE Throughout Canada and the United States except the Southeast.

POINT OF FACT It often dies back during summer or times of drought, and then unfurls new fronds when moisture returns.

I SPOTTED IT!

WHEN I SAW IT
DATE

WHERE I SAW IT
SPECIFIC LOCATION, INCLUDE STATE

NOTES

....

....

CLUBMOSSES & HORSETAILS
Common Clubmoss
(Lycopodium clavatum)

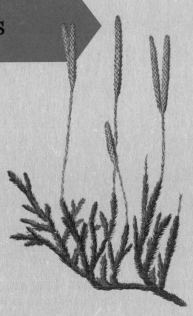

REGIONAL NAME Running Pine

PLANT SIZE 4–10 inches (10-25.5 cm) tall

PLANT SHAPE Creeping evergreen with clustered, branched, upright green stems that are densely covered in small, pale green leaves.

SPORES September to October (cone-shaped cases in clusters on the ends of a tall stalk that extends from a branch).

HABITAT Open fields, thickets, and moist woods.

RANGE Eastern and Northern United States and Canada.

POINT OF FACT It's rare in some areas due to past over-collecting for winter holiday decorations and herbal remedies.

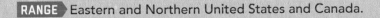

◖ I SPOTTED IT! ▷

WHEN I SAW IT
DATE

WHERE I SAW IT
SPECIFIC LOCATION, INCLUDE STATE

NOTES

....

....

Field Horsetail

(Equisetum arvense)

PLANT SIZE 1–2 feet (0.5 m) tall

PLANT SHAPE Green, hollow, jointed stems with whorls of thin, ridged branches.

SPORES March to May (separate stalk with a cone-like top).

HABITAT Fields, woods, marshes, roadsides, and empty lots.

RANGE Throughout Canada and the United States except the Gulf Coast and Florida.

POINT OF FACT Its genus name comes from the Latin words *equus* meaning a horse, and *seta* meaning a bristle.

I SPOTTED IT!

WHEN I SAW IT
DATE

WHERE I SAW IT
SPECIFIC LOCATION, INCLUDE STATE

NOTES

....

....

Cord Moss
(Funaria hygrometrica)

PLANT SIZE 0.5 inch (1.5 cm) tall

PLANT SHAPE & LEAVES Pale, yellow-green mat with tightly overlapping leaves that have bud-like heads.

SPORE CAPSULES Numerous, large, and pear-shaped; hang from the end of a long, curled stalk.

HABITAT Disturbed or bare places, moist and shady rocks, and plant pots.

RANGE Throughout the United States and Canada.

POINT OF FACT It's also called bonfire moss because it grows where fire has burned the ground.

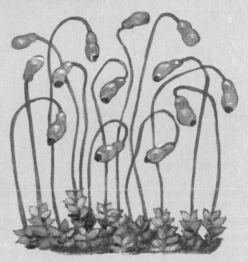

I SPOTTED IT!

WHEN I SAW IT
DATE

WHERE I SAW IT
SPECIFIC LOCATION, INCLUDE STATE

NOTES

....

....

Star Moss
(Mnium cuspidatum)

REGIONAL NAME Woodsy Thyme

PLANT SIZE 1–1.5 inches (2.5–4 cm) tall

PLANT SHAPE & LEAVES Upright or creeping, unbranching stems with whorls of light green, oval-shaped leaves.

SPORE CAPSULES Oval-shaped with a cone-shaped lid and rounded tip with droops on the stalk.

HABITAT Woods on rotting logs and tree trunks, fields, lawns, and roadsides.

RANGE Throughout the United States and Canada except in the Arctic.

POINT OF FACT Warblers, wrens, thrushes, and other songbirds line their nests with it.

I SPOTTED IT!

WHEN I SAW IT
DATE

WHERE I SAW IT
SPECIFIC LOCATION, INCLUDE STATE

NOTES

Common Liverwort
(Marchantia polymorpha)

PLANT SIZE 2–3 inches (5–7.5 cm) wide

PLANT SHAPE & LEAVES Leathery, dark green, ribbonlike branching structure with diamond-shaped marks on its upper surface.

SPORE CAPSULES Umbrella-like shape on stalks; male's is disc-shaped and female's is star-shaped with 9 fingerlike structures.

HABITAT Moist soil and rocks along stream banks, bogs, marshes, and gardens.

RANGE Throughout the United States and Canada.

POINT OF FACT There are separate male and female plants, but both produce plant buds that are spread by water.

I SPOTTED IT!

WHEN I SAW IT
DATE

WHERE I SAW IT
SPECIFIC LOCATION, INCLUDE STATE

NOTES

PART V

MUSHROOMS AND
OTHER FUNGI

J. DAWSON

What would
YOU do?

The rain has stopped, the tent's up, and Dad's lighting a fire. Day 2 of your autumn backpacking trip is almost in the "win" column. But where's Sadie? Here she comes, wagging her tail and trotting out from behind some trees. What's that in her mouth?

You kneel down and take something white and slobber-covered out of your dog's mouth. It's a large mushroom cap with a Sadie-size bite missing. Oh no! She ate a wild mushroom! Will it make Sadie sick?

How can you tell if the mushroom is poisonous? It's not red, so does that mean it's okay to eat? The car is parked at the trailhead fifteen or so miles from here. Should you start hiking out now? Does Sadie need a vet? *What would you do?*

SHAGGY PARASOL
(NONPOISONOUS)

GREEN-SPORED MUSHROOM
(POISONOUS)

CHAPTER 1

Spotting Mushrooms and Other Fungi

Mushrooms are both mysterious and magical. The strange, squishy, umbrella-shaped things seem to appear in an instant! Dozens of little toadstools can show up overnight, where yesterday there was only grass. There are mushrooms that glow in the dark, turn colors when touched, and carry enough poison to kill a cow. Mushrooms can grow out of stumps, sprout in wet basements, and thrive in places without soil or sunshine. What sort of plant lives like this? None, actually. That's because mushrooms aren't plants—they are fungi.

PUFFBALLS   CAP MUSHROOMS   BRACKET FUNGUS

CUP FUNGI   JELLY FUNGI   MORELS   LICHEN

Fungi, like plants, are living organisms that don't move around, which makes them easy to spot. Unlike plants, fungi can't make their own food with air and sunlight through photosynthesis. Fungi must eat to survive, like animals do. The food of fungi is other living things—or things that were once living.

Scavenge, Harm, Share

Mushrooms are mouthless. They eat other organisms with long, threadlike filaments, called *hyphae*, that grow from their bodies. Hyphae spread under leaf litter or inside an old log. The threads carry enzymes that dissolve animal and plant cells so the fungus can soak up the nutrients, which is how it feeds itself.

Many mushrooms consume dead or rotting things. They are nature's decomposers, with the essential job of turning fallen leaves, old stumps, dead bugs, and poop into rich soil. Scientists use the term *saprophytes* to describe mushrooms that live on decaying stuff. There are other mushrooms, as well as many kinds of fungi, that instead feed on living plants and animals. They're parasites. You've likely already seen parasitic fungi. Mildews and rusts that sicken plants are examples of parasitic fungi, as well as athlete's foot, ringworm, and other fungal infections! Some bracket fungi harm the living trees they grow on, which makes them parasitic fungi as well.

Infecting living things and eating dead ones aren't the only ways mushrooms earn a living. Some mushrooms grow and feed on plant roots in a way that actually helps the plant. The plant

FUNGAL TROPHS

SAPROPHYTE

PARASITE

SYMBIOSIS

and fungus live in a kind of symbiosis called *mutualism*, which is a relationship that benefits both of them. The mushroom hyphae can help tree roots soak up water and minerals from the soil, while the fungus eats some of the stored food in the tree's roots. Some kinds of mushrooms have symbiotic relationships with particular tree types. Slippery jack mushrooms usually grow around conifers, for example, while common morel mushrooms prefer deciduous forests. The kind of tree a mushroom grows under is often a big clue to identification.

Fungal "Flower"

The umbrella-shaped, easily seen part of a mushroom isn't the entire organism. It's just a tiny, short-lived part of the fungus that's only a spore-making structure, called a *fruiting body*. Most of the organism, called the *mycelium*, lies beneath the ground or inside a rotting log.

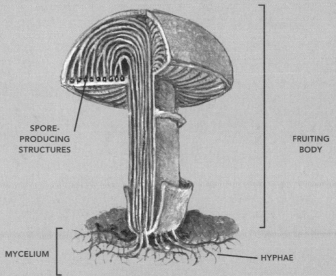

SPORE-
PRODUCING
STRUCTURES

FRUITING
BODY

MYCELIUM

HYPHAE

The continual work of absorbing nutrients and staying alive is the mycelium's job, while the fruiting body's purpose is reproduction—just like flowers! Also like flowers, mushrooms have terrific distinct characteristics that make them essential for fungi identification.

Life of a Mushroom

No matter its size, a mushroom starts out as a too-tiny-to-see micro-scopic spore. A spore will germinate if it lands on a suitable place with enough food and moisture. Hyphae sprout, lengthen, and branch out from the spore to create an underground or under-bark web that grows into a mycelium. You've probably seen white, weblike fungus mycelium if you've ever turned over a rotting log, pulled bark off a dead tree, or poked around in the soil near a cluster of mushrooms.

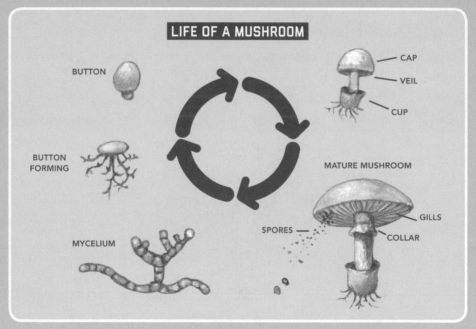

LIFE OF A MUSHROOM

BUTTON

BUTTON FORMING

MYCELIUM

CAP

VEIL

CUP

MATURE MUSHROOM

SPORES

GILLS

COLLAR

When conditions are favorable, knots or swellings form in the mycelium. These tiny buttons are baby mushrooms. As an egg-shaped button swells, it pushes above the surface. A cap and stalk develop and stretch out the button, tearing it in two. The bottom half becomes a cup, and the top half becomes the cap. The spore-producing gills of the cap are protected by a skin-like covering called a *partial veil*. As the mushroom matures, the veil peels away.

Some mushrooms retain a portion (or a lot) of their veil, which becomes the collar that's so important for mushroom identification.

Once mature, the gills release their spores and the mushroom dies. The entire mushroom cycle happens very quickly, often after a rainfall. The hyphae soak up the rainwater, and a mushroom pops up in a matter of hours. Most mushrooms grow to their maximum height within a day or two. That's why mushroom spotting is a now-or-never activity—they might not be there tomorrow!

Fungus Among Us

All mushrooms are fungi, but not all fungi are mushrooms. Learn to spot and identify other sorts of strange and wonderful fungi you come across outside, as well as mushrooms. Here are seven general types of fungi and mushrooms to look for while out and about in shady, damp places, which you can also find represented in the identification section (pages 374–405).

GILLED CAP MUSHROOMS or agarics, are mushrooms with spore-producing structures on the underside of their caps, which are shaped like gills or fleshy slits. While many are umbrella-shaped, some are vase-shaped, like chanterelles. Mushrooms for salads and pizzas are gilled mushrooms.

HORSE MUSHROOM

KING BOLETE

SPONGY CAP MUSHROOMS also called tubed or pored cap mushrooms, have spongy caps with no gills. Instead, the spores are produced inside tubes that end in little openings (pores) on the underside of the cap.

BRACKET FUNGI also called polypores or conks, are tough or woody and often grow like small, half-moon shelves on tree trunks or stumps. They also make spores in tubes that end in pores on their undersides. Unlike mushrooms, the fruiting bodies of many kinds of bracket fungi live for months or years.

ARTIST'S FUNGUS

CUP or **BALL-SHAPED FUNGI** are usually stalkless. The surface inside the cup or ball produces spores.

SCARLET CUP

JELLY FUNGI are rubbery fungi that come in many colors and shapes including globs, earlike, discs, and glistening lobes.

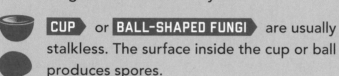

CLUB-SHAPED FUNGI like morels and stinkhorns have thick stalks and wear their spore-producing surfaces on the outside.

WITCHES'-BUTTER

COMMON MOREL

LICHEN is a living thing made up of a fungus and another kind of simple organism—usually a photosynthesizing alga or cyanobacteria that feeds the fungi in exchange for water. Lichens are small and can live on rocks, bark, or soil. Fruticose lichens look like dry miniature plants or shrubs. Foliose lichens are leaflike. Crustose lichens are flat and look like a crusty coating.

MAP LICHEN (CRUSTOSE)

DOG LICHEN (FOLIOSE)

BRITISH SOLDIERS (FRUTICOSE)

Poisonous Mushrooms

The saying among people who forage for edible mushrooms is: "There are old mushroom hunters and bold mushroom hunters. But there are no old, bold mushroom hunters." That's because eating wild mushrooms can kill you. Mushrooms like deadly galerina, autumn skullcap, death cup, destroying angel, and deadly dapperling carry caution in their names.

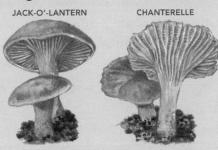

JACK-O'-LANTERN   CHANTERELLE

One of these look-alikes is a treat and the other is a dangerous trick. Can you tell them apart?

North America is home to wild mushrooms full of organ-destroying poisons, vomit-inducing toxins, and hallucination-causing substances. It's also home to all sorts of dead-wrong myths about how to tell edible mushrooms from poisonous ones. Here are a few of the more famous falsehoods:

→ All white mushrooms are edible. (False! A destroying angel mushroom is white.)

→ If it grows on wood, it's edible. (Absolutely untrue.)

→ You can test a mushroom's poison level by checking if it tarnishes a silver spoon. (False.)

→ If other animals eat it, so can people. (Not so. Think of all the poisonous berries and other stuff animals eat.)

→ Mushrooms that grow in meadows and pastures are all edible. (Nope.)

How can foragers be 100 percent sure that a mushroom is safe to eat? Simply, they can't. Most poisonous mushrooms look very similar to edible ones. And positive identification of the mushroom itself is only part of the task. Typically-edible mushrooms can become toxic if they're growing in soil with heavy metals or on certain kinds of trees, such as eucalyptus. Some kinds of mushrooms are safe to eat if cooked a certain way, while others can poison you with their cooking fumes. Plus, what one person eats without a problem can send another person to the hospital. NEVER eat wild mushrooms unless they've been identified by an experienced and trusted mycologist.

Talk Like a Mycologist

Here are some terms to know for fungi identification.

AGARIC a gilled mushroom

ANNULUS the collar or ringlike structure on a stalk left over from a partial veil; ring

BRACKET FUNGI fungi with a shelflike shape; polypore

BUTTON a young mushroom

MEADOW MUSHROOM

CAP the top part of the fruiting body of a mushroom; pileus

COLLAR the remnants of the veil on a stipe (stalk); ring; annulus

CONK the woody, fruiting body of a bracket or polypore fungus

CUP the cuplike base of certain fungi; volva

FAIRY RINGS a naturally occurring ring of mushrooms; elf circle

FERTILE SURFACE the layer of spore-bearing cells on a fungus; hymenium

GILLS the platelike structures on the undersides of the fruiting bodies of gilled fungi

HYMENIUM fertile surface

HYPHAE the threadlike filaments (strands) that make up the mycelium

LAMELLAE gills (the platelike structures on the undersides of the fruiting bodies of gilled fungi)

LATEX the liquid that oozes from cut surfaces of certain fungi

MUTUALISM a symbiotic relationship between two organisms that benefits both

MYCELIUM the mass of threadlike hyphae that is the fungus's body

MYCORRHIZA a symbiotic relationship between a fungus and plant roots

PARASITE a symbiotic relationship between two organisms where one benefits and the other is harmed

PILEUS the cap of a mushroom fruiting body

POLYPORE FUNGUS bracket fungus

PORES the open tips of spore-making tubes in some fungi

RING the remnants of the veil on a stipe; collar; annulus

SAPROPHYTE an organism that lives and feeds on dead or decaying things

SPORE a microscopic reproductive cell of a fungus

SPORE PRINT a powdery deposit of spores from a fungus fruiting body

STIPE stalk; stem

SYMBIOSIS a close and long-term relationship between two different organisms that can be mutualistic or parasitic

TOADSTOOL an inedible mushroom

VEIL the tissue that covers the young gills of certain fungi

VOLVA the cuplike base of some fungi; cup

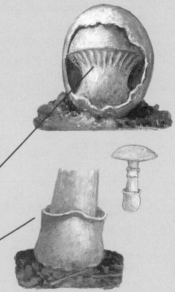

BUTTON

TRY IT → Fun Fungus Search

Put your fungus smarts to the test where it counts—outdoors! Review and find as many of the seven types of fungi as you can (information on page 353–354). And don't touch unfamiliar mushrooms without wearing gloves—they might be poisonous.

> **WHAT YOU'LL NEED**
>
> ➤ A pencil or pen, a hand lens, gloves (optional).

STEP 1 Head outside to an area with lots of damp, shady spots. (Note: Fall and spring are the best seasons for fungal finds.)

Check off any of the seven fungi types you see:

☐ gilled cap mushroom   ☐ spongy cap mushroom

☐ bracket fungus   ☐ jelly fungus

☐ cup- or ball-shaped fungus   ☐ club-shaped fungus

☐ lichen (circle one: fruticose   foliose   crustose)

STEP 2 Pick two examples of your found fungi types and note down some information about them on the next page. Which of the seven types from the groups above is it? If it's a lichen, include whether it's fruticose, foliose, or crustose.

HORSE MUSHROOM

DATE .... LOCATION ....

Time of Day ....

What fungus type is it?

Describe the fungus's shape, color, and features.

Can you identify its name?

DATE .... LOCATION ....

Time of Day ....

What fungus type is it?

Describe the fungus's shape, color, and features.

Can you identify its name?

I DID IT! DATE:

TRACK IT ↘ Draw and Compare Fungi Types

Take a closer look at and draw the two types of fungi you found.
How are they similar? What makes them different?

WHAT YOU'LL NEED

➤ Colored pencils or pens, a hand lens,
gloves (optional).

STEP 1 Write about and draw each fungus type. Use colored
pencils or pens to record their colors.

FUNGUS #1	FUNGUS #2
Type:	Type:

STEP 2 What characteristics do these two organisms share?
How are they distinct from each other?

STEP 3 Identify either of the fungi you drew using the
Mushrooms and Fungi Identification section on pages
374–405. Write the name in the chart, and then check off its
I SPOTTED IT! box and fill in the blanks.

I DID IT!   DATE:

Local Hazardous Mushrooms

Research what kinds of poisonous mushrooms are common in your neck of the woods. County extension offices and state universities often have information on local hazardous plants and animals, including mushrooms. Make "Toxic Toadstools" flash cards to help you learn to recognize them. Write the common name, species name, and description on one side, and draw what it looks like on the other side. Take your cards in your backpack, along with this book, on your mushroom hunting adventures. Then you'll be armed with information to help keep yourself, others, and pets safe.

I DID IT! DATE:

JACK-O'-LANTERN

GREEN-SPORED MUSHROOM

CHAPTER 2

Identifying Mushrooms and Other Fungi

You're likely to spot a familiar fungus while wandering through the woods or a meadow on a foggy, damp fall morning. You may find bracket fungus and lichen on trees, cup and jelly fungi on stumps and fallen branches, and mushrooms poking up through grass and leaf litter. But while identifying a lichen from a puffball is easy, figuring out how to identify all the different umbrella-shaped mushrooms is not always that simple.

Most of us picture a gilled cap mushroom whenever someone says "mushroom." Iconic gilled cap mushrooms have thin, delicate gills under their rounded caps—but there are thousands of different species of these gilled mushrooms in North America alone. That makes them an exciting identification challenge.

Mastering gilled mushroom identification takes keen observation skills. Let's focus only on mushrooms with gill-filled caps and what you should look for when spotting one.

FAIRY RING

Colorful Clues

Mushrooms come in a wider variety of colors than you might think. Parrot mushrooms are green, brick tops are red-brown, and destroying angels are white. Cap color and stalk color are sometimes the same, but not always. The famously red-capped fly agaric mushroom has a white stalk, for example. The color of a particular type of mushroom often darkens or lightens during its short life. And the environment it lives in matters, too. Most mushrooms that grow in full-shade habitats are darker than those in sunnier spots.

FLY AGARIC

Some mushrooms can be identified by the color they turn into when they are bruised or when they bleed. The cap, stalk, and gills of various mushrooms change color when cut, pinched, nicked, or otherwise "bruised." For example, white horse mushrooms bruise yellow, while white grocery-store button mushrooms bruise pink. A few kinds of mushrooms "bleed" a milky liquid, or latex, when cut. Milky cap mushrooms are famous bleeders. The color of the latex can help identify the mushroom, as well as whether the latex changes color. The indigo milk cap mushroom bleeds blue latex that slowly turns green once exposed to air.

INDIGO MILK CAP MUSHROOM

When identifying gill cap mushrooms, don't forget to observe spore print color, because it will often differ from the colors of the cap, stalk, latex, or bruise. The blue latex-oozing indigo milk cap mushroom has plain white spores. And white-colored horse and meadow mushrooms have dark spores. That's why spore prints are so essential in mushroom identification!

Caps Are Key

Not all gilled mushrooms have an umbrella shape. Mushroom caps come in a range of shapes and sizes. Some are shaped like pointed hats, while others are flat or have upturned edges. Mycologists have special words to describe up to a dozen cap shapes. But being able to tell an upside-down bowl (convex)–shaped cap from a flat one will get you a long way. Cap shape can change with the age of the mushroom, just like its color. Young mushroom caps are almost always rounder and narrower than mature ones.

Mushroom caps of any shape can be covered in scales or warts.

MUSHROOM CAP SHAPES

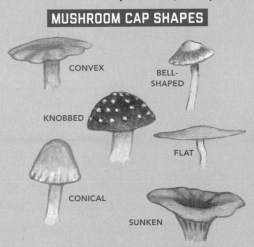

CONVEX

BELL-SHAPED

KNOBBED

FLAT

CONICAL

SUNKEN

These spots, flakes, or protrusions are terrific clues for identification. The brown scales on the cap of a shaggy parasol mushroom are an important characteristic to look for, as are the iconic white warts of a poisonous fly agaric mushroom. Caps and stalks also have varying textures. Some are rough or hairy, while others are slimy or smooth.

Go for the Gills

All mushroom gills are not alike. Every group of gilled mushrooms has its own distinctive gill characteristics—which makes gill observation important for fungi identification.

When you spot a gilled mushroom, check out the density of the gills on the underside of the cap. The gills may be super crowded, just close together, or separated from each other.

Pay close attention to how the gills attach to the stalk of the mushroom, also. The gills of haymaker's and glistening inky cap mushrooms attach directly to the stalk. In contrast, the gills of shaggy parasol and horse mushrooms are "free" and don't attach at all. Some mushrooms have gills that extend past the cap and down the stalk, like chanterelle and oyster mushrooms do, which mycologists call *decurrent gill attachment*.

GILL SPACING

CROWDED

CLOSE

DISTANT

GILL ATTACHMENT

FREE

ATTACHED

EXTENDING DOWN STALK

The stalk itself can also hold clues to the mushroom's identity. Some are short and thick, while others are long and thin. There are hollow mushroom stalks, bulb-shaped ones, and some stalks that attach to the cap off to one side, such as with oyster mushrooms. Always check if a mushroom stalk has a collar. A collar is a leftover from

CHANTERELLE

the veil, the membrane that covers the gills of young mushrooms. A collar around a stalk can be a faint band, a ruffled skirt like the fly agaric mushroom wears, or anything in between. Also observe the volva, or cup, that the stalk sits in. Some kinds of mushrooms have a noticeable volva (such as the grisette mushroom), while others have none at all.

Time and Place

When and where you spot a gilled mushroom also aids in its identification. Most mushrooms have a preferred time of year when they will pop up. Some are common in spring, while others show up only after autumn rains.

GRISETTE

Fairy ring mushrooms aren't the only mushrooms that form rings.

Habitat and particular tree type are also big identification clues for mushrooms. Good spotters know which kinds of mushrooms grow on oak stumps, which kinds can grow on the ground near pine trees, which types form fairy rings, and which types shun the sunlight.

What's that Smell?

Mushrooms aren't known for their sweet smells and fine fragrances. However, there are several mushrooms with smells so distinctive that their scents are helpful in identification.

Here are some well-known mushrooms with noticeable scents:

CHANTERELLES (*Cantharellus spp.*) smell fruity, like apricots.

FENUGREEK MILK CAP MUSHROOMS (*Lactarius helvus*) have a burned maple syrup odor, especially when dried.

GARLIC MUSHROOMS (*Mycetinis scorodonius*) smell and taste like garlic.

STINKHORN FUNGI (*Phallus spp.*) have a horrible rotting smell that attracts flies and other bugs that spread their spores.

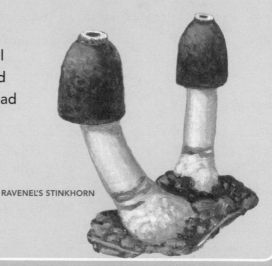

RAVENEL'S STINKHORN

TRY IT →

Mystery Mushroom Spore Print

Find out the color of a mushroom's spore print by making your own!

CAUTION Always wear gloves to handle wild mushrooms, and remember to wash your hands after finishing.

WHAT YOU'LL NEED

➢ Gloves, waxed paper (optional), white paper, a knife, a jar or container larger than mushroom.

STEP 1 Find and collect a mature gilled or spongy cap mushroom (it will have a fully opened cap where you can see the gills or open pores in the spongy area).

STEP 2 Carefully cut off the stalk. Then gently wrap the mushroom cap in waxed paper until you return home.

STEP 3 Choose a flat place for your spore print where it can sit overnight and not get disturbed, especially by pets and younger siblings. Set a sheet of white paper down in place.

STEP 4 Place the mushroom cap on the paper with the gills or spongy side down. Cover the mushroom cap with an upside-down jar or other container to keep the spores from escaping. Leave the mushroom overnight.

STEP 5 Remove the jar or container and carefully lift off the mushroom cap.

What color is the spore print?
Draw the pattern left by the gills or pores.

STEP 6 Does the spore print color match any of the mushrooms in the identification section on pages 374–405? Which ones? Check off the I SPOTTED IT! box if you're able to identify the mushroom.

I DID IT! DATE:

TAKE IT TO THE NEXT LEVEL ↗

My Mycelium

Mushroom spawn is any material that has mycelium growing in it. Growers of edible mushrooms use spawn to "seed" growth beds that produce harvestable mushrooms. Try making mushroom spawn yourself.

WHAT YOU'LL NEED

➢ Clean, corrugated cardboard; fresh oyster mushrooms with stems; a clean bucket; a plastic bag; water; a knife; a hammer and nail.

STEP 1 Tear cardboard (without printing or tape) into small pieces to fit in the bucket. Use enough pieces to completely fill the bucket.

STEP 2 Dump the cardboard pieces into a clean tub or sink filled with warm water. Let soak for at least an hour.

STEP 3 Turn over the bucket so its base faces up. Then cut, drill, poke, or hammer some drainage holes into the base. Then turn the bucket right side up.

STEP 4 Drain the water from the soaking cardboard.

STEP 5 Carefully and gently cut off the bottom inch of the mushroom stems.

STEP 6 Tear off the papery layers of a soaked piece of cardboard (and keep them on the side). Cover the bottom of the bucket with the remaining wavy, corrugated, soaked cardboard.

STEP 7 Place the mushroom stem ends on the corrugated paper a few inches apart. Cover with papery or corrugated soaked cardboard. Make additional layers in the bucket until all the stem ends are used.

STEP 8 Gently compress the layers with your hand so the stems are touching the cardboard but air can still circulate. Then cover the bucket with a plastic bag.

STEP 9 Set the bucket out of the sun in an area that stays shady. Remove the plastic regularly for air exchange. With luck, you'll see white mycelium growing on the cardboard in a few weeks to a month.

I DID IT! DATE:

Plant Spotter Deep Dive: Profile a Fungus

Put all your fungus knowledge together and dive deeper!
Choose a favorite fungus or mushroom and profile it.

WHAT YOU'LL NEED

➤ A pencil or pen, a ruler or measuring tape,
a hand lens, gloves for handling fungus.

DATE

LOCATION

Is it a
- [ ] gilled cap mushroom
- [ ] spongy cap mushroom
- [ ] bracket fungus
- [ ] cup- or ball-shaped fungus
- [ ] jelly fungus
- [ ] club-shaped fungus

What kind of habitat does it live in?

How tall or wide is the mushroom or fungus
(including units)?

Draw the entire mushroom or fungus and label its
parts.

Describe its color.

Describe its spore print color.

Describe its texture:

☐ rough ☐ slimy ☐ warty ☐ scaly

If there's a cap, what shape is it?

☐ convex ☐ bell-shaped ☐ conical
☐ knobbed ☐ flat ☐ sunken

Does it have gills? ☐ yes ☐ no

If yes, how are the gills spaced?

☐ crowded ☐ close together ☐ distantly separated

How are the gills attached to the stalk?

☐ free ☐ attached ☐ extending down stalk

If it doesn't have gills, where are the spores made?

Describe the stalk, if there is one.

Note any other unique characteristics:

Mushroom or Fungus Name:

Check off its I SPOTTED IT! box in the identification section and fill in the blanks. Marvelous effort, fungus spotter!

I DID IT! DATE:

MUSHROOM AND FUNGUS IDENTIFICATION

Welcome to your Mushroom and Fungus Identification guide!

Here are some tips to get started, and where in the book you'll find more info:

These pages have two groups. **MUSHROOMS & FUNGI** is first up, followed by **LICHENS**.

PARTS OF A MUSHROOM

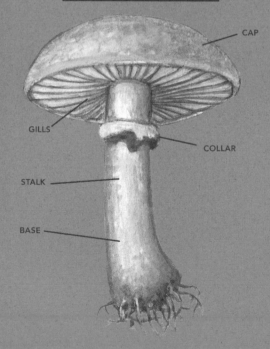

CAP

GILLS

COLLAR

STALK

BASE

SHAPE is shown as one of eight icons next to the mushroom or fungus name (pages 353–354).

GILLED CAP　SPONGY CAP　BRACKET　CLUB SHAPE　CUP SHAPE　JELLYLIKE　BALL SHAPE　VASE

The lichens' icons represent the three types:

CRUSTOSE　FOLIOSE　FRUTICOSE

COLOR is found on the shape icon and represents the mushroom's or fungus's overall main color. Fungi colors can vary, so there are only four color categories: yellow to brown, white to gray, reddish, and greenish. If you're looking for a yellowish mushroom and don't find it among the yellow to brown, try white to gray.

SIZE given is the largest height or width a mushroom usually grows to.

CAP includes various details about the mushroom cap, including color and shape.

GILLS/SPORE-BEARERS is a description of where spores are made and how gills are spaced and attached to the stalk (pages 366–367).

STALK includes color, relative thickness, and presence of a collar.

SPORE PRINT describes the spore color inside a mushroom's gills or other spore-producing surface (pages 369–370).

SEASON refers to the general time of year when you're most likely to spot the mushroom, which varies by geography and weather.

RANGE is within the United States and Canada. Many mushrooms grow across multiple continents.

Orange Milk Cap
(Lactarius deliciosus)

VASE

SIZE Up to 3 inches (7.5 cm) tall

CAP Orange with bands of color that stain green with age. It has a sunken center that becomes vase-shaped as the mushroom matures, and it is slimy when wet.

GILLS/SPORE-BEARERS Gills crowded, attached, and partially extended down the stalk.

STALK Thick and orange with a white, powdery coating.

SPORE PRINT Cream.

SEASON Late summer to autumn.

HABITAT Conifer forests, especially pines.

RANGE Throughout the United States and Canada.

POINT OF FACT When this mushroom is cut or bruised, an orange, milky latex oozes out and stains things green.

I SPOTTED IT!

WHEN I SAW IT
DATE

WHERE I SAW IT
SPECIFIC LOCATION, INCLUDE STATE

NOTES

....

....

Honey Mushroom
(Armillariella mellea)

GILLED CAP

SIZE Up to 6 inches (15 cm) tall

CAP Yellow-brown, oval-shaped, and sticky with fine hairs over its center, and a slightly sunken center that's nearly flat.

GILLS/SPORE-BEARERS Gills distantly separated that are attached or somewhat extended down the stalk.

STALK Yellow with a collar near its cap.

SPORE PRINT White.

SEASON Autumn.

HABITAT Woodlands, clusters near tree stumps and logs, and sometimes tree bases.

RANGE Throughout the United States and Canada.

POINT OF FACT This honey-colored mushroom grows on wood and has underground spreading runners that reach 30 feet (9 m).

I SPOTTED IT!

WHEN I SAW IT
DATE

WHERE I SAW IT
SPECIFIC LOCATION,
INCLUDE STATE

NOTES

....

....

Jack-O'-Lantern
(Omphalotus illudens)

VASE

REGIONAL NAME False Chanterelle

SIZE Up to 8 inches (20.5 cm) tall

CAP Yellow to orange with a sunken or vase-shaped center.

GILLS/SPORE-BEARERS Gills closely spaced and sharp-edged that extend down the stalk.

STALK Yellow to orange, long, curved, and smooth.

SPORE PRINT Pale cream.

SEASON Midsummer to autumn.

HABITAT Mixed forests, with large clusters at bases of stumps and over buried roots of oaks and other deciduous trees.

RANGE Eastern United States, California, and Canada.

POINT OF FACT This poisonous mushroom causes vomiting, cramps, and diarrhea if eaten, and is sometimes confused with edible chanterelles.

I SPOTTED IT!

WHEN I SAW IT
DATE

WHERE I SAW IT
SPECIFIC LOCATION,
INCLUDE STATE

NOTES

....

....

King Bolete
(Boletus edulis)

SPONGY CAP

REGIONAL NAMES Porcini, Penny Bun

SIZE Up to 10 inches (25.5 cm) tall

CAP Large, thick, smooth, and red-brown with a convex shape.

GILLS/SPORE-BEARERS Spore-producing, spongy surface under its cap with small, round pores.

STALK Thick and bulb-shaped; white near the top that darkens to brown-tan toward the bottom; netlike ridges.

SPORE PRINT Olive-brown.

SEASON Summer to autumn.

HABITAT Mixed and coniferous forests, and on the ground under trees.

RANGE Throughout the United States and Canada.

POINT OF FACT Called porcini mushrooms in cookbooks, these are a favorite of chefs and are sold dry in gourmet markets.

I SPOTTED IT!

WHEN I SAW IT
DATE

WHERE I SAW IT
SPECIFIC LOCATION,
INCLUDE STATE

NOTES

Slippery Jack
(Suillus luteus)

SPONGY CAP

SIZE Up to 4 inches (10 cm) tall

CAP Large, yellow to red-brown, slimy, smooth, and convex-shaped.

GILLS/SPORE-BEARERS Spore-producing, spongy white surface that yellows with age under its cap with small round pores.

STALK Thick, pale yellow with brown dots and a draping collar.

SPORE PRINT Cinnamon (dull red-brown).

SEASON Autumn to early winter.

HABITAT Coniferous forests and on the ground under pine and spruce trees.

RANGE Eastern North America.

POINT OF FACT Young mushrooms have a veil over the bottom of the cap that becomes the collar.

I SPOTTED IT!

WHEN I SAW IT
DATE

WHERE I SAW IT
SPECIFIC LOCATION,
INCLUDE STATE

NOTES

....

....

Haymaker's Mushroom
(Panaeolus foenisecii)

GILLED CAP

REGIONAL NAME Mower's Mushroom

SIZE Up to 3 inches (7.5 cm) tall

CAP Conical to bell-shaped, brown, and smooth.

GILLS/SPORE-BEARERS Brown to purple gills are attached to the stalk, with varied gill separations.

STALK Slender, brittle, and dingy-white to tan.

SPORE PRINT Dark purple-brown.

SEASON Spring through late autumn and warm winters.

HABITAT Grassy areas, lawns, and fields.

RANGE Throughout the United States and Canada.

POINT OF FACT You've likely stepped on this small, common mushroom that grows in damp grass.

I SPOTTED IT!

WHEN I SAW IT
DATE

WHERE I SAW IT
SPECIFIC LOCATION,
INCLUDE STATE

NOTES

....

....

Glistening Inky Cap
(Coprinus micaceus)

GILLED CAP

REGIONAL NAME Mica Cap

SIZE Up to 3 inches (7.5 cm) tall

CAP Egg- to bell-shaped and brown.

GILLS/SPORE-BEARERS White gills that can turn into an inky gray color are closely spaced and attached to the stalk.

STALK Slender, white, and hollow.

SPORE PRINT Black.

SEASON Spring to autumn.

HABITAT Woodlands and dense clusters on logs and stumps.

RANGE Throughout the United States and Canada.

POINT OF FACT The name comes from its very young caps that have shiny white speckles that darken with age.

○ I SPOTTED IT!

WHEN I SAW IT
DATE

WHERE I SAW IT
SPECIFIC LOCATION,
INCLUDE STATE

NOTES

....

....

Fairy Ring Mushroom

(Marasmius oreades)

GILLED CAP

SIZE Up to 3 inches (7.5 cm) tall

CAP Knobbed bell-shape and tan to red-brown with a grooved edge that turns upward with age.

GILLS/SPORE-BEARERS Yellow-white gills are distantly separated and free or partly attached to the stalk.

STALK Slender, white to tan, and hairy at the base.

SPORE PRINT White to light tan.

SEASON Late spring to summer.

HABITAT Grassy areas and lawns.

RANGE Throughout the United States and Canada.

POINT OF FACT Grows in groups, arcs, and rings that get larger each year as the mycelium spreads outward in search of food.

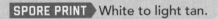

I SPOTTED IT!

WHEN I SAW IT
DATE

WHERE I SAW IT
SPECIFIC LOCATION, INCLUDE STATE

NOTES

....

....

Waxy Laccaria
(Laccaria laccata)

GILLED CAP

REGIONAL NAME Common Laccaria, Deceiver

SIZE Up to 4 inches (10 cm) tall

CAP Brown to pink when grown; smooth to rough in texture; convex to flat in shape with a dent in the center.

GILLS/SPORE-BEARERS Pink gills are distantly separated and attached or partially extended down the stalk.

STALK Thick, fibrous, dry, and brown to pink.

SPORE PRINT White.

SEASON Summer to autumn.

HABITAT Woodlands, open areas, and empty lots.

RANGE Throughout the United States and Canada.

POINT OF FACT This common mushroom, known as "the deceiver," can be tough to identify because its caps vary so greatly in size, color, and shape.

I SPOTTED IT!

WHEN I SAW IT
DATE

WHERE I SAW IT
SPECIFIC LOCATION, INCLUDE STATE

NOTES

....

....

Witch's Hat

(Hygrophorus / Hygrocybe conicus)

GILLED CAP

REGIONAL NAME Conical Wax Cap

SIZE Up to 4 inches (10 cm) tall

CAP Orange-red, conical-shaped, sticky when moist, and smooth.

GILLS/SPORE-BEARERS White gills that turn yellow to orange in color are closely separated, and free or partially attached to the stalk.

STALK Thick, hollow, and darker red or yellow near the base.

SPORE PRINT White.

SEASON Midsummer to early autumn.

HABITAT Grows alone or in a scattered group under conifer trees in coniferous forests.

RANGE Throughout the United States and Canada.

POINT OF FACT This mushroom can sometimes turn poisonous as it ages, while its cap, gills, and stalk turn black when bruised or cut.

◎ I SPOTTED IT!

WHEN I SAW IT
DATE

WHERE I SAW IT
SPECIFIC LOCATION, INCLUDE STATE

NOTES

....

....

MUSHROOMS & FUNGI

Horse Mushroom
(Agaricus arvensis)

GILLED CAP

SIZE Up to 8 inches (20.5 cm) tall

CAP White, smooth, and convex-shaped; bruises yellow.

GILLS/SPORE-BEARERS White to gray gills are closely spaced and freely attached to the stalk.

STALK Thick and white; bruises yellow with a skirtlike collar.

SPORE PRINT Black-brown.

SEASON Summer to autumn.

HABITAT Meadows, fields, grassy areas, and near spruce trees.

RANGE Throughout the United States and Canada.

POINT OF FACT It's often found growing in fairy rings around horse stables and pastures, which is how it got its name.

I SPOTTED IT!

WHEN I SAW IT
DATE

WHERE I SAW IT
SPECIFIC LOCATION, INCLUDE STATE

NOTES

386

Meadow Mushroom
(Agaricus campestris)

GILLED CAP

SIZE Up to 2 inches (5 cm) tall

CAP White to tan, mostly smooth or sometimes frilly-edged, and convex-shaped.

GILLS/SPORE-BEARERS Pink gills that darken with age are crowded and freely attached to the stalk.

STALK Short, stout, and white with a thin, temporary collar.

SPORE PRINT Black-brown.

SEASON Late summer to early autumn, and sometimes in spring.

HABITAT Grassy areas.

RANGE Throughout the United States and Canada.

POINT OF FACT A long time ago in Scotland, slices of this mushroom were placed on burns to soothe the skin.

I SPOTTED IT!

WHEN I SAW IT
DATE

WHERE I SAW IT
SPECIFIC LOCATION,
INCLUDE STATE

NOTES

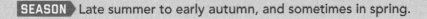

Chanterelle
(Cantharellus cibarius)

VASE

SIZE Up to 4 inches (10 cm) tall

CAP Bright yellow to orange with wavy edges; vase-shaped and apricot-scented.

GILLS/SPORE-BEARERS The spore-producing fertile surface is gill-like, with distantly separated, narrow, forked ridges that extend down the stalk.

STALK Stout, smooth, somewhat fibrous, and the same color as the cap.

SPORE PRINT Cream.

SEASON Late summer to early autumn.

HABITAT Grows under trees on the ground in oak and conifer forests.

RANGE Throughout the United States and Canada.

POINT OF FACT An unfortunate look-alike to the poisonous jack-o'-lantern mushroom, it's a prized find for wild mushroom foragers.

◖ I SPOTTED IT! ▷

WHEN I SAW IT
DATE

WHERE I SAW IT
SPECIFIC LOCATION,
INCLUDE STATE

NOTES

....

....

388

Grisette

(Amanita vaginata)

GILLED CAP

SIZE Up to 5 inches (12.5 cm) tall

CAP Gray with white patches, lined edges, and a wide, conical shape.

GILLS/SPORE-BEARERS Gills are close together and freely attached to the stalk.

STALK White and smooth with a large, sack-like cup (volva) at the base.

SPORE PRINT White.

SEASON Summer.

HABITAT Grows on the ground in open woods and near trees.

RANGE Throughout the United States and Canada.

POINT OF FACT The name means "little gray one" in French.

I SPOTTED IT!

WHEN I SAW IT
DATE

WHERE I SAW IT
SPECIFIC LOCATION,
INCLUDE STATE

NOTES

....

....

Fly Agaric

(Amanita muscaria)

GILLED CAP

SIZE Up to 5 inches (12.5 cm) tall

CAP Orange-red to deep red with white warts, a convex to flat shape, and a sunken center.

GILLS/SPORE-BEARERS White gills are crowded and freely attached to the stalk.

STALK White to cream with frills and a skirtlike collar.

SPORE PRINT White.

SEASON Midsummer to autumn.

HABITAT Grows on the ground in oak, birch, and coniferous forests.

RANGE Throughout the United States and Canada.

POINT OF FACT People used to make housefly poison by mixing this dangerous mushroom with milk.

◖ I SPOTTED IT! ▷

WHEN I SAW IT
DATE

WHERE I SAW IT
SPECIFIC LOCATION, INCLUDE STATE

NOTES

....

....

Shaggy Parasol
(Chlorophyllum rhacodes)

GILLED CAP

SIZE Up to 8 inches (20.5 cm) tall

CAP Covered in pink to brown, large, coarse, curled scales, with a convex to flat shape.

GILLS/SPORE-BEARERS White gills are closely separated and freely attached to the stalk.

STALK Stout and white with a fringed collar that bruises yellow when cut.

SPORE PRINT White.

SEASON Late summer to autumn.

HABITAT Woodlands, grassy areas, gardens, mulch, and compost piles.

RANGE Throughout the United States and Canada.

POINT OF FACT It's easily confused with the poisonous "false" parasol or green-spored parasol mushroom, but its bruising color and spore print tell it apart.

I SPOTTED IT!

WHEN I SAW IT
DATE

WHERE I SAW IT
SPECIFIC LOCATION, INCLUDE STATE

NOTES

....

....

Green-Spored Mushroom

(Chlorophyllum molybdites)

REGIONAL NAMES False Parasol, Vomiter

SIZE Up to 10 inches (25.5 cm) tall

CAP White with brown scales near its center and a convex to flat shape.

GILLS/SPORE-BEARERS White gills that become gray-green as the mushroom matures are closely separated and freely attached.

STALK Smooth and white that browns with age or bruising.

SPORE PRINT Green.

SEASON Late summer.

HABITAT Grows in fairy rings in lawns, pastures, meadows, and other grassy areas.

RANGE Most of the United States except the upper plains and Northwest.

POINT OF FACT Those who eat this poisonous mushroom become violently ill for days and learn why it's nicknamed "vomiter"!

I SPOTTED IT!

WHEN I SAW IT
DATE

WHERE I SAW IT
SPECIFIC LOCATION, INCLUDE STATE

NOTES

Common Morel
(Morchella esculenta)

CLUB

REGIONAL NAMES Yellow Morel, Honeycomb Morel

SIZE Up to 4 inches (10 cm) tall

CAP Light yellow to tan with a long oval shape that's covered in a honeycomb-like pattern of rounded ridges and pits.

GILLS/SPORE-BEARERS None. Its spore-making surface is outside the cap.

STALK White and hollow.

SPORE PRINT Cream to yellow.

SEASON Spring to early summer.

HABITAT Grows on the ground in deciduous woods and old orchards.

RANGE Throughout the United States and Canada.

POINT OF FACT Compared with most mushrooms, morels' caps are turned inside out—the fertile surface that makes and ejects spores is on the outside of the cap.

I SPOTTED IT!

WHEN I SAW IT
DATE

WHERE I SAW IT
SPECIFIC LOCATION, INCLUDE STATE

NOTES

....

....

Ravenel's Stinkhorn

(Phallus ravenelii)

CLUB

SIZE Up to 8 inches (20.5 cm) tall

CAP Olive-green and conical with a white, ringed hole on the top.

GILLS/SPORE-BEARERS Spores cover the cap in a smelly green slime.

STALK White to yellow, thick, and long with a bulbous cup around the base.

SEASON Late summer to autumn.

HABITAT Wooded areas (including cities) with rotting stumps, wood debris, or sawdust.

RANGE Eastern United States and Southeastern Canada.

POINT OF FACT The slime around the spores smells like poop and attracts flies and other insects, which help the spores spread to other food sources.

I SPOTTED IT!

WHEN I SAW IT
DATE

WHERE I SAW IT
SPECIFIC LOCATION, INCLUDE STATE

NOTES

Bird's-Nest Fungus

(Cyathus striatus)

CUP

REGIONAL NAME Splash Cups

SIZE Up to 0.5 inch (1.5 cm) tall

FUNGUS Bowl-shaped and brown, with a shaggy outer cup and grooved, shiny inner cup.

GILLS/SPORE-BEARERS Spores are inside tiny, egg-shaped sacs within the cap.

SEASON Summer to early autumn.

HABITAT Grows in clusters on dead tree branches and other wood debris in open woodlands.

RANGE Throughout the United States and Canada.

POINT OF FACT When raindrops splash into its cup, the egg-shaped sacs are ejected and their spores are spread around.

I SPOTTED IT!

WHEN I SAW IT
DATE

WHERE I SAW IT
SPECIFIC LOCATION, INCLUDE STATE

NOTES

....

....

Giant Puffball

(Calvatia gigantea)

BALL

SIZE Up to 1.6 feet (0.5 m) wide

FUNGUS Huge, smooth white ball that cracks and yellows with age.

GILLS/SPORE-BEARERS Its spongy, spore-making surface is inside the ball.

SPORE PRINT Brown.

SEASON Late summer to autumn.

HABITAT Grows on the ground in open woods, pastures, and grassy areas.

RANGE Eastern United States and Southeastern Canada.

POINT OF FACT Puffballs make trillions of spores that spread outward like powdery smoke.

I SPOTTED IT!

WHEN I SAW IT
DATE

WHERE I SAW IT
SPECIFIC LOCATION, INCLUDE STATE

NOTES

Artist's Fungus
(Ganoderma applanatum)

BRACKET

REGIONAL NAME Artist's Conk

SIZE Up to 1.6 feet (0.5 m) wide

CAP Hard, woody, and pale to dark brown or gray, with ridges, furrows, and a white edge; flattened semicircle or fan shape.

GILLS/SPORE-BEARERS Its spore-producing surface is white with a spongy underside.

SPORE PRINT Brown.

SEASON Year-round.

HABITAT Grows on dead wood or in wounds of living trees in deciduous forests.

RANGE Southern Canada and most of Northern and Central United States.

POINT OF FACT The undersides of young fungi are soft enough to etch an image into them that becomes permanent when it dries.

I SPOTTED IT!

WHEN I SAW IT
DATE

WHERE I SAW IT
SPECIFIC LOCATION,
INCLUDE STATE

NOTES

....

....

Turkey Tail

(Trametes versicolor)

BRACKET

SIZE ▶ Up to 4 inches (10 cm) wide

CAP ▶ Clusters of overlapping small, leathery, thin, fan-shaped caps with bands of multiple colors on top and white or yellow underneath.

GILLS/SPORE-BEARERS ▶ Its spore-producing surface is on the spongy underside of the fungus.

SPORE PRINT ▶ White.

SEASON ▶ Late spring to early winter (though sometimes survives year-round).

HABITAT ▶ Grows on dead wood or in wounds of living trees in deciduous and coniferous forests.

RANGE ▶ Throughout the United States and Canada.

POINT OF FACT ▶ It's named for its similarity to the multicolored tail of a male wild turkey.

◉ I SPOTTED IT! ▶

WHEN I SAW IT
DATE

WHERE I SAW IT
SPECIFIC LOCATION, INCLUDE STATE

NOTES

....

....

Red Belt Fungus

(Fomitopsis pinicola)

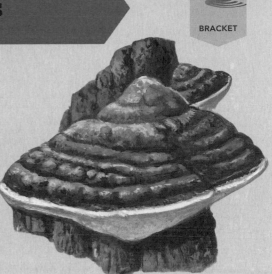

BRACKET

REGIONAL NAME Red-Belted Conk

SIZE Up to 1.3 feet (0.5 m) tall

CAP Hard, woody, dark brown, and hoof-shaped with a red, resinous crust near the edges.

GILLS/SPORE-BEARERS Its white to yellow, spore-producing surface is on the spongy underside of the fungus.

SPORE PRINT White.

SEASON Year-round.

HABITAT Grows on dead trees, stumps, logs, and sometimes living trees in deciduous and coniferous forests.

RANGE Throughout Canada and most of the United States except the Southeast.

POINT OF FACT This fungus grows on more than 100 species of trees.

I SPOTTED IT!

WHEN I SAW IT
DATE

WHERE I SAW IT
SPECIFIC LOCATION,
INCLUDE STATE

NOTES

....

....

Witches' Butter

(Tremella mesenterica)

JELLY-LIKE

REGIONAL NAMES Yellow Brain, Golden Jelly Fungus

SIZE Up to 4 inches (10 cm) wide

FUNGUS Yellow, firm, gelatin-looking mass with a lobed, brain-like shape.

GILLS/SPORE-BEARERS The entire surface produces spores.

SPORE PRINT Yellow-white.

SEASON Year-round.

HABITAT Grows on stumps, logs, and dead branches in deciduous forests.

RANGE Throughout the United States and Canada.

POINT OF FACT These jellylike fungi dry out for weeks or months and then revive when water returns.

I SPOTTED IT!

WHEN I SAW IT
DATE

WHERE I SAW IT
SPECIFIC LOCATION, INCLUDE STATE

NOTES

Bear's Head Tooth
(Hericium americanum)

BRACKET

SIZE Up to 1 foot (0.5 m) wide

CAP Large white mass made up of many small tufts tipped with hanging, icicle-like "teeth."

GILLS/SPORE-BEARERS None. Its spores are made on the outside of hanging strands called teeth.

SPORE PRINT White.

SEASON Late summer to autumn.

HABITAT Grows on old stumps and logs, and on wounds of some living trees in deciduous forests.

RANGE East of the Great Plains.

POINT OF FACT Its genus name means hedgehog in reference to its spiny-shaped, pointed, spore-bearing structures.

I SPOTTED IT!

WHEN I SAW IT
DATE

WHERE I SAW IT
SPECIFIC LOCATION, INCLUDE STATE

NOTES

....

....

Scarlet Cup
(Sarcoscypha coccinea)

CUP

REGIONAL NAME Scarlet Elf Cap

SIZE Up to 2 inches (5 cm) wide

CAP Cup-shaped with curved edges, a red inside, and a white outside.

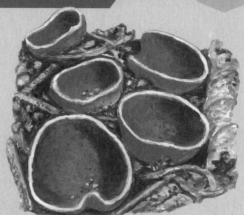

GILLS/SPORE-BEARERS Its spores are produced on the inside surface of the cup.

STALK White and very short, if present at all.

SPORE PRINT White.

SEASON Early to late spring.

HABITAT Grows on fallen branches in wet places and deciduous forests.

RANGE Eastern, Midwestern, and Northwestern United States, California, and Southern Canada.

POINT OF FACT It's one of the very first fungi to appear in early spring, and its bright color makes it easy to spot.

I SPOTTED IT!

WHEN I SAW IT
DATE

WHERE I SAW IT
SPECIFIC LOCATION, INCLUDE STATE

NOTES

....

....

Dog Lichen

(Peltigera canina)

FOLIOSE

SIZE 2.5–8 inches (6.5–20.5 cm) long

BODY Leathery sheet with ruffled edges, with a blue-gray to brown top surface and a woolly and tan underside.

HABITAT Grows in most woods and other damp, shady places such as leaf litter, among mosses, on bases of trees, and on rotting wood.

RANGE Throughout the United States and Canada.

POINT OF FACT The fruiting bodies form on the edges of the leaflike structures and look a bit like dog teeth.

◖ I SPOTTED IT! ◗

WHEN I SAW IT
DATE

WHERE I SAW IT
SPECIFIC LOCATION,
INCLUDE STATE

NOTES

....

....

Map Lichen
(Rhizocarpon geographicum)

CRUSTOSE

SIZE 0.5–4 inches (1.5–10 cm) wide

BODY Bright yellow to green patches of crust surrounded by black outlines and crack lines.

HABITAT Grows on exposed rocks in upland and mountain regions.

RANGE United States and Canadian mountain ranges.

POINT OF FACT Its patches grow next to one another to create a maplike pattern.

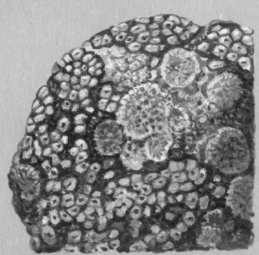

I SPOTTED IT!

WHEN I SAW IT
DATE

WHERE I SAW IT
SPECIFIC LOCATION, INCLUDE STATE

NOTES

....

....

British Soldiers
(Cladonia cristatella)

FRUTICOSE

SIZE 1–1.5 inches (2.5–4 cm) tall

BODY Tiny, bright red cups on the ends of lumpy, scaly, hollow, green to gray stalks or branches.

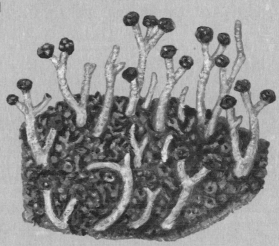

HABITAT Grows on decaying wood, mossy logs, and tree stumps in dry, sunny places.

RANGE Eastern United States and throughout most of Canada.

POINT OF FACT It's named after the red coats of British soldiers during the American Revolutionary War.

I SPOTTED IT!

WHEN I SAW IT
DATE

WHERE I SAW IT
SPECIFIC LOCATION, INCLUDE STATE

NOTES

....

....

101 OUTDOOR SCHOOL
TREE, WILDFLOWER, AND MUSHROOM SPOTTING ACHIEVEMENTS

1 Reviewed the Plant Spotting Rules and Reminders

2 Found plant with taproot and fibrous root

3 Made a line transect

4 Identified local plant life

5 Practiced plant terminology

6 Profiled a weed

7 Labeled the parts of a plant

8 Conducted a leaf survey

9 Magnified a leaf

10 Observed plant transpiration

11 Collected burrs/clingy seeds

12 Went on a seed search

13 Started a seed log

14 Planted a mysterious seed

15 Identified plant defenses

16 Researched local problem plants

17 Learned local plants to avoid

18 Scouted plant habitats

19 Compared plant habitats

20 Completed the plant habitat observation tracker

21 Identified local tree

22 Learned dendrologist terms

23 Estimated tree height

24 Determined tree shape

25 Found all 5 tree shapes

26 Identified simple leaf and compound leaflets

27 Identified a leaf in the fall

28 Went on a tree leaf scavenger hunt

29 Compared leaf characteristics

30 Profiled a tree leaf

31 Collected leaf specimen

32 Started a leaf collection

33 Identified a tree bark sample

34 Found all 8 types of tree bark

35 Practiced tree bark comparison

36 Made a bark rubbing

37 Examined state tree bark

38 Counted tree rings to estimate age

39 Measured tree circumference to estimate age

40 Identified twig

41 Went on a winter twig walk

42 Identified all 6 parts of a twig

43 Found carnivorous plant

44 Adopted a local branch

45 Identified a conifer tree

46 Found 5 species of conifer trees

47 Used an identification key

48 Examined a conifer cone

49 Profiled first tree

50 Found 5 species of trees

51 Identified and sized a shrub

52 Found 4 soil types

53 Identified wildflower

54 Examined a flower

55 Found all 6 parts of a flower

56 Memorized remedies for local plants to avoid

57 Documented a wildflower from bud to seed

58 Found all 6 flower shapes

59 Practiced flower terminology

60 Completed a wildflower shape survey

61 Practiced seeing symmetrically

62 Pressed wildflowers

63 Examined wildflower leaves

64 Went on a wildflower walk

65 Identified all wildflower leaf characteristics

66 Found 4 examples of plant damage

67 Made a quadrat

68 Studied local plant habitats

69 Profiled a wildflower

70 Identified 5 species of wildflower

71 Found 5 types of grass

72 Learned nonflowering plant terms

73 Located a nonflowering plant

74 Found 5 species of nonflowering plants

75 Compared nonflowering plants

76 Made a fern spore print

77 Grew fern spores

78 Identified first moss

79 Identified first fern

80 Went on a fern and moss scavenger hunt

81 Identified 10 types of ferns and mosses

82 Compared vertical and horizontal mosses

83 Made a moss terrarium

84 Profiled a moss or fern

85 Identified all parts of a moss

86 Identified all parts of a fern

87 Identified first fungus

88 Learned fungi vocabulary

89 Found 3 pinnate and 3 palmate compound leaves

90 Found 7 types of mushrooms and fungi

91 Compared fungi types

92 Researched local hazardous mushrooms

93 Found 5 different gill-capped mushrooms

94 Made toxic toadstool flash cards

95 Found 3 kinds of leaf edges

96 Found 5 different spongy-cap mushrooms

97 Collected mushroom

98 Made a mushroom spore print

99 Grew mushroom spawn

100 Profiled a mushroom or fungus

101 Found 10 types of mushrooms and fungi

INDEX

About the Creators

Mary Kay Carson is the author of more than fifty books for young people about wildlife, space, weather, nature, and history—including *Outdoor School: Animal Watching*. After studying biology in college and a stint in the Peace Corps, she began her writing career working on the Scholastic classroom magazine *SuperScience*. Her books have received more than a dozen starred reviews as well as multiple awards. She lives in Cincinnati, Ohio, with her husband in a century-old house surrounded by urban greenspace, deer, hawks, woodchucks, coyotes, and songbirds. Visit marykaycarson.com for more information on the author.

John D. Dawson has created art spanning over four decades, from early years in advertising art to freelance work for the US Postal Service, National Park Service, United Nations, National Wildlife Federation, National Geographic Society, the Audubon Society, and the Golden Guide books. He and his wife, Kathleen, have lived on the Big Island of Hawaii since 1989.